IMAGES
of America

Ada

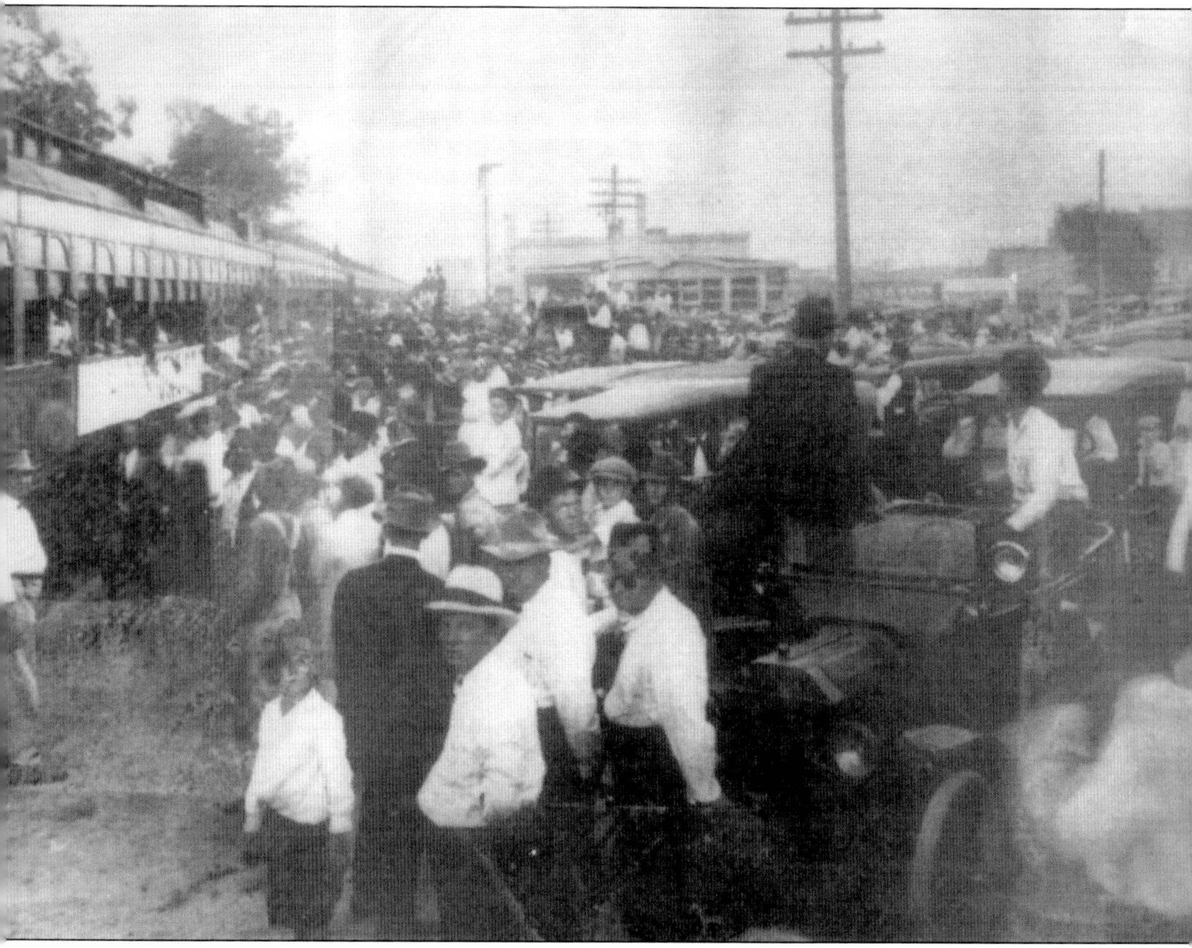

The city of Ada turned out to see its boys off to World War II. Quite a crowd gathered to wave the soldiers goodbye. The cars tell the era, and the fedora hats seal this spot in time. Brave Oklahomans were leaving home to proudly defend the United States. Passenger trains used to be a way of life for many people; however, people today view them simply as a fanciful way to tour the country. (Courtesy of Alberta Blackburn.)

ON THE COVER: One of Ada's Junior League baseball players went on to Major League Baseball. Harry Brecheen (back row, second from left) pitched for the St. Louis Cardinals and was the winning pitcher for three of their World Series games in 1946. (Courtesy of Bud Throne.)

IMAGES
of America

ADA

Dare Strickland

ARCADIA
PUBLISHING

Copyright © 2010 by Dare Strickland
ISBN 978-0-7385-8436-2

Published by Arcadia Publishing
Charleston, South Carolina

Printed in the United States of America

Library of Congress Control Number: 2010930540

For all general information, please contact Arcadia Publishing:
Telephone 843-853-2070
Fax 843-853-0044
E-mail sales@arcadiapublishing.com
For customer service and orders:
Toll-Free 1-888-313-2665

Visit us on the Internet at www.arcadiapublishing.com

To Dustin for his computer whizziness, Sterling for his levity, and my brother-in-law, Leon Thompson, for his excellent memory.

Contents

ACKNOWLEDGMENTS

First I would like to thank Ted Gerstle, my editor, for his patience with a first time author. Deciphering my inquiries could not have been easy. You have become a faceless friend that I hope to meet someday. Bless you, Ted. And also, I would like to thank my infrequent contact, John Pearson, who substituted admirably.

Without Alberta Blackburn with her pictures, stories, and encouragement, I would have had nowhere to lean when discouraged. Her pure joy, her beautiful face, encouragement, and smile will not go unmentioned. Love you, Alberta.

Bud Throne was so very helpful with his wonderful pictures, one of which became the whimsical cover depicting serious participants in America's favorite pastime. Having baseball legend Harry Brecheen on the cover while he was in Ada Junior League baseball was so unexpected. Thank you so much, Bud, for pointing him out in the picture.

A serious collector of old memorabilia, Gary Haney, trusted me with many of his Ada postcards. His contribution to the pictorial aspect of this book was invaluable. Thank you, Gary, for the encouragement. It was heart warming.

The Ada Public Library was a great help to me. Such cooperation in a public facility is vital. Ada's library is excellent. Thank you so very much.

And thank you, sister Zeddra, for keeping me up on where I needed to go and stop. Your knowledge of the computer was a net for me more than once, as were your flying fingers. I love you.

Introduction

Oklahoma is where the wind comes sweeping down the plains. The territory's name was derived from a Native American word that means, "Land of the Red Man." Yet the treaty that was signed for the benefit of the Native Americans and their homeland was written with vanishing ink. Whatever the government did, or did not do, to assist the merging of different cultures in the wild country of Oklahoma is the stuff of history.

In 1889, Ada began to emerge from land that belonged to Native Americans. Since the beginning, parts of Ada's history have made national news. One story that hit headlines in 1909 was the lynching of four men. These men were killed in a stable by a mob of people whose names are still unknown. This incident changed the course of history.

Decades later in 1984, a young woman was kidnapped and presumed dead. Two men were accused of the kidnapping and were convicted of murder—even though there had never been a body found. Writer Robert Mayer came to Ada, took notes on the crime, and wrote a book entitled *Dreams of Ada*. Years later in 1988, another young woman was murdered in her home, and two men were found guilty in the same Ada courtroom. John Grisham, a famous author of popular mystery books, came to Ada when, many years later, the two men were proven innocent when DNA testing became available. The court system was questioned, and the book *The Innocent Man* was written, which was Grisham's first non-fiction book. The guilty man was found and is now in prison for life.

In 1889, Tom Hope sold his profitable general store in Geary, Indian Territory, and set out in a buckboard to find a suitable place in the Oklahoma Territory to start a new town and open a bank of his own. He came upon Daggs Flat, a small gathering of dilapidated businesses on the prairie, which, surprisingly, included a post office. After a short visit, Hope decided to move on and, in less than a day's ride, he found his reward. In the distance, he could see several wagons and pioneers gathered around a spring, and the land surrounding the spring was just what Tom Hope was looking for to begin his new life.

John Beard was among the characters enjoying the gathering and the water. Beard, a land agent, set to work immediately by placing his desk out in front of his tent in heavy mud. He sold prime lots of land that soon became Ada, Oklahoma.

Many lots were sold to excited new settlers and business owners in Daggs Flat, who readily signed an agreement to move their small businesses to prime spots in the new town, just a few miles from Daggs Flat.

Ada is named after the eldest daughter of Jeff Reed, who was a supporter of Tom Hope and many other hopeful citizens involved in similar activities. The town grew quickly and businesses and homes were erected. It had a bank and a post office, and soon Ada was known as a booming town in the territory.

Native Americans were not only cheated out of their government-issued acreage but also shoved out of the way by swindlers with a little cash and a lot of firewater. After illegally elected officials got Native American land owners sufficiently intoxicated, greedy residents took advantage of the corrupt situation and bought the land off these Native Americans for little more then $50. Some pioneers were not proud of this; however, the manner in which this procedure was transacted was considered legal, and most people, especially local ranchers Jesse West and Joe Allen, did not care to change the procedure.

Gus Bobbitt was a respected former U.S. marshal who retired to his ranch outside of Ada. After seeing the unjust land deals made by Ada officials, he decided to stop the dishonest treatment of Native Americans. His intention to find honest land agents who treated Native Americans fairly was soon known to Jesse West and Joe Allen. The greedy ranchers decided to put a stop to Bobbitt's plan, and there was only one way to do it.

B. B. Burrell was sent to deliver payment to ensure their chosen assassin, Jim Miller, would come to Ada and kill the former marshal.

Deacon Jim Miller, a deadly assassin known to be one of the most notoriously heartless killers in the territory, left Fort Worth, Texas, and traveled to Ada to kill do-gooder Gus Bobbitt.

Miller and his favorite weapon for killing, a shotgun, were settled in the fork of a roadside tree, not far from Bobbitt's Lightning Ridge Ranch. As Bobbitt drove his wagon past the tree, Miller ambushed the unsuspecting rancher with two shots. Miller then rode away from the dying man, leaving a wagon driver, hired to follow Gus Bobbitt, as a witness.

Through word of mouth and with the help of the investigation performed by the resident deputy, U.S. Marshal Bob Nestor, it became known that the killer was Deacon Jim Miller. The manner of the killing went according to his reputation. Deacon Jim's history was full of unresolved and deadly happenings. When he was around six years old, his parents died mysteriously. As the boy was sent from home to home, the mysterious deaths followed him. He was considered as a possible suspect in these murders, but people discounted him because he was just a boy, so he was eventually sent to live with his sister and her husband.

When he was 17 years old, Miller came upon his brother-in-law as he slept on the porch and killed him with a shotgun. This time he was tried and found guilty, but with the loose Western laws, he rode away without any punishment. He was well known for getting away with these murders unscathed. He somehow lied his way into being a U.S. marshal for a while and was also a preacher and a deacon in several churches. He was, for some reason, well respected by many.

A one-block area at the western end of Ada was named "The Bucket of Blood" for good reason. Scum of the territory had begun to take refuge in Ada. Thirty-eight murders stemmed from the area in 1908. The law didn't dare interfere with the block for fear of their lives.

Ollie's Blind Pig Saloon was a favorite meeting place on West Main, located among other unsavory bars and hotels. No decent person was safe on that end of Ada's Main Street. Gus Bobbitt had come out of retirement to rid the town of the unjust purchasing of Native American land, and he had been killed in cold blood. The violence had to stop. Ada citizens' choices were whittled down to one. And that choice would dramatically change the history of the wild and woolly west.

All the facts came together, and the four men involved in Bobbitt's murder, which included B. B. Burrell, who delivered the payment, were put in Ada's jail and a trial date was set. Miller wasn't worried, and townspeople soon found out why.

It was soon learned that he had hired the most unscrupulous and unprincipled lawyer known in the west, Moman Pruiett. He was well known for his antics in a courtroom that were used to sway minds. He had no problem defending someone who was known to be outright guilty. Defending Jim Miller was a challenge worth meeting for the flamboyant lawyer. But he was never to meet Deacon Jim. What happened in the town of Ada, Oklahoma, on the morning of April 19, 1909, became the old west's most talked-about, historic event in its short history. The courage that it took to help set the west on the right track was phenomenal.

During the night just prior to the trial a large group of men had the lights turned out in Ada and marched quietly to the jail. They overpowered the guards and took the four men known to have been involved in the killing of Gus Bobbitt. Without disturbing anyone sitting in the darkened houses, they hung the men one by one from the rafters of the stable. Jim Miller was the last to die.

In the next morning's twilight, N. B. Stall set up his camera at the scene and took a picture of the grizzly sight. The image became nationally famous as a postcard and put Ada's name in the history books. To this day, not a soul has spoken up about the act that literally cleared out the scum of the west from "The Bloody Bucket" area. Many fled for fear of receiving the same fate. Ada was no longer a safe haven from the law.

In 1906, several out-of-state businessmen, such as James Wintersmith, became interested in the natural mineral ingredients that were used for making cement. A quarry was developed in Lawrence, just a few miles south of Ada. The Portland Cement Company became one of the most prominent suppliers of cement in the country.

Land southeast of Ada was dammed off for a lake in order to supply water for the venture. The lake turned into a beautiful and serviceable addition to the city. It became a natural park. It was dedicated and named after James Wintersmith's wife, Frances, who campaigned and led a cultural push for Ada to be all it could be instead of just a wild cow town with a history of violence. She was known citywide for her strength of character and determination to bring culture to Ada. To this day, Frances Wintersmith Park is a beautiful social spot on the outskirts of Ada.

Ada acquired an ice plant and a bottling company that soon became a Coca-Cola enterprise. Cotton became king, and huge cotton crops were shipped out on the three railroads that built depots in close proximity to the business area. The railroad companies included the Sante Fe, the Katy, and the Frisco.

Oil was discovered a few miles from Ada in Fittstown and it brought much commerce to the area. The Aldridge and the Harris Hotels were known for catering to businessmen who were making deals furthering the city's growth. A Fittstown resident, Julia Ann Smith, profited greatly from the oil boom. She moved to Ada, bought the Harris Hotel, and added another floor to the top. The hotel was renamed the Julianna, and a fancy neon bellboy swinging a suitcase was added to the high corner of the building. This sight was enjoyed by all who saw it. In its older days, the Julianna became known for bawdy antics on the top floor.

In the 1960s, a fire destroyed a large part of the block starting on the corner of Broadway Avenue and Main Street, destroying several businesses. They were rebuilt and became even more prosperous than before.

Ada, being the county seat, drew people from surrounding towns to shop. Several movie houses on Main Street and a drive-in theater north of town, "The Tower," also entertained them. Close to the ticket booth was a huge spotlight that could be seen for many miles, heralding the outskirts of Ada.

Small downtown parks were built in spots where there had been a fire or a building had been condemned. They added a hometown flavor and beauty. The Chickasaw Nation has enhanced its headquarters in Ada with many beautiful buildings and landscaped areas.

Several famous people came from Ada including Robert S. Kerr, former governor and U.S. senator. There is a water lab named after him honoring his contributions to his town, state, and country.

Many athletes including Harry "the Cat" Brecheen, a famous pitcher for the St. Louis Cardinals, were raised in or near Ada. Don Kaiser from the area just outside Ada pitched for the Chicago Cubs, and Jerry Walker pitched for the Baltimore Orioles. Popular country singer Blake Shelton was raised here. Garth Brooks's piano player, Dave Gant, was raised in Ada.

Ada hosted the second largest rodeo in the country, which brought world-class cowboys and celebrities to town. They stayed mainly in the Aldridge Hotel and frequented the Aldridge Coffee Shop. Minnie Pearl and Smiley Burnett sat in a corner booth during one of the rodeos of the early 1950s and signed autographs.

The largest theater in Ada, the McSwain, started out as a vaudeville theater. Years later, after decades of being the most popular movie house in Ada, it closed for economic reasons. It later was bought and became a country music theater to rival Branson. It has been renovated again by the Chickasaw Nation and proudly stands on its corner, looking as it did in its vaudeville heyday.

Over the years, the Chickasaw Nation has brought prosperity to Ada with its many housing additions and business buildings that are wonders for all to see. The pride of the Chickasaws is clearly seen in the city where they have built many unique and earthy buildings that portray their heritage. The mixture of this natural beauty into Ada's surroundings has made a unique blend that has clearly brought the Native American mystique back home.

The majestic Pre-Paid Legal Building sits on a hill south of town. The company was founded by Harold Stonecipher from Ada and has spread nationwide, offering an insurance plan for future legal needs. It is totally an Ada phenomenon.

In 1910, the first building of East Central Normal School was built. It is now a well-respected university, bringing many students into Ada.

The Chickasaw Nation set up its headquarters in Ada under the remarkable leadership of Gov. Bill Anoatubby. Their success has brought American Indian pride to the forefront by providing jobs and opportunities not known before.

The uniting of the Chickasaws and others in Ada's population brought new beauty to the city. The Chickasaw land is returning to them in peace to beautify this city in east central Oklahoma. Ada has combined the past and the future within the Red Man's land and is thriving because of an acceptance that was both honorable and inevitable.

One

Ada, Indian Territory

The land was a compliment to nature. It was a mixture of hills and valleys, tall and short grass, and flatlands that were waiting for cultivation. Spread out before the impatient land seekers, the morning sun displayed what would soon be their future. Winds flapped the Conestogas' worn canvas. Pioneers had come from far and wide to participate in what was recorded in history as "The Land Run."

Fifty acres of land that was to belong to each Native American had been chosen before the run. Native Americans watched as the only home they had ever known disappeared from view with the sound of a gunshot. When the dust cleared, they could no longer sit on their ponies atop the highest hill and take pride in the one thing they valued more than any other, their freedom.

Pioneers scattered all over the land and took what they could. Lot jumpers were confronted, and confusion grew, but soon a handshake and a man's word was the equivalent of a contract. The pioneers knew to depend on each other to make Ada what they wanted it to become.

The 200 tents in the area looked oddly prosperous in 1902, and, as houses and businesses rose from the Oklahoma soil, Ada began to appear. Early pioneer Henry Blackburn built the first cotton gin, and cotton became king. When the new railroad was built in 1900, the township of Ada moved closer to the rail area to make shipping more convenient.

But Ada began to be a safe haven for criminals, and in 1908, there were 36 murders. Although deaf as a post, Bob Nestor, an old-time lawman, did try to keep the peace. Bob once left to hunt down a witness and eventually sent a telegram back that read, "Witness dead and gone to hell, horse give out and can't foller." Ada was destined to make history.

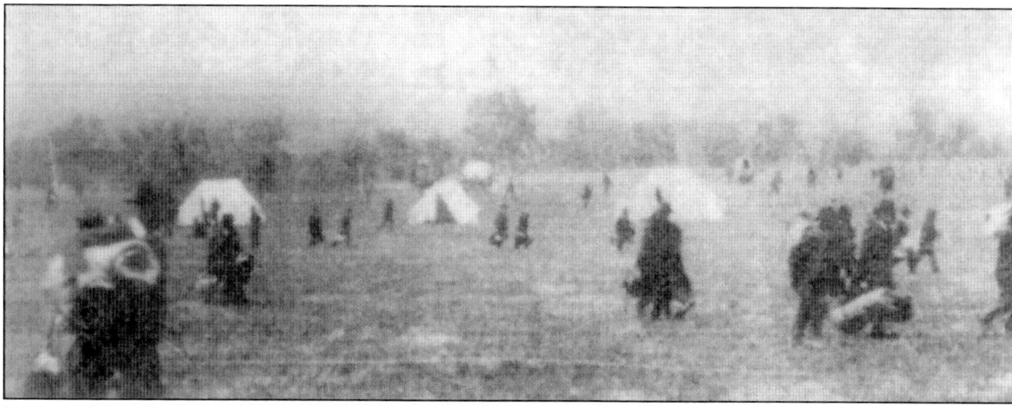

Scenes like this were commonplace after the April 22, 1889, land run. Tents served as the first homes. It didn't take long for saloons to find a home among the pioneers. (Courtesy of Alberta Blackburn.)

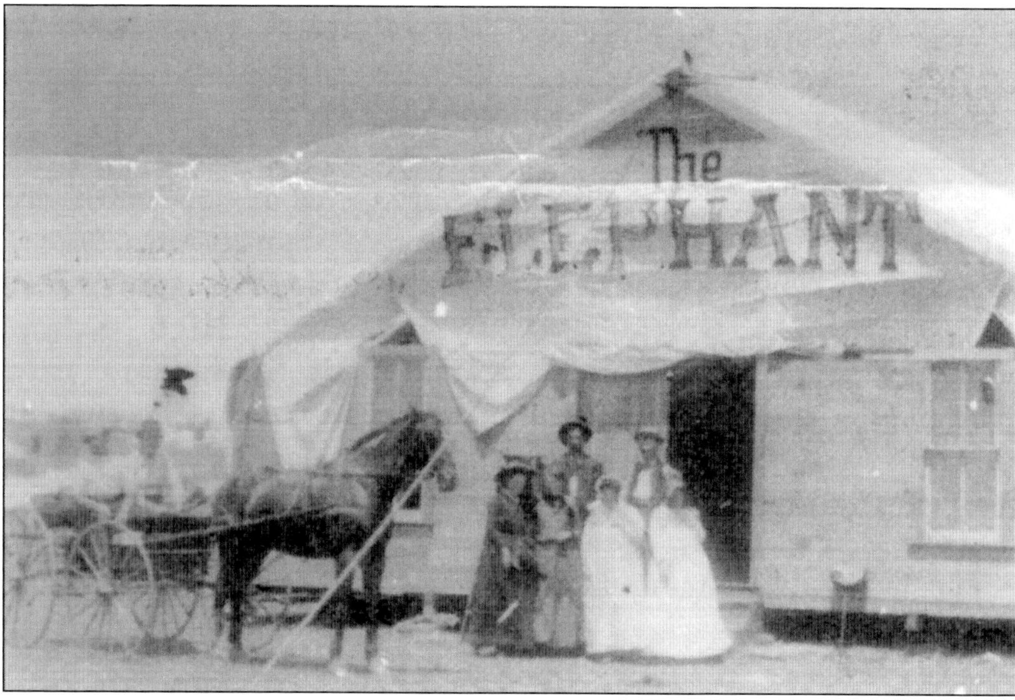

This scene was recorded soon after the April 22, 1889, land run. Tents and makeshift camps were set up on chosen lots. Even after the panic of jockeying for land, there was little peace in this new town. Saloons were quickly set up for wetting whistles and providing entertainment of a female nature. It didn't take long for saloons to make a profit from the tired and anxious settlers, and employees at the "Elephant" were even proud enough to pose for a rare picture. (Courtesy of Alberta Blackburn.)

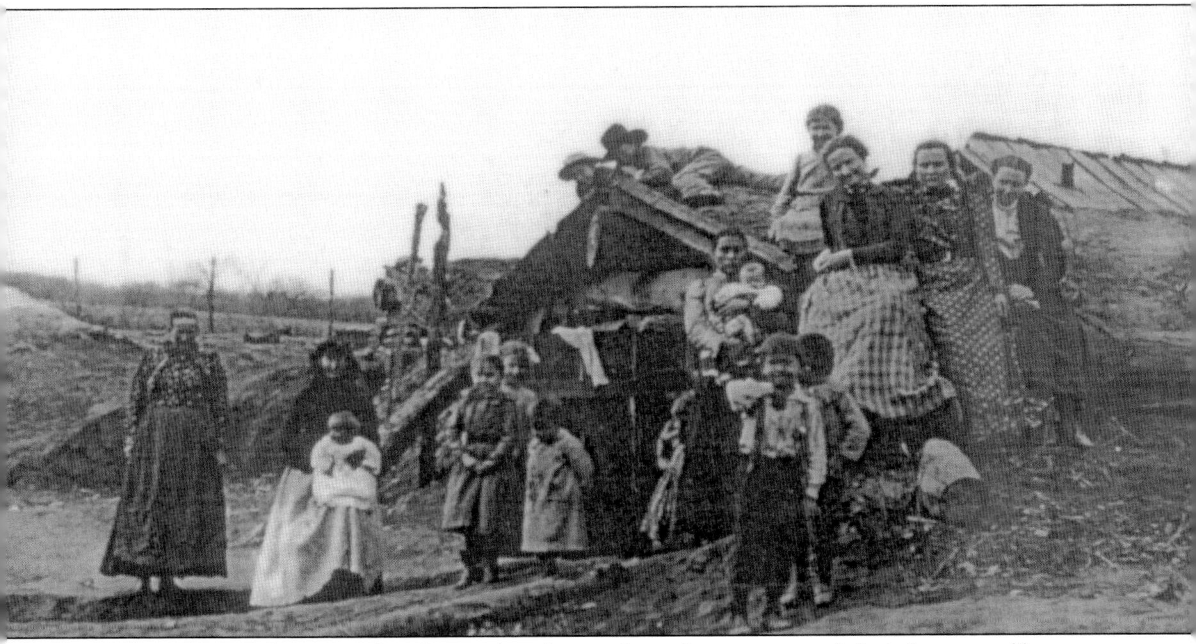

Three generations of Cannon family members lounge happily on or around their dugout sod home in Indian Territory. From the elderly to the infant, they all seem at home. There weren't many trees to climb on the prairie, so children resorted to climbing the house. This wasn't hard to do in this scenario. These people give the word "pioneer" a deeper meaning. Pure grit, determination, and an exceptional amount of love put the Cannon family to bed at night, but the occasional visit from a pet mole kept the kids awake. These were admirable, brave people who were very proud for a chance at a new beginning. It would be rather difficult for lot jumpers to take their territory. (Courtesy of Alberta Blackburn.)

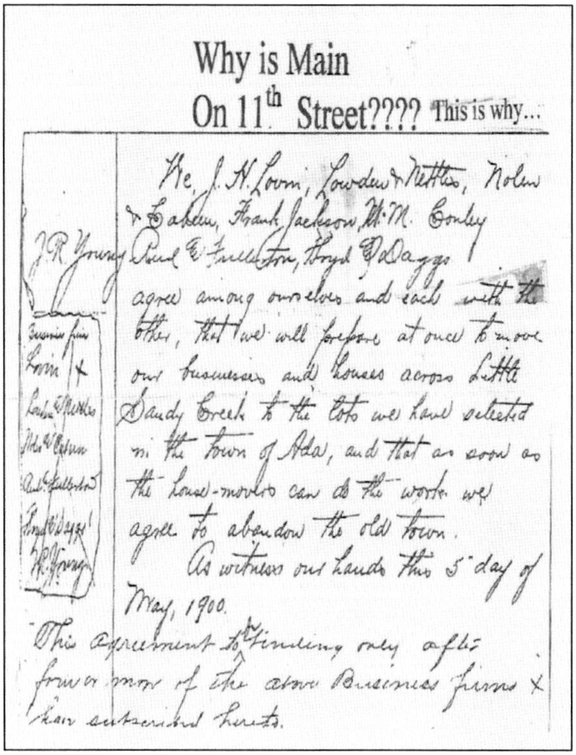

When Jeff Reed and John Beard started the settlement of Ada, they invited the businesses of Daggs Flat to move over and be a part of the new town. This is the contract haphazardly signed by some business owners. All signed and moved except for the owner of the post office and a general store, John Hodges. His decision caused a series of very interesting and almost comical events. (Courtesy of Alberta Blackburn.)

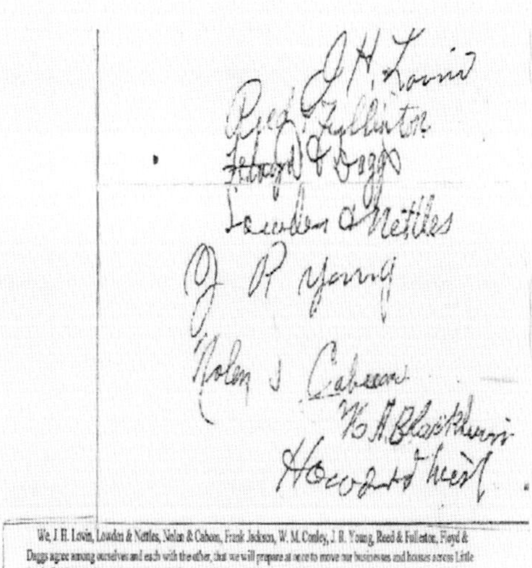

We, J. H. Lovin, Lowden & Nettles, Nolen & Cabeen, Frank Jackson, W. M. Conley, J. R. Young, Reed & Fullerton, Floyd & Daggs agree among ourselves and each with the other, that we will prepare at once to move our businesses and houses across Little Sandy Creek to the lots we have selected in the town of Ada, and that as soon as the house-movers can do the work we agree to abandon the old town.

As witness our hands this 5th day of May, 1900.

This agreement to be binding only after four or more of the above Business firms have subscribed hereto.

(Signed by) J. H. Lovin, Reed & Fullerton, Floyd & Daggs, Lowden & Nettles, J. R. Young, Nolen & Cabeen, H. A. Blackburn, Howard West

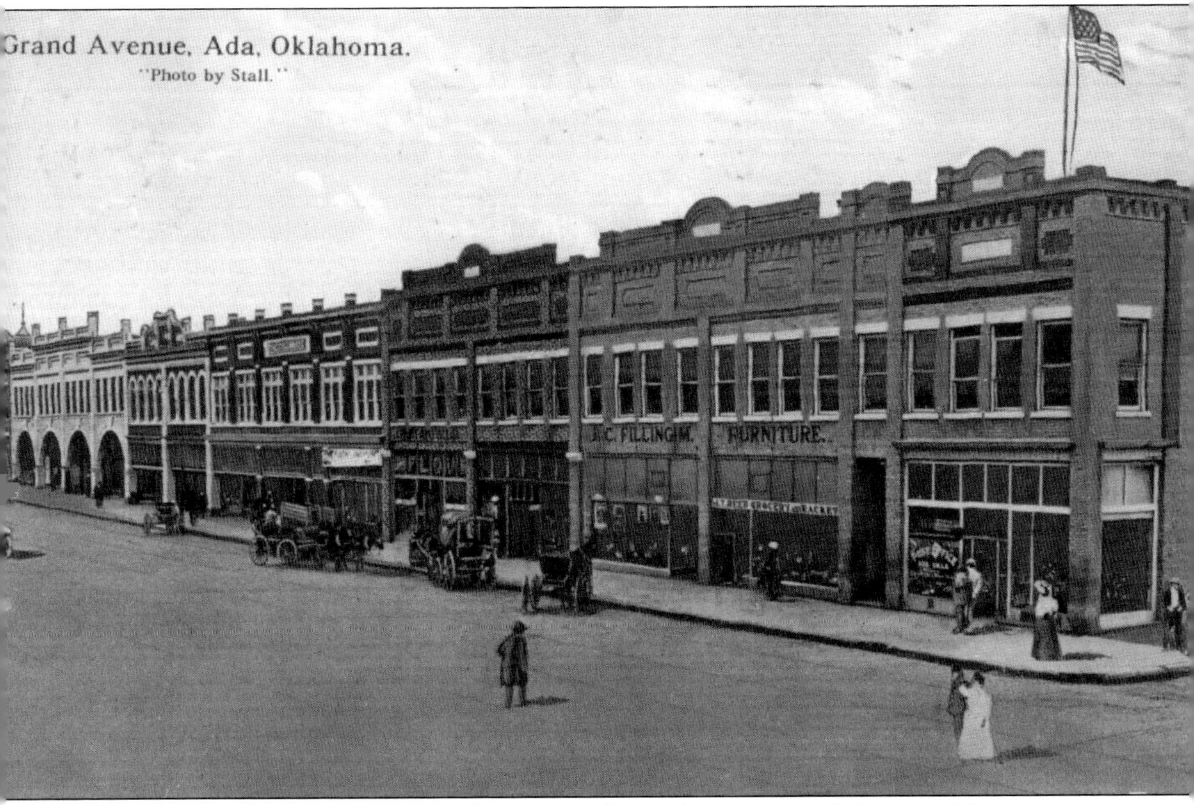

The small post office shown here on the corner of Grande Avenue and Townsend Street was put in business from a small shack that came from the area of Fourth Street, which was where Ada began. The shack was in Daggs Flat when it was literally picked up and moved by 25 new Adans and a team of horses. They transplanted the post office because the postmaster of the doomed community, John Hodges, wouldn't move, even though all the other businesses from the area had signed a contract to do so. He said, "I'll move when I'm daid and in my Diamond Willow coffin." The coffin was on display in his small general store, so the men decided to secure Hodges in it while they moved the shack to Ada. They changed the sign immediately to "Post Office, Ada, Indian Territory." So much for being "daid." Later when Ada moved its business district closer to the railroad, the shack was deserted and a new post office was placed on Grande Avenue. The Ada Post Office is now located on the corner of Twelfth and Rennie Streets. (Courtesy of Gary Haney.)

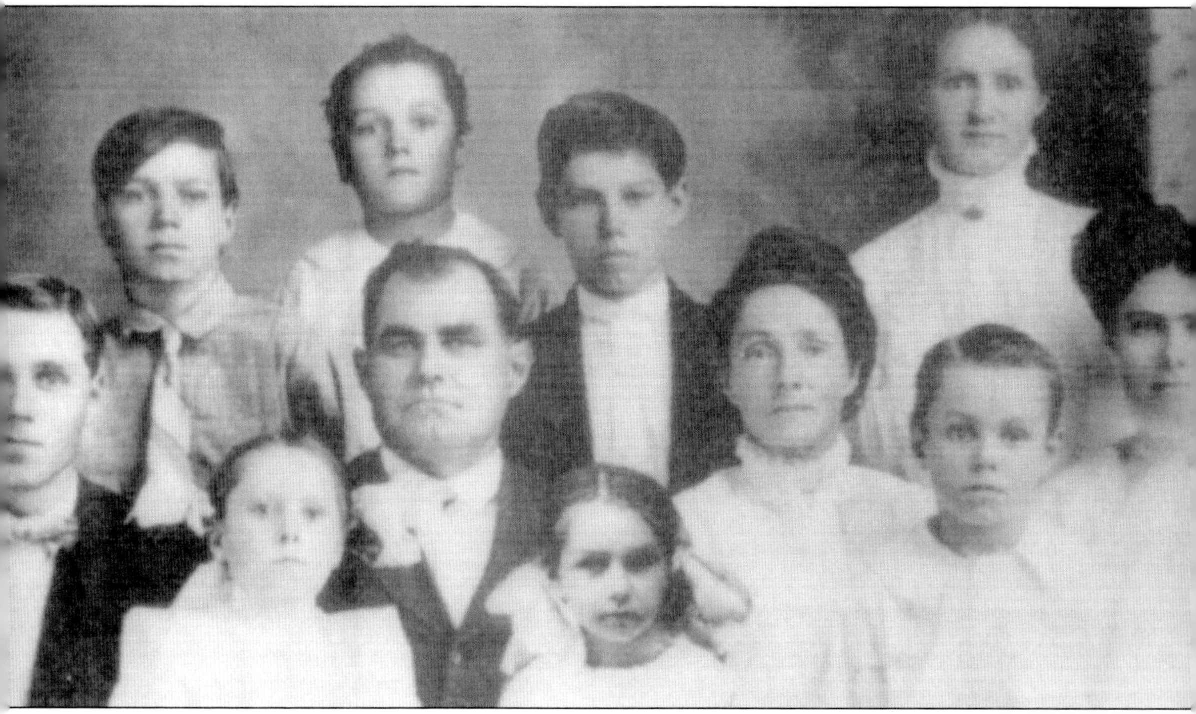

The father of this pioneer family had the honor of having the town named after his eldest daughter. On the far right sits Ada Reed. Her mother, Joanna Reed, selected a site for their home at 522 West Fourth Street. Their home was first a tent and then a log house. Jeff Reed was an important founder of the city of Ada. (Courtesy of Alberta Blackburn.)

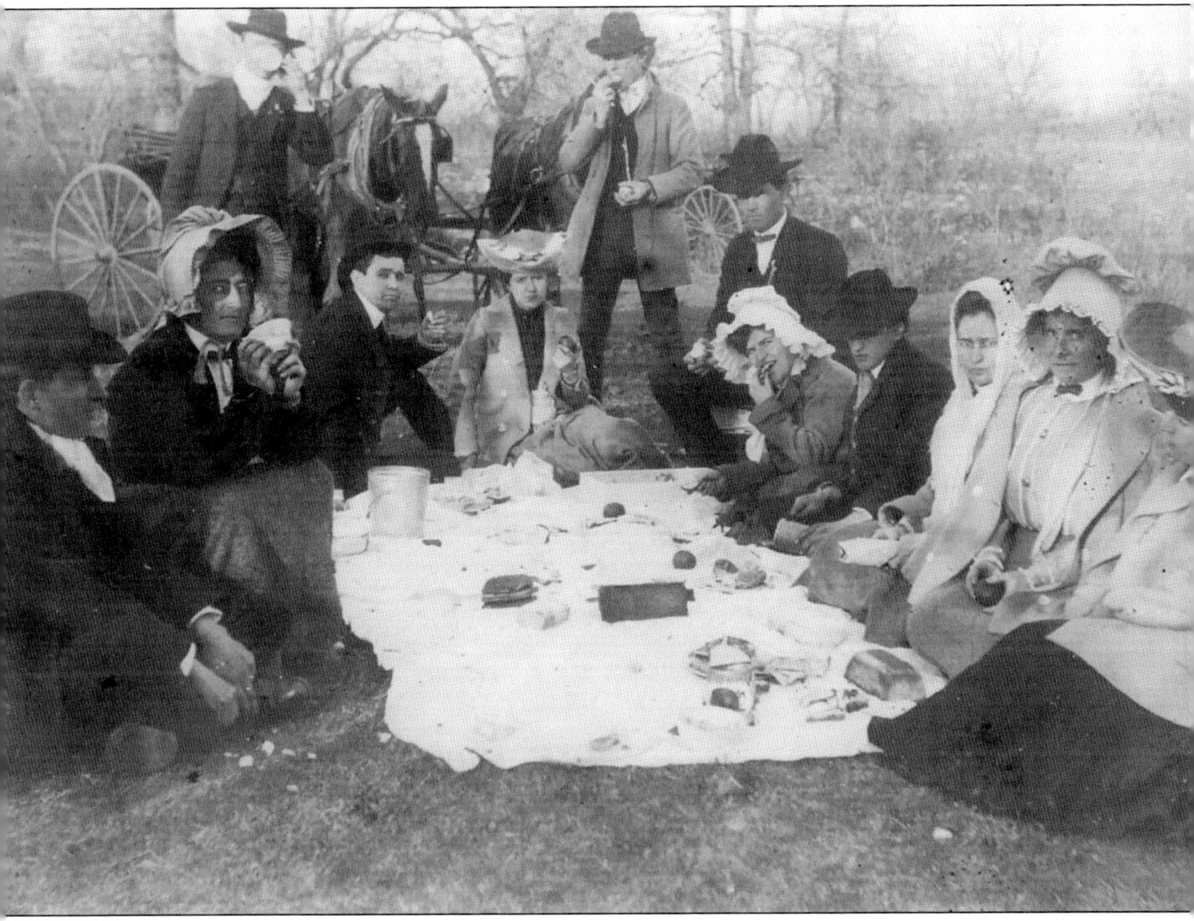

Decked out in their Sunday best, this group spread out their blanket near an apple tree, which suggests that they all have a taste for the sweet, wild fruit. Picnicking was a favorite outing at that time. It is a forgotten pastime that would be nice to revive. (Courtesy of Bud Throne.)

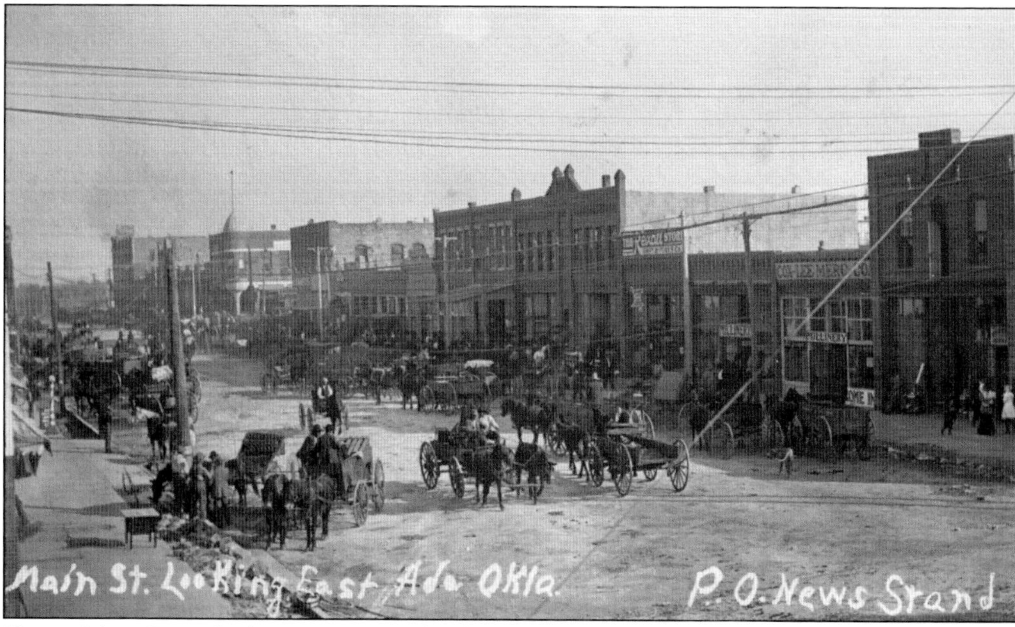

Here is Main Street looking east. Some landmarks are still recognizable today. Broadway Avenue crossed Main Street, which is marked by the rounded, corner building. To this day, Adans keep time by the clock that was later hung from the corner of the bank building. Farther back in the photograph stands the Harris Hotel. Cox-Lee Mercantile Company invites people to come in and check out its millinery selection. (Courtesy of Gary Haney.)

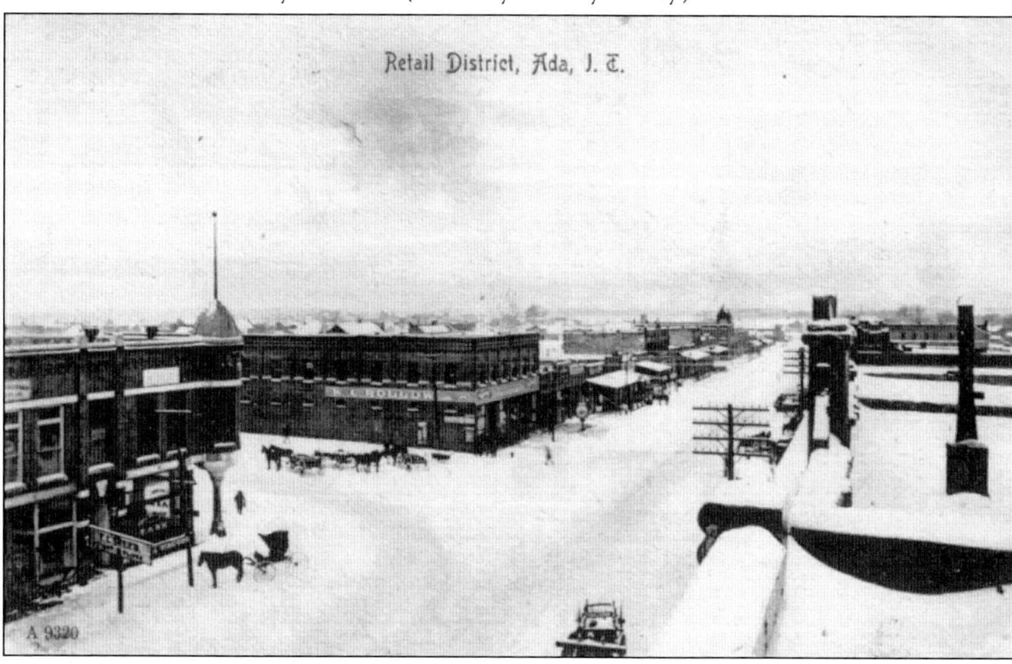

This photograph shows a snowy day in the retail district at the intersection of Main Street and Broadway Avenue. Rollows is across the street, west of the bank building corner, which is where Gem Jewelers is now. S&Q Clothiers occupied that corner for several years until it burned down in 1961. (Courtesy of Gary Haney.)

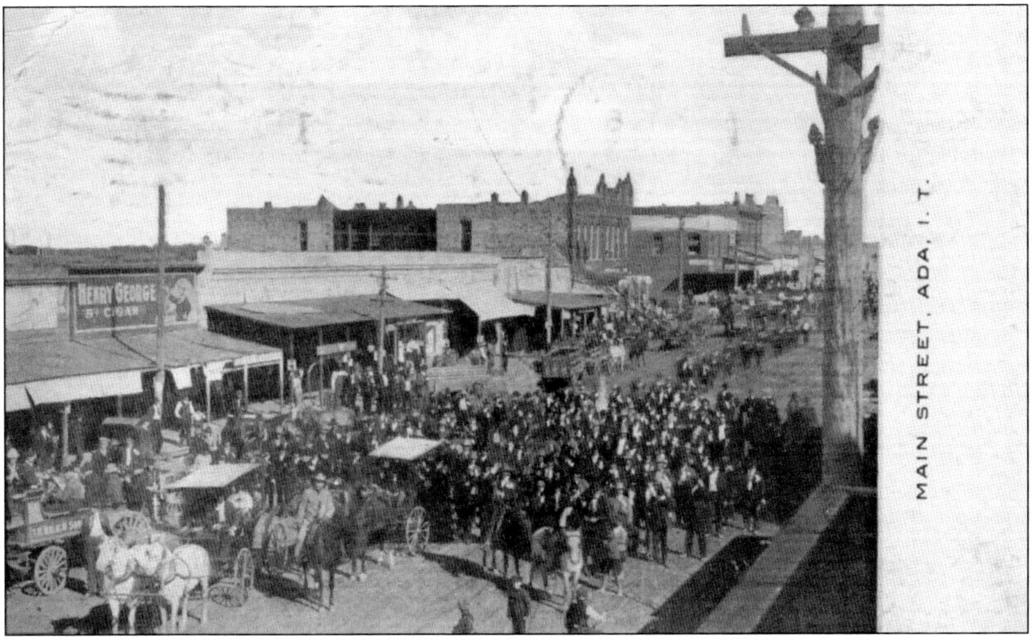

This shot of Main Street shows a large mob of settlers in front of a store advertising Henry George cigars for a nickel. (Courtesy of Gary Haney.)

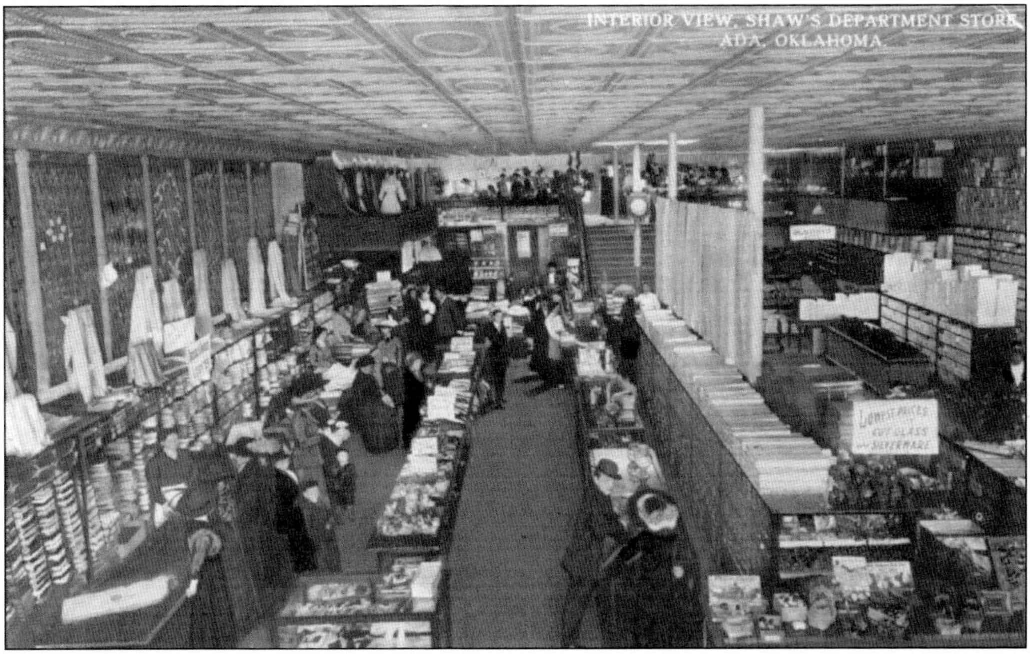

Shaw's Nickel Store was full to the brim with merchandise. Notice the embossed tin ceiling that was popular at that time. The store offered the lowest prices in cut glass and silverware. Shaw's Nickel Store was usually a very busy place. (Courtesy of Gary Haney.)

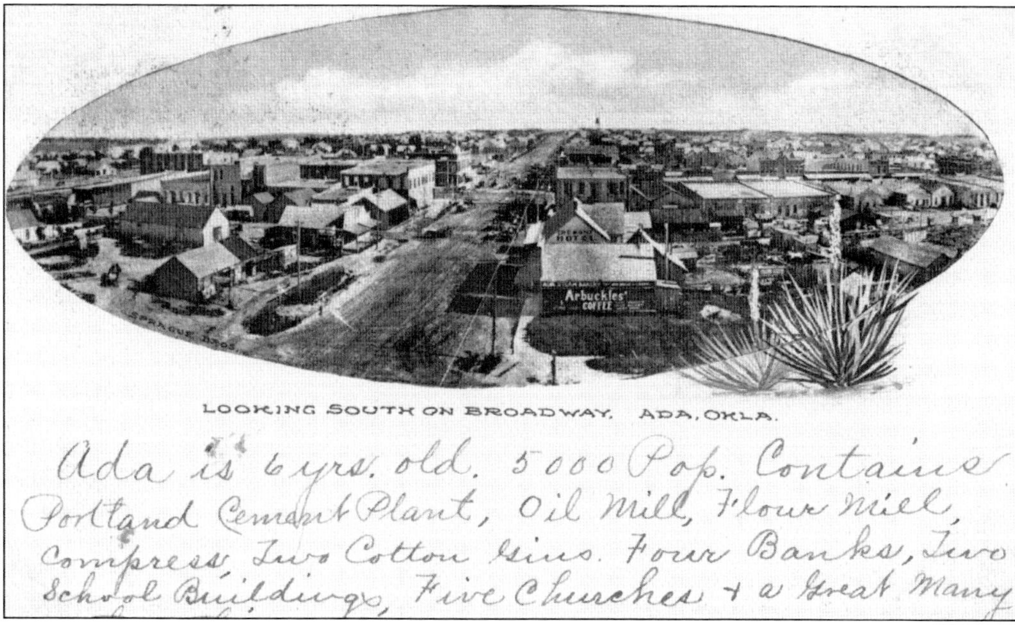

This is a very interesting postcard. At six years of age, Ada had 5,000 people employed at Portland Cement, a cotton oil mill, a flour mill, a cotton compress, and two gins. It had four banks, two schools, five churches, and much more to come. The Tremont Hotel was settled against a bakery that advertised Arbuckle coffee. The far water tower overlooks the small community. (Courtesy of Gary Haney.)

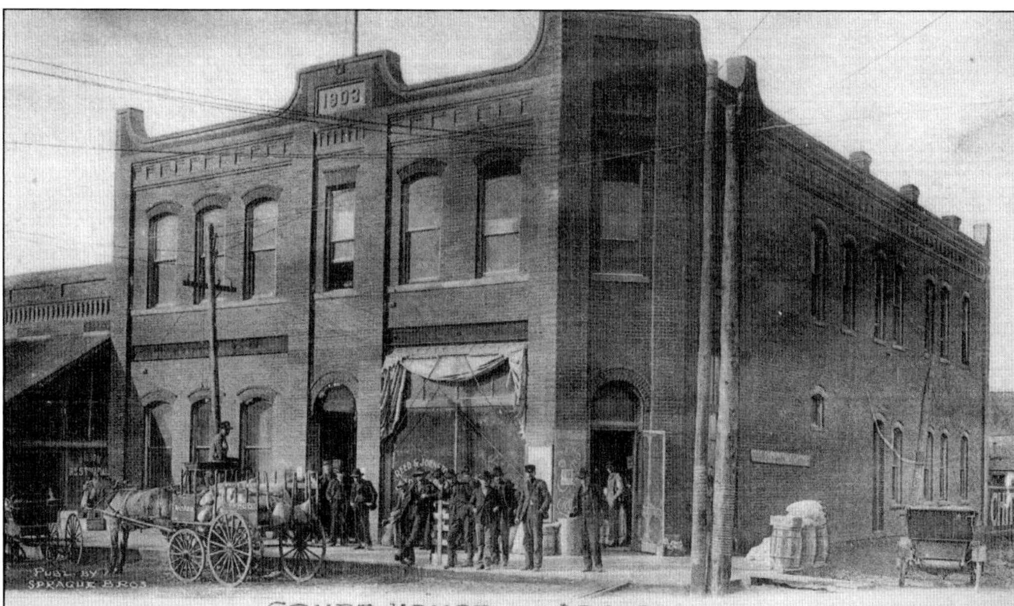

This building, later O.K. Furniture and the Ada Hotel, was the courthouse on the corner of Townsend Avenue and Main Street. The lynching took place a block north in a stable. Crime drew a crowd in those days, and the courthouse at that time was on the northeastern corner of the block referred to as "The Bloody Bucket" and not very far from the infamous Ollie's Blind Pig Saloon, which was fronted with a corset shop. (Courtesy of Gary Haney.)

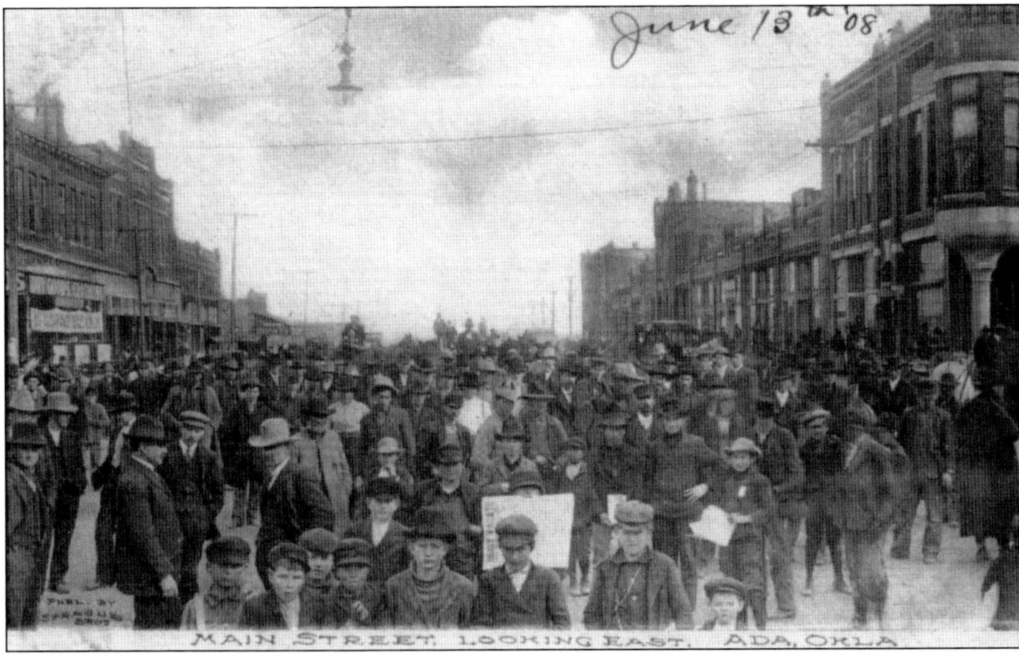

This 1908 view of Main Street is looking east from Broadway Avenue. The women must have stayed home. The bank pedestal corner is to the right. A clock was later hung on the outside corner. The Harris Hotel is on the right, second from last. (Courtesy of Gary Haney.)

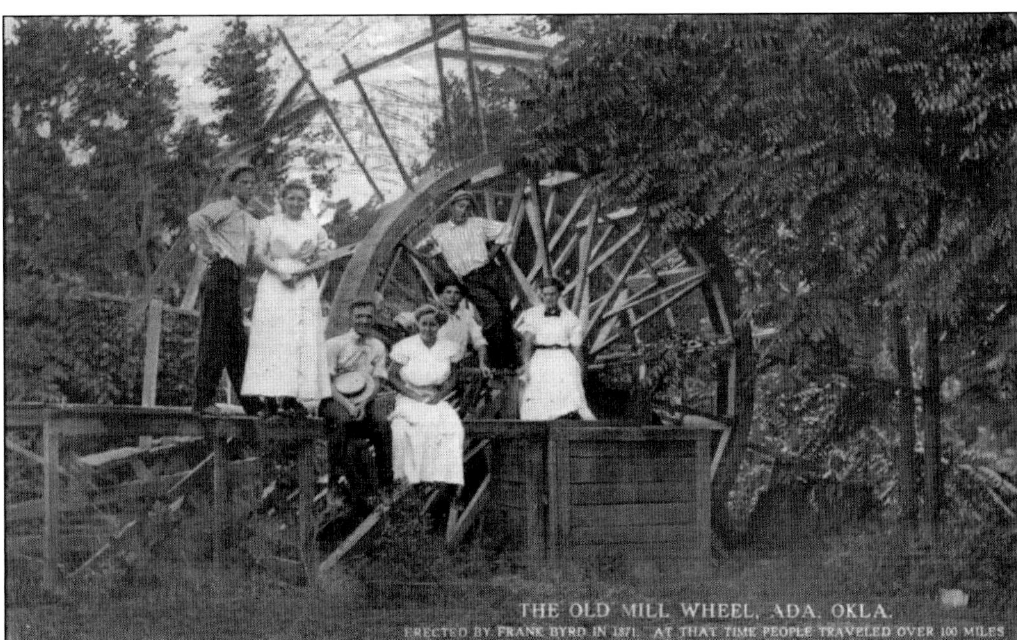

Erected in 1871 by Frank Byrd, the old mill wheel worked for people from over 100 miles away. It was a good location to take a picture with some friends, and these people seem to respect the old mill's reputation. (Courtesy of Gary Haney.)

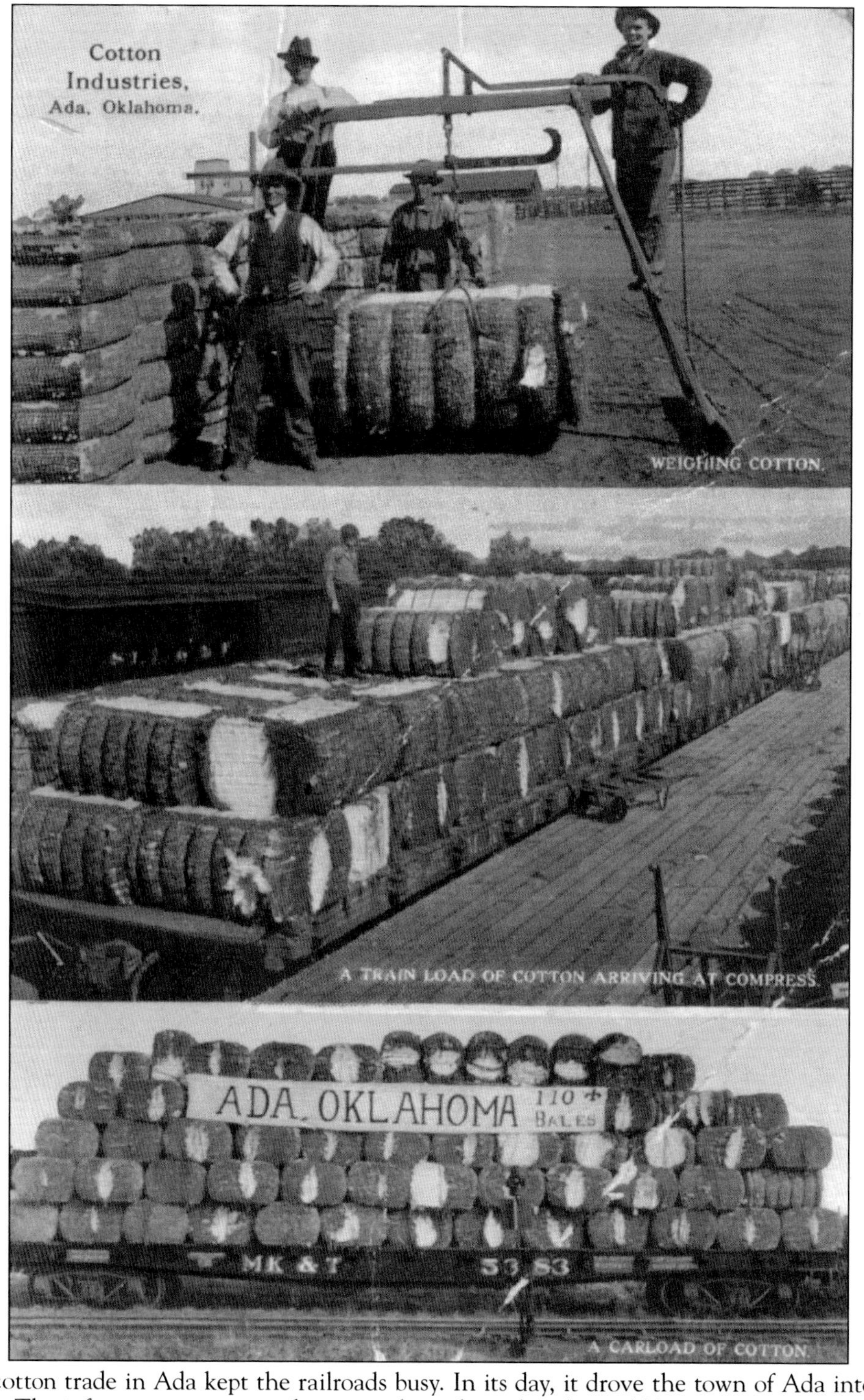

The cotton trade in Ada kept the railroads busy. In its day, it drove the town of Ada into the future. The infant town was moved over to where the railroads would be more accessible for the transport of cotton. This postcard shows that there was an abundance of cotton. (Courtesy of Gary Haney.)

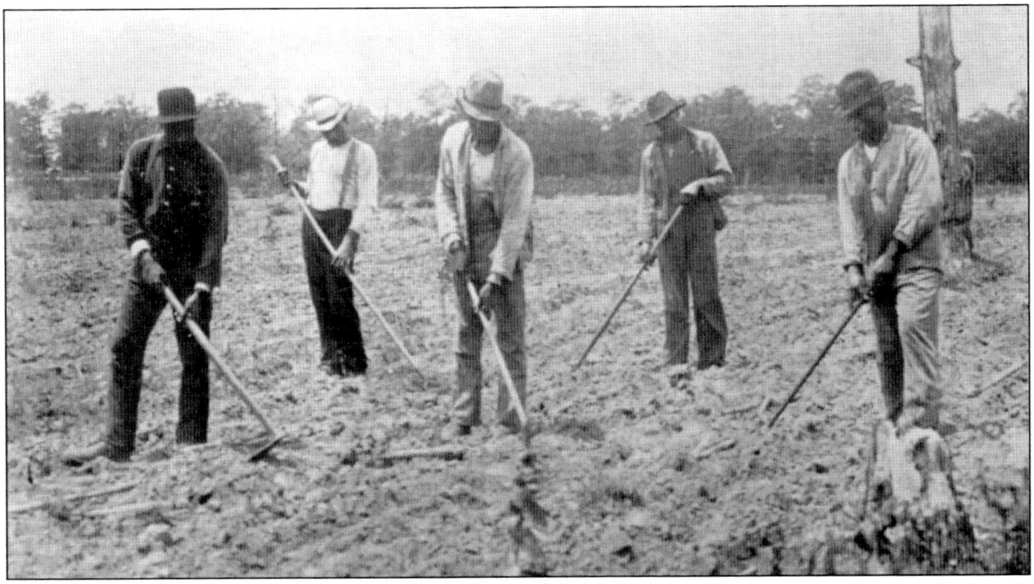

Without the machinery now available, all the work of cultivating the cotton was done by hand. Harvesting it was relatively easy, but chopping and weeding the soil was a long, hard job. (Courtesy of Gary Haney.)

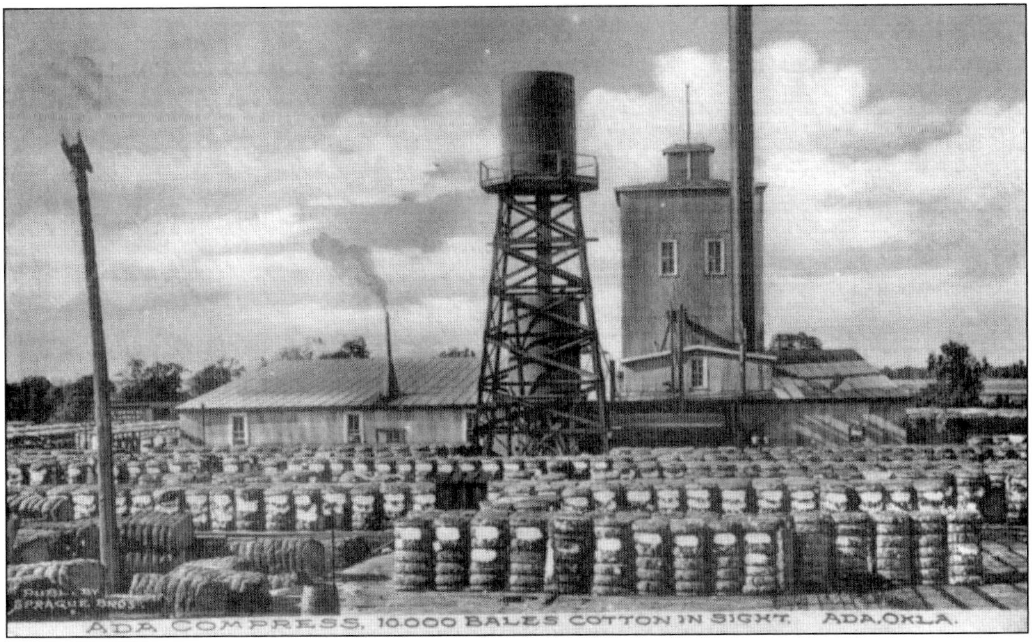

At this time at the Ada Cotton Compress, there were over 10,000 bales in sight. That was a lot of cotton in one place, which made it Ada's bread and butter at that time. (Courtesy of Gary Haney.)

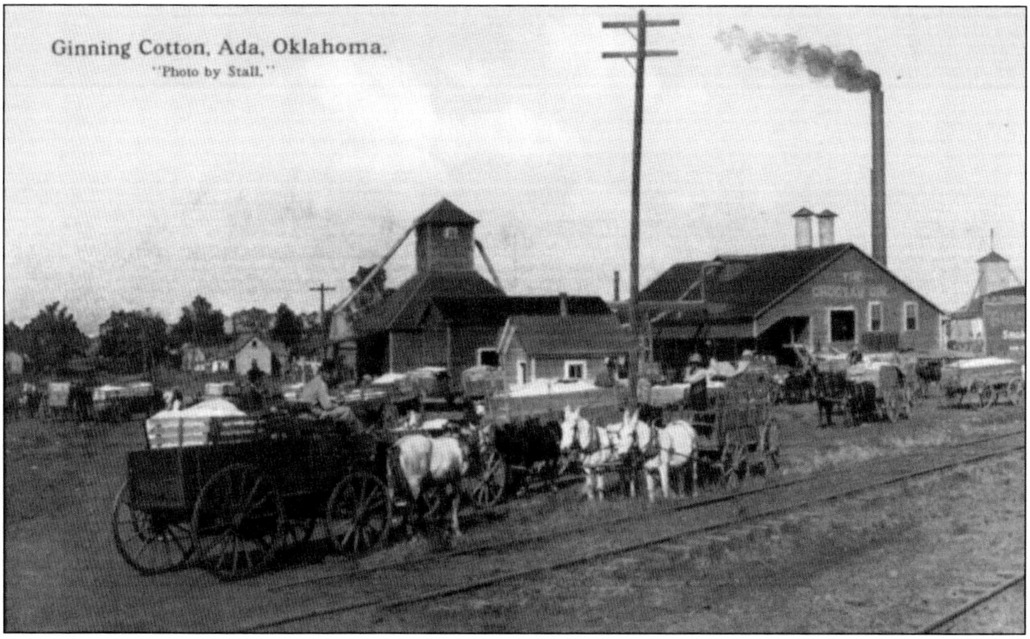

Ginning the cotton was a constant job. Wagon after wagon came to get the job done. Cotton was key to the pioneers' livelihood and survival. (Courtesy of Gary Haney.)

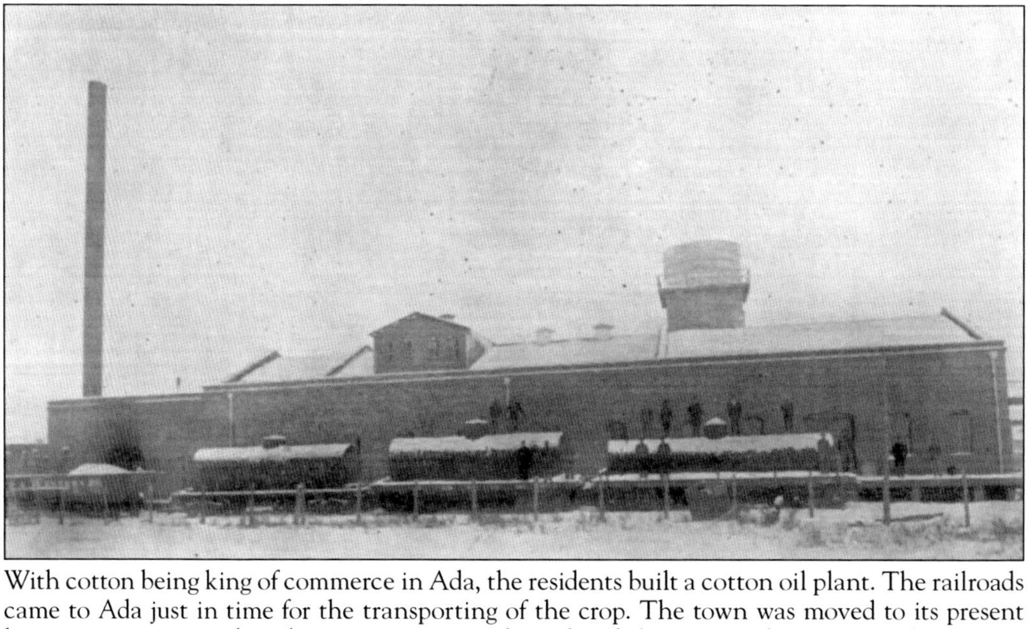

With cotton being king of commerce in Ada, the residents built a cotton oil plant. The railroads came to Ada just in time for the transporting of the crop. The town was moved to its present location to accommodate shipping cotton via the railroad. (Courtesy of Gary Haney.)

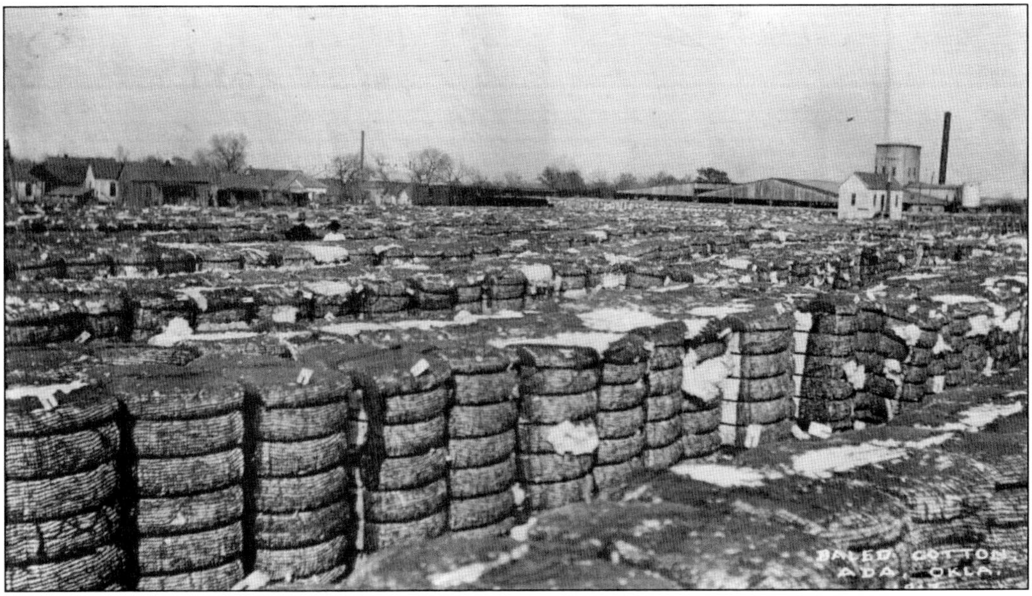

These huge bales of freshly picked cotton sit in bundles in the sunshine, just waiting for the train. The harvest that year was obviously overwhelming. (Courtesy of Gary Haney.)

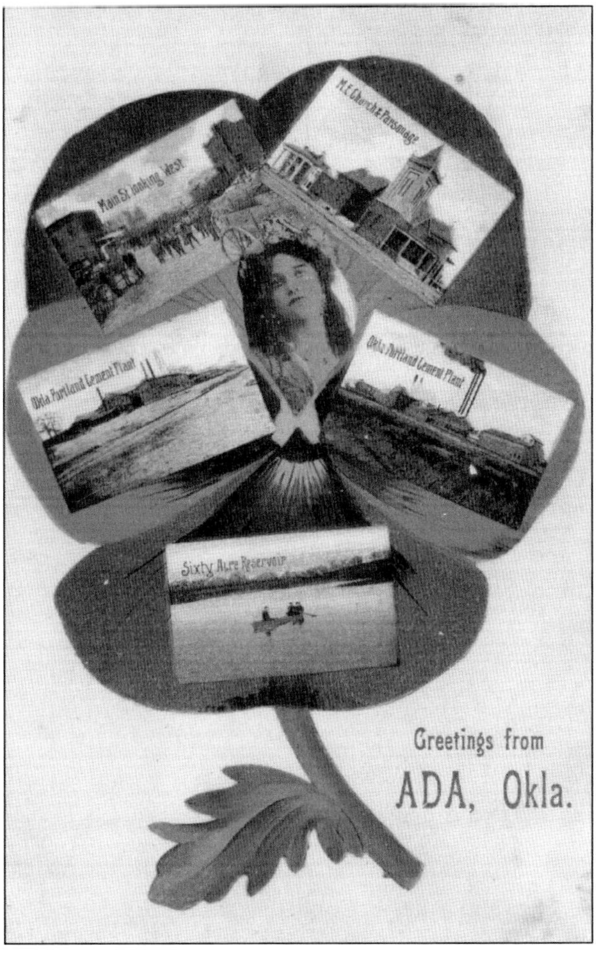

Cards were a popular way to advertise, and some of the unusual ones are especially valuable to collectors today. This one shows four of Ada's reasons for success: Main Street, the Methodist parsonage, the Portland Cement plant, and the reservoir. (Courtesy of Gary Haney.)

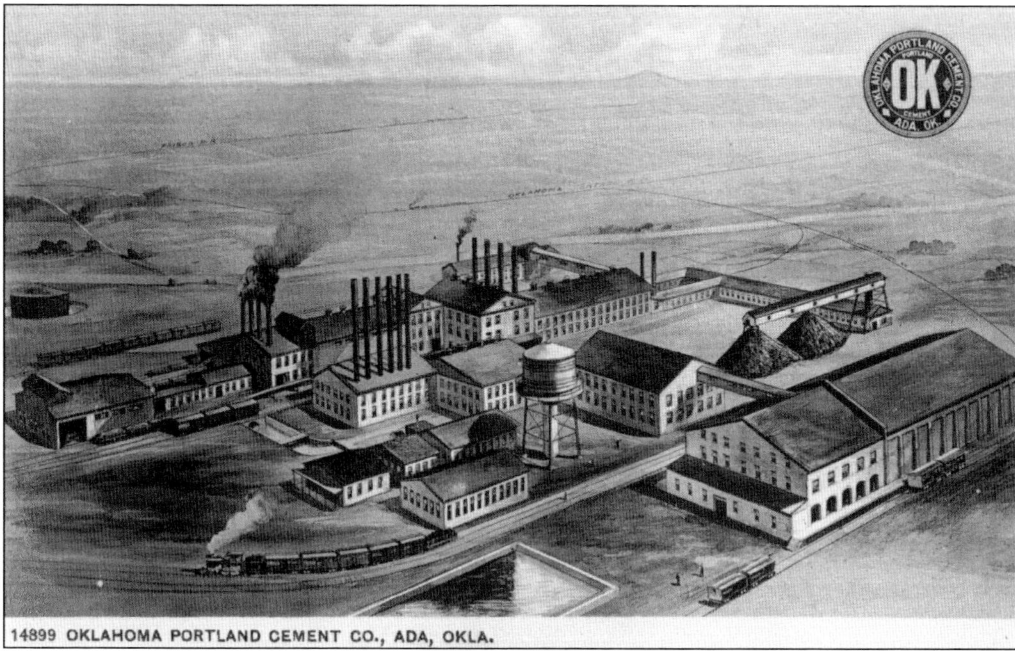

This rendition of what was to come was used by the businessmen who attracted the Portland Cement plant to Ada. This let the city officials see a progressive vision of what they were investing in. (Courtesy of Gary Haney.)

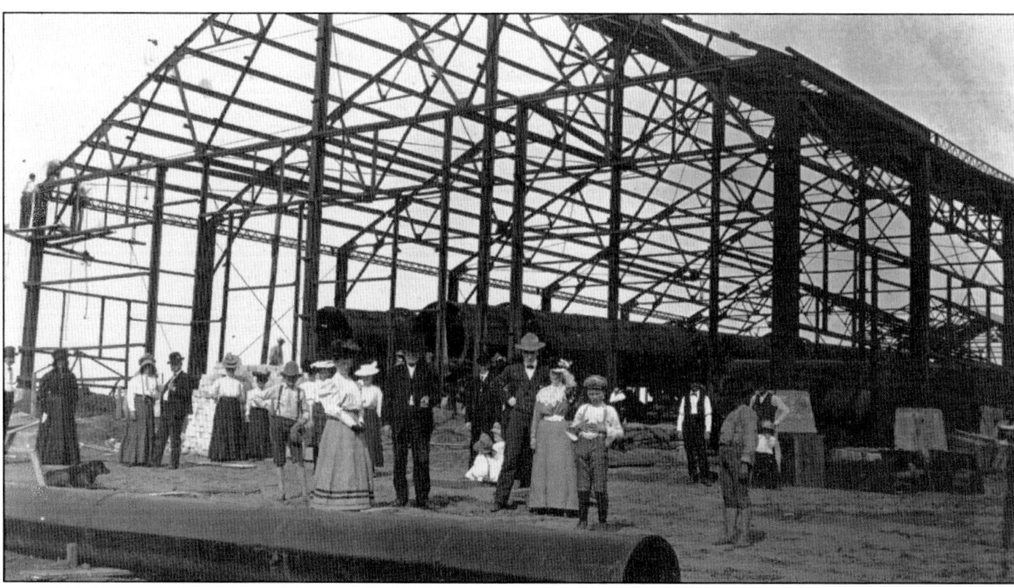

The curious people of Ada came to see the construction of the Portland Cement plant. The coming of the large plant gave hope for workers and for Ada's economy. It was a huge step forward for the town. Although the ownership has changed to Holcim, the plant still exists. (Courtesy of Gary Haney.)

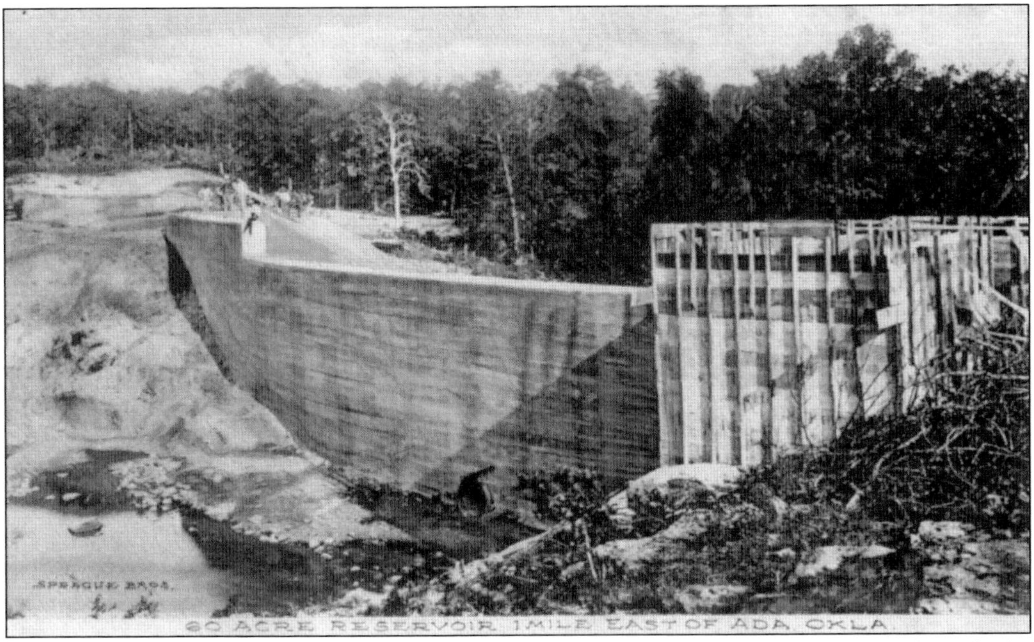

Wintersmith Lake began with the construction of a large reservoir. It was meant to furnish the water needed for the cement plant. The lake and park that followed were named after Francis Wintersmith. She convinced Ada philanthropist P. A. Norris to contribute the land for the reservoir, which also served as a swimming pool for Ada's citizens. She was the wife of one of the founders of the plant, James Wintersmith. (Courtesy of Gary Haney.)

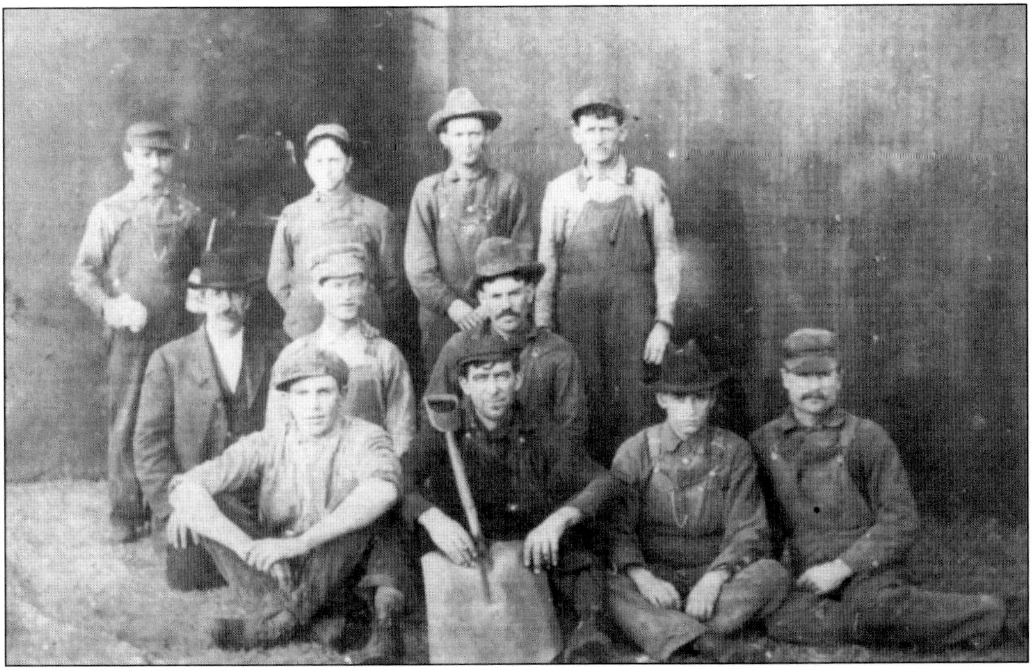

A group of Portland Cement workers take a break. The plant building became a familiar landmark when Adans returned home from trips. When they saw the smoke stacks, it was like a lighthouse waiting for their arrival. (Courtesy of Gary Haney.)

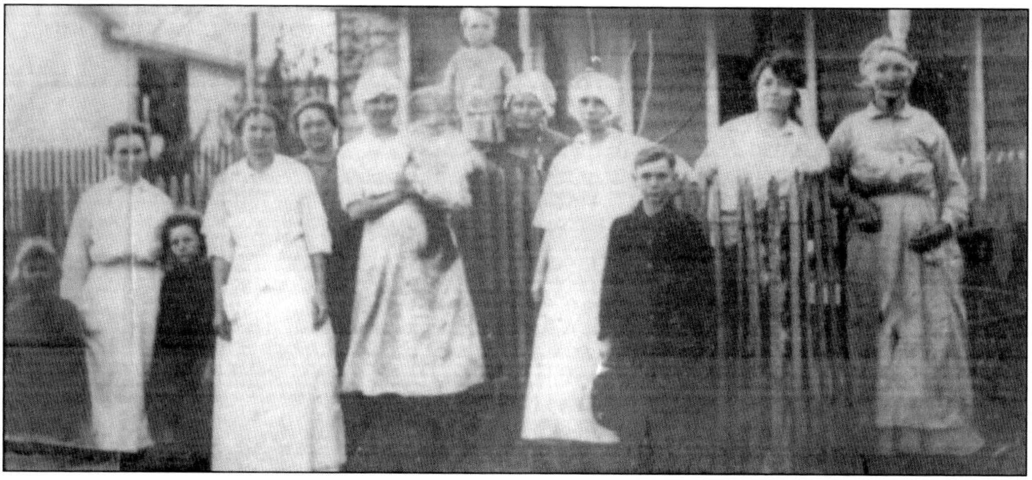

The Rogers-Johnson family gathers for a photograph in Portland Park. Portland Park was a small community, located across from the cement company. It was a popular neighborhood for those who worked at the plant. Today, however, its residents' occupations aren't necessarily related to the plant. (Courtesy of Alberta Blackburn.)

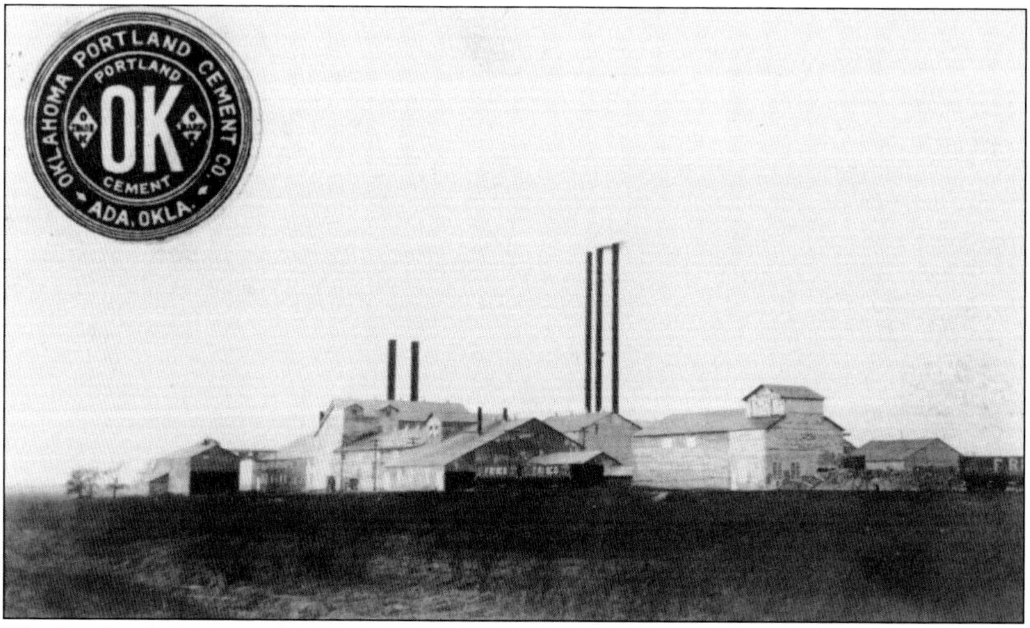

The Portland Cement plant puts its seal of approval on its products and is proud of the plant's productivity. It is one of the largest cement plants in the United States. (Courtesy of Gary Haney.)

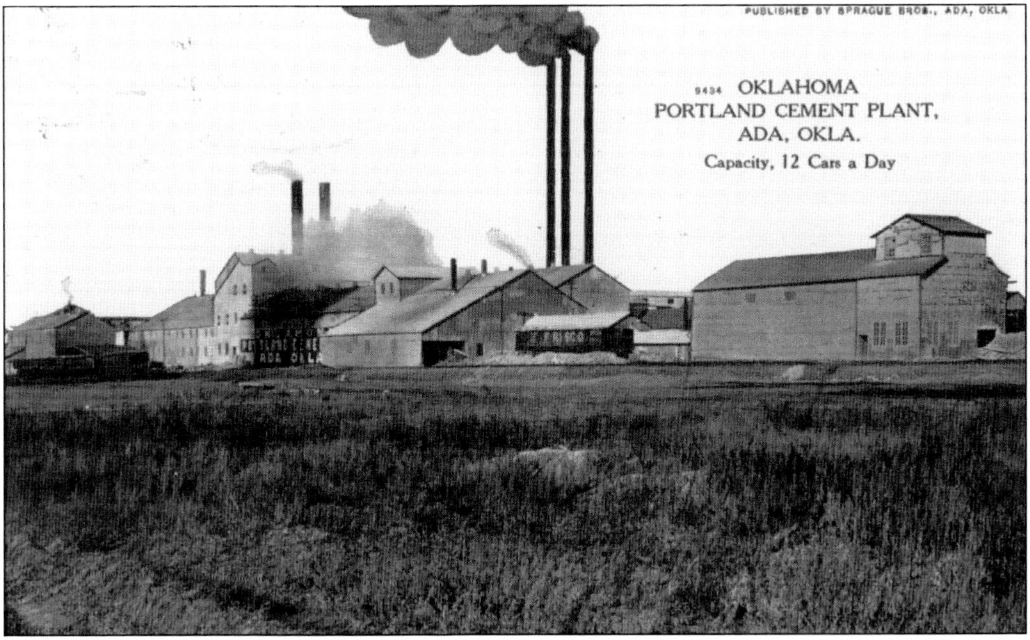

At the time this photograph was taken, the Portland plant was in full swing with the capability of filling 12 railroad cars a day. No one understood that the smokestacks were an environmental issue; they merely represented an obvious sign of prosperity for Ada. (Courtesy of Gary Haney.)

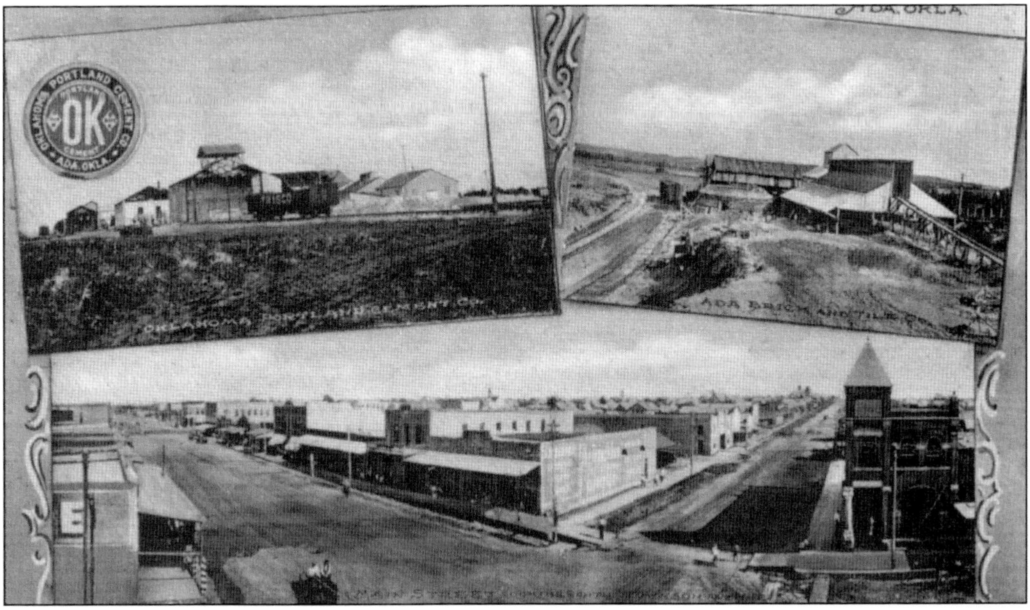

This postcard advertises Ada with three pictures of prosperity, which included the Cement company, the Ada brick plant, and an overview of downtown. The intent of this postcard was to make people take Ada seriously as a town that had expansion in its future. (Courtesy of Gary Haney.)

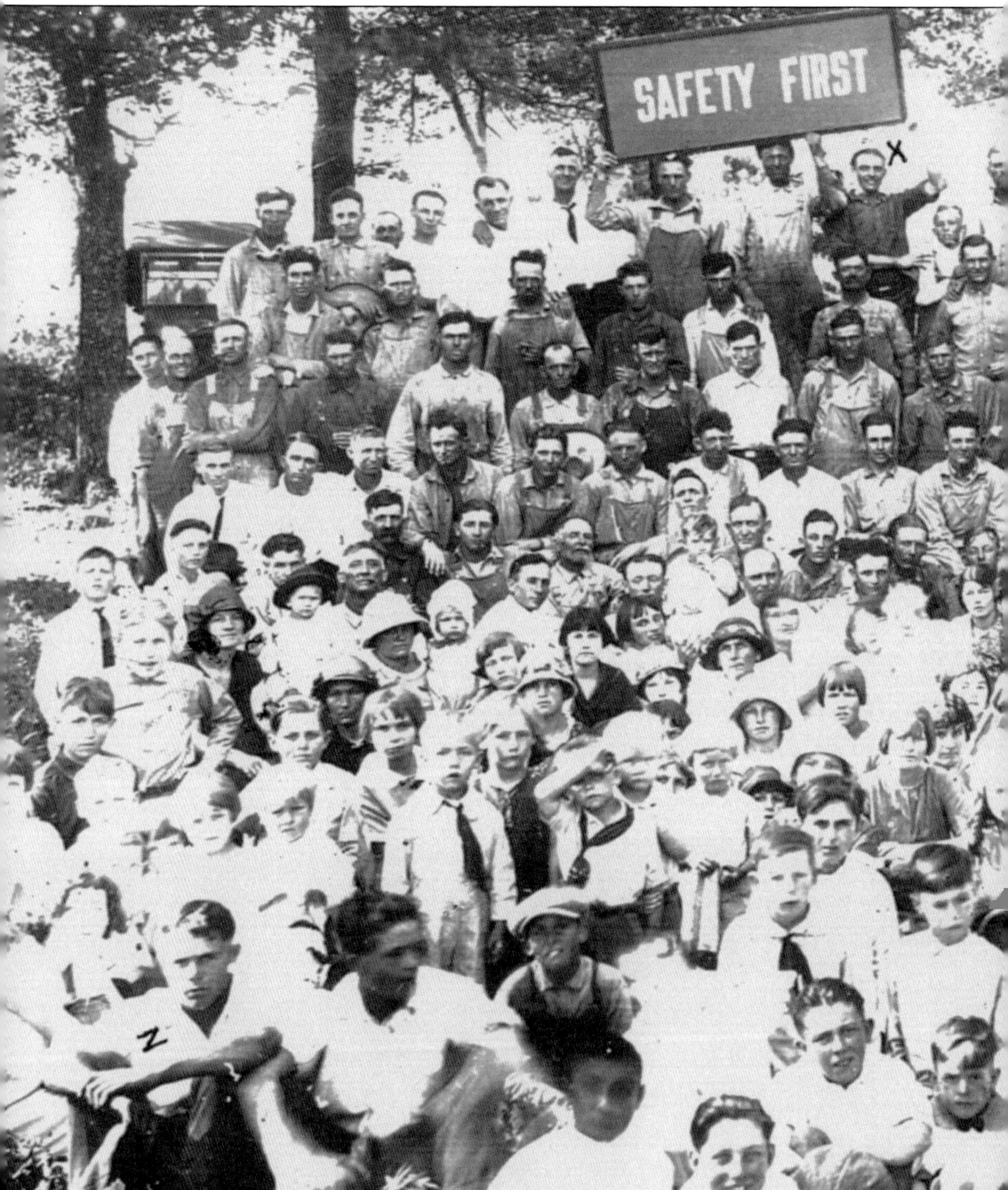

The Portland Cement plant gave many Adans a place to work, and this annual picnic shows how much they appreciated it. The plant was the reason for Wintersmith Park, a recreational area southeast of Ada. A lake that was made to supply water for industrial needs was turned into

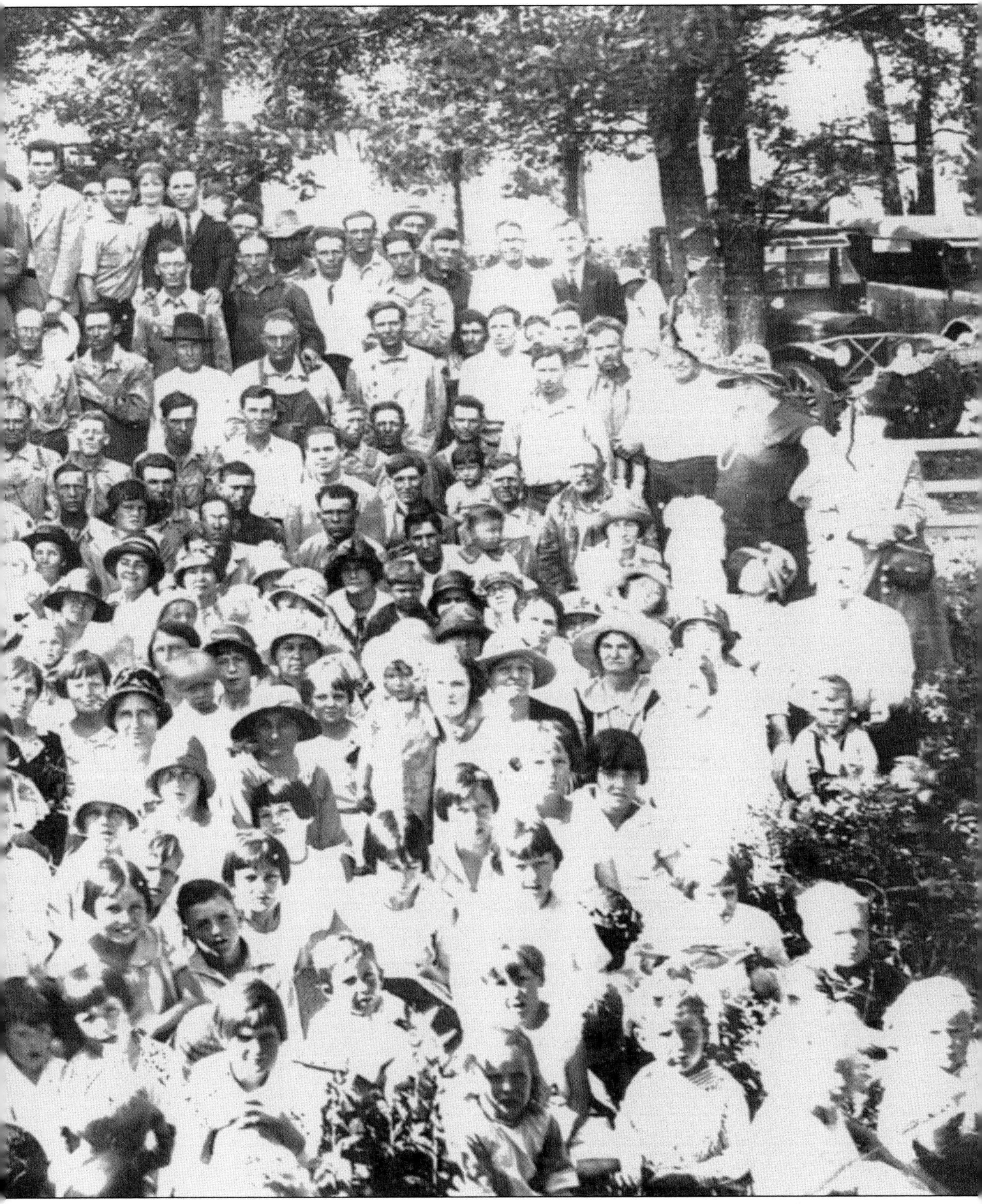

a beautiful park for many outdoor activities. With cement tables and benches, bridges over a meandering stream, several playgrounds, and cement walking paths, it is today one of the most beautiful spots for recreation in Oklahoma. (Courtesy of Gary Haney.)

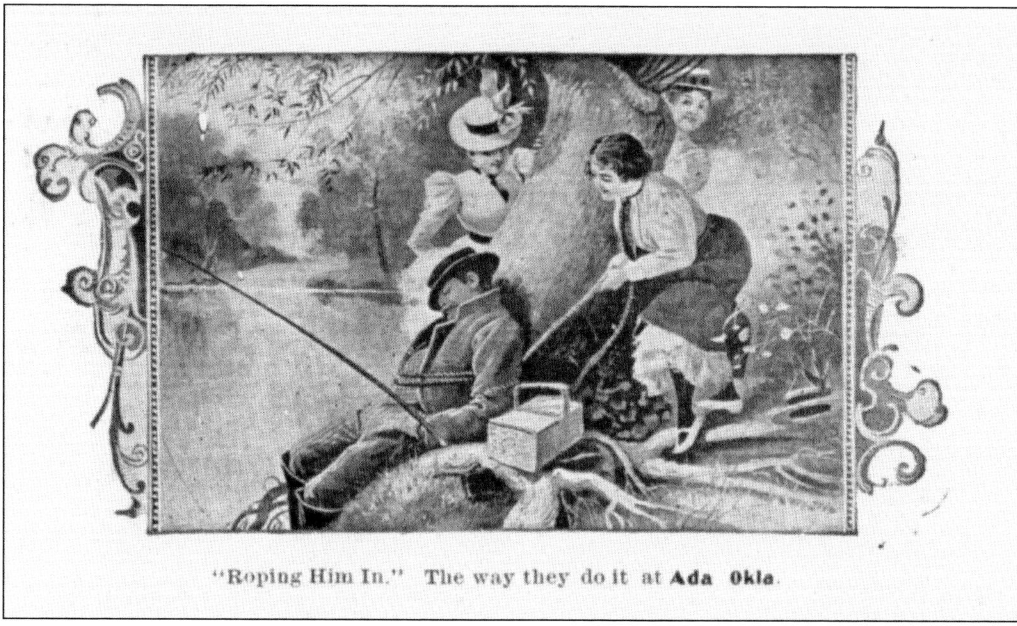

This postcard shows a sleeping fisherman with women lassoing him from behind a tree. Under the picture is the statement: "Roping Him In. The way they do it in Ada, Okla." This must have been a popular postcard during Rodeo week. Creative postcards like this were very popular before the time of easily accessible photography. (Courtesy of Gary Haney.)

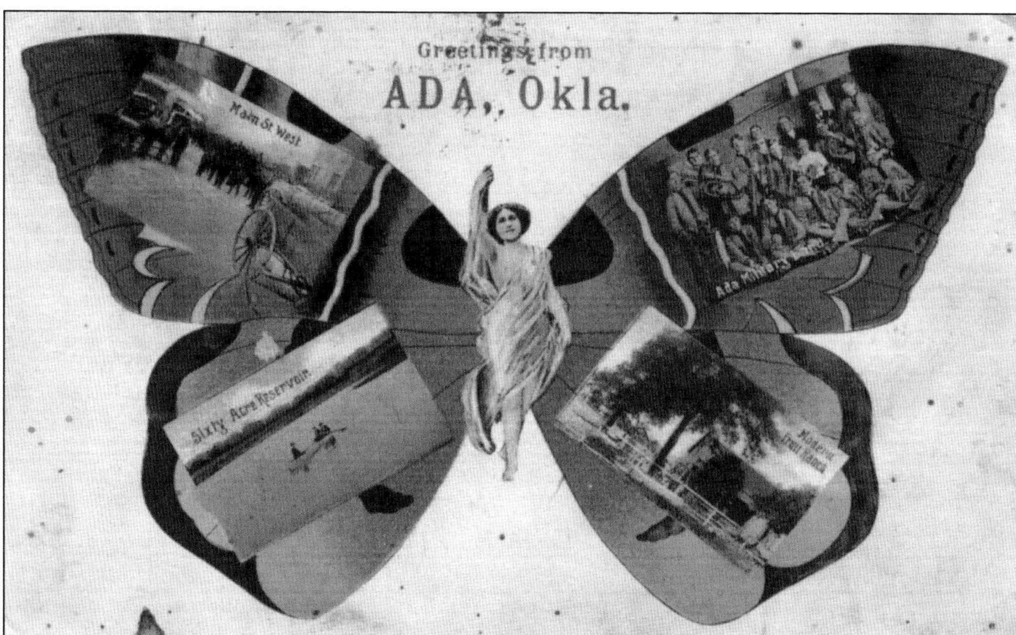

Here is a postcard that artfully advertises a full spectrum of Ada attractions: Main Street West, the reservoir, the military band, and a modern fruit ranch. Gary Haney, the collector of many of these cards, has approximately 10,000 pieces of Ada memorabilia. (Courtesy of Gary Haney.)

Two

Exodus

The *Ada Evening News* was started in 1901, and for 50¢ a year, people could buy subscriptions to it. The newspaper vowed to give away the paper to families that were too poor to afford it. On Broadway Avenue, between Main Street and Tenth Street, the news was gathered and printed. It is still in the same location, even after fires destroyed previous buildings.

The lack of much law enforcement made Ada a good place to harbor criminals. Ada's law, Bob Nester, a U.S. marshal, did all he could do, but despite his efforts, the west end of Ada's Main Street became known as "The Bucket of Blood." The scourge of the west took refuge on the block and did whatever they pleased with no retribution. It was the perfect place for undesirables to hide.

A retired U.S. marshal, Gus Bobbitt lived outside of Ada on his Lightning Ridge Ranch. Disturbed by the dangerous criminal activity in Ada and the conniving way the Native Americans were being cheated out of their land, he vowed to change the land agent elections and elect honest men to assist the Native Americans in keeping their land.

Some of the greedy ranchers weren't happy with Bobbitt's interference and hired a notorious assassin, Jim Miller, from Texas, to come to Ada and kill Bobbitt. Deacon Miller was known to ambush his victims. He welcomed the price he was offered to kill Bobbitt.

The murder was accomplished, with four men being pointed out as collaborators. They were all jailed and awaited trial. However, on April 19, 1909, the night before a questionable trial, a well prepared group of men physically took the four men from the jail and lynched them in a stable not far away. No one, to this day, knows who made up the mob that changed the history of the wild west. The exodus of the outlaws in "The Bucket of Blood" has been attributed to this brave act.

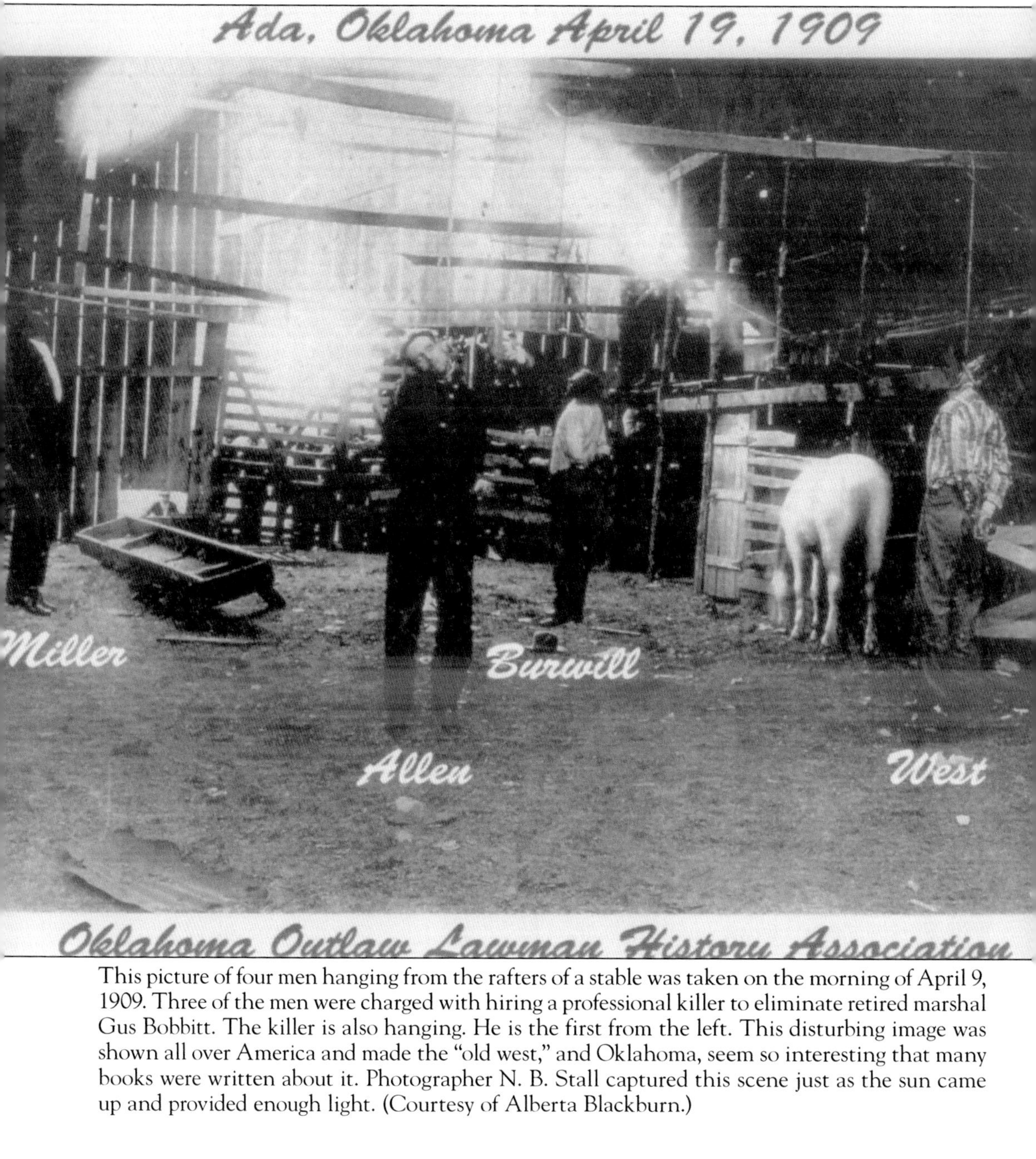

This picture of four men hanging from the rafters of a stable was taken on the morning of April 9, 1909. Three of the men were charged with hiring a professional killer to eliminate retired marshal Gus Bobbitt. The killer is also hanging. He is the first from the left. This disturbing image was shown all over America and made the "old west," and Oklahoma, seem so interesting that many books were written about it. Photographer N. B. Stall captured this scene just as the sun came up and provided enough light. (Courtesy of Alberta Blackburn.)

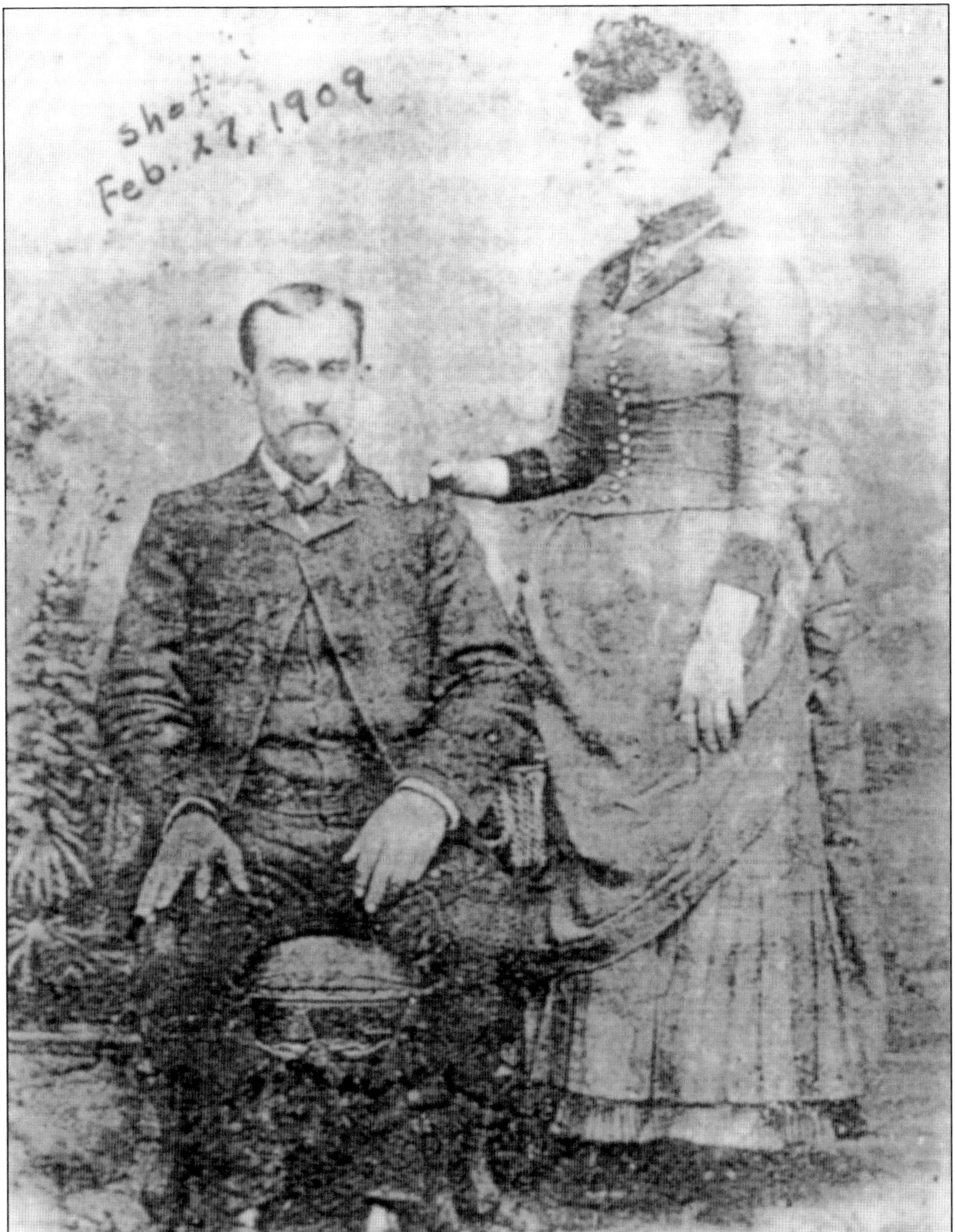

Prior to his untimely death, Gus Bobbitt was well respected and was getting ready to put a stop to all the corruption in Ada. He was a retired U.S. marshal who still tried to keep the peace. Bobbitt and a few of his brave friends, including Bob Nester, went down to Ollie's Blind Pig Saloon, stood along the bar, and had a cowboy stare-down just to prove his point. He was a brave man and did not deserve to be shot from behind a tree by a coward. (Courtesy of Alberta Blackburn.)

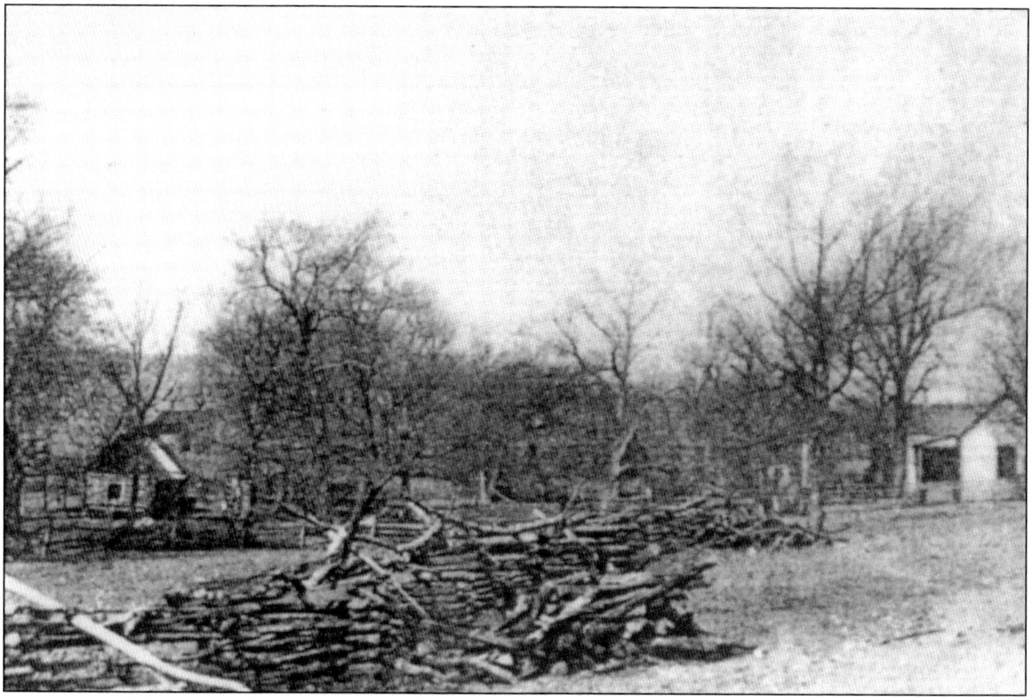

This is Gus Bobbitt's Lightning Ridge home, located southwest of Ada. He was just a few miles from home when Jim Miller ambushed him. Gus was in a wagon, bringing home supplies. He died from the shotgun blast, but his wife made it to his side just before he passed away. The hired killer rode away from the scene immediately. (Courtesy of Alberta Blackburn.)

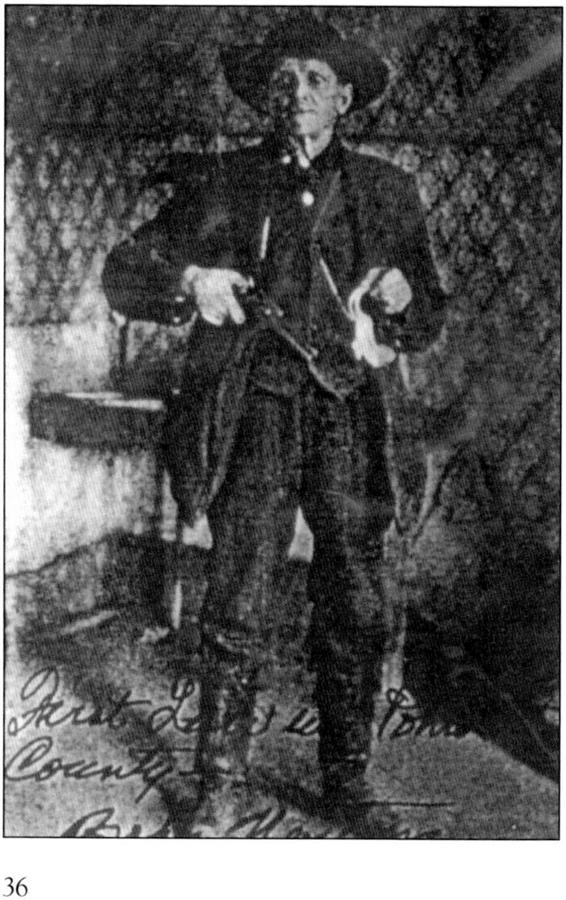

Bow-legged, short, and deaf, Bob Nester was a U.S. deputy in early Ada. A loyal servant of the law, he was even wounded during the removal of the men who were taken to be lynched. (Courtesy of Alberta Blackburn.)

Moman Pruiett, the notorious, unscrupulous lawyer who was hired to defend Jim Miller, was a major reason for the lynching. He truthfully boasted of defending 343 criminals charged with murder, with a total of 303 of these cases ending with acquittals. President Roosevelt gave Pruiett's only client sentenced to death clemency. (Courtesy of Alberta Blackburn.)

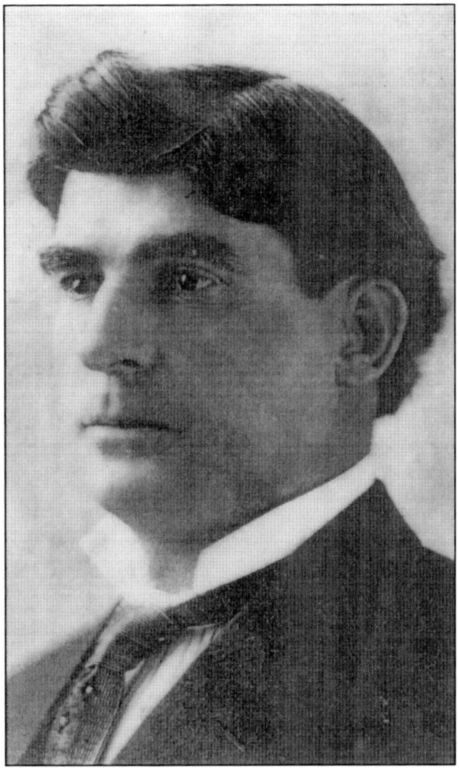

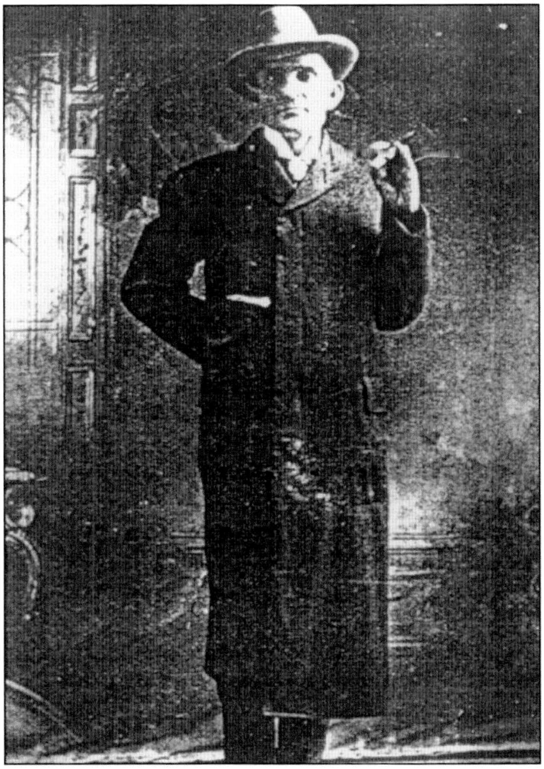

Cocky and proud, Jim Miller had this portrait taken in his infamous trench coat. He wore it at all times, and nobody knew that he had fashioned a breastplate of metal to wear under it. This is one reason why he lived through all his gunfights. He was one of the most feared killers of the era; however, he was also a deacon in his church and was well liked in many places. (Courtesy of Alberta Blackburn.)

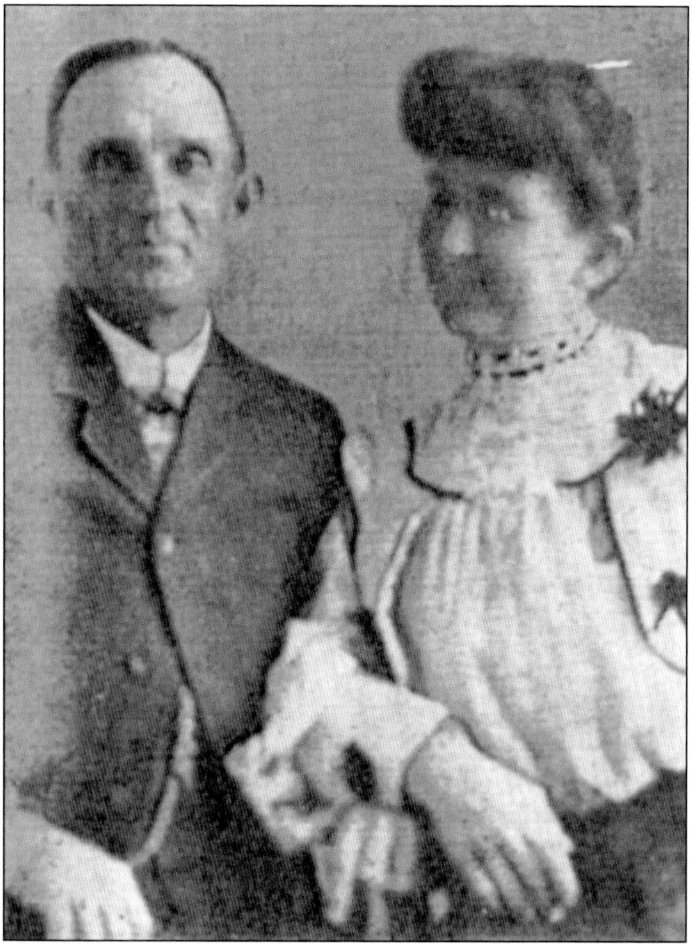

Miller liked his looks and was proud of his fastidious appearance. While in jail, he had a local laundry supply him with fresh shirts daily, and his meals were delivered from a cafe across the street. He thought that the pompous lawyer, Moman Pruiett, would get him off—and he probably would have—but what Miller did not know was that the people of Ada were determined to put an end to him. (Courtesy Alberta Blackburn.)

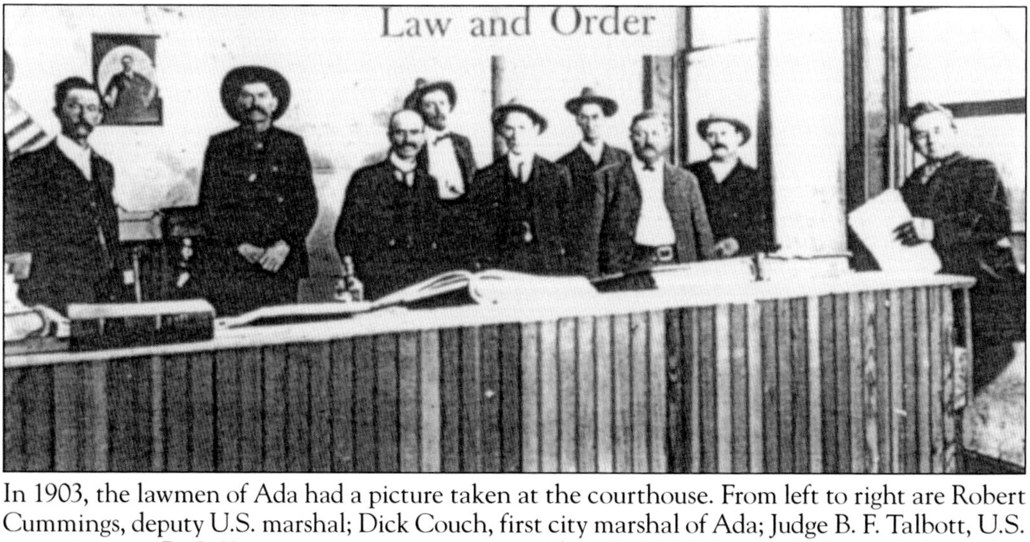

In 1903, the lawmen of Ada had a picture taken at the courthouse. From left to right are Robert Cummings, deputy U.S. marshal; Dick Couch, first city marshal of Ada; Judge B. F. Talbott, U.S. commissioner; B. C. King, pioneer attorney; two unidentified; T. F. Brents, U.S. marshal; rancher A. A. (Gus) Bobbitt; and attorney Sid Tolbert. (Courtesy of Alberta Blackburn.)

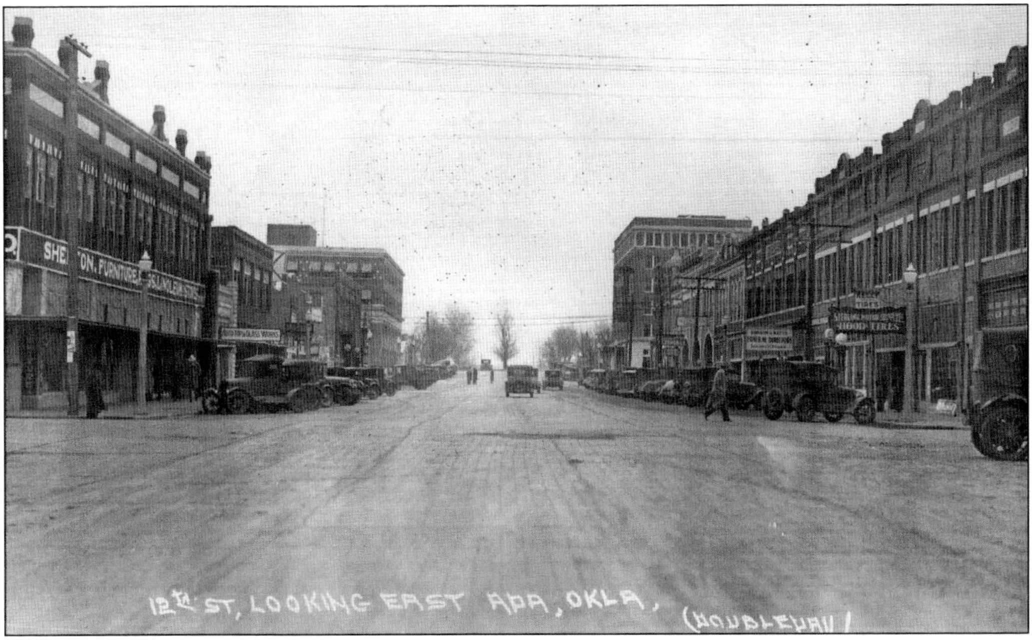

This is a view of Twelfth Street looking east. It was a very full street at the time. Before Eleventh Street became Main Street because the businesses there were in greater demand, this street was the main road and was called Grande Avenue. (Courtesy of Gary Haney.)

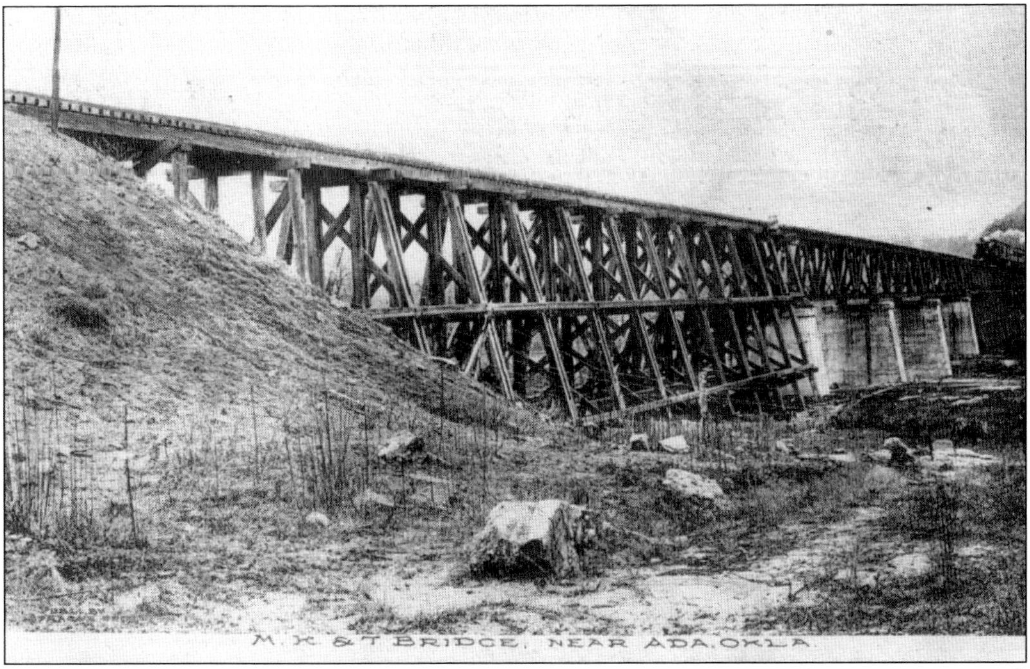

The MK&T railroad trestle, located south of Ada, had two lanes going to the town of Stonewall and on to Texas. The long bridge was considered dangerous because it had a hill to its north and a curve to its south. A road just north of the bridge turned west and led across approximately 5 miles to the community of Latta, which was just southwest of Ada. (Courtesy of Gary Haney.)

HEADQUARTERS ADA POLICE DEPARTMENT

——$50 REWARD——

For recovery 1926-27 Model Buick Coupe, Oklahoma 1927 License No. 589-142, Serial No. 1649301, Motor No. 1700905, dark blue duco body, black running gear, glass in motor meter cracked, crank that raises glass in right hand door was off and lying on shelf behind seat, left rear fender dented on rim. Stolen from South Broadway Avenue, Ada, Oklahoma, at about 8:00 P. M., October 17, 1927. Car equipped with four Goodyear balloon tires, size 31x5.25, non-skid new tread; two spare tires, one Goodyear 31x5.25, non-skid new tread and one Goodrich 31x5.25. Paint, top, fender and lamps in good condition.

NOTIFY SAM HARGIS, CHIEF OF POLICE,

October 18, 1927 Ada, Oklahoma

The Ada chief of police in 1927, Sam Hargis, had his 1926–1927 model Buick Coupe stolen. He must have been proud of it, considering how many details he was able to list in this reward notice. Hopefully he found it and jailed the thief. (Courtesy of Gary Haney.)

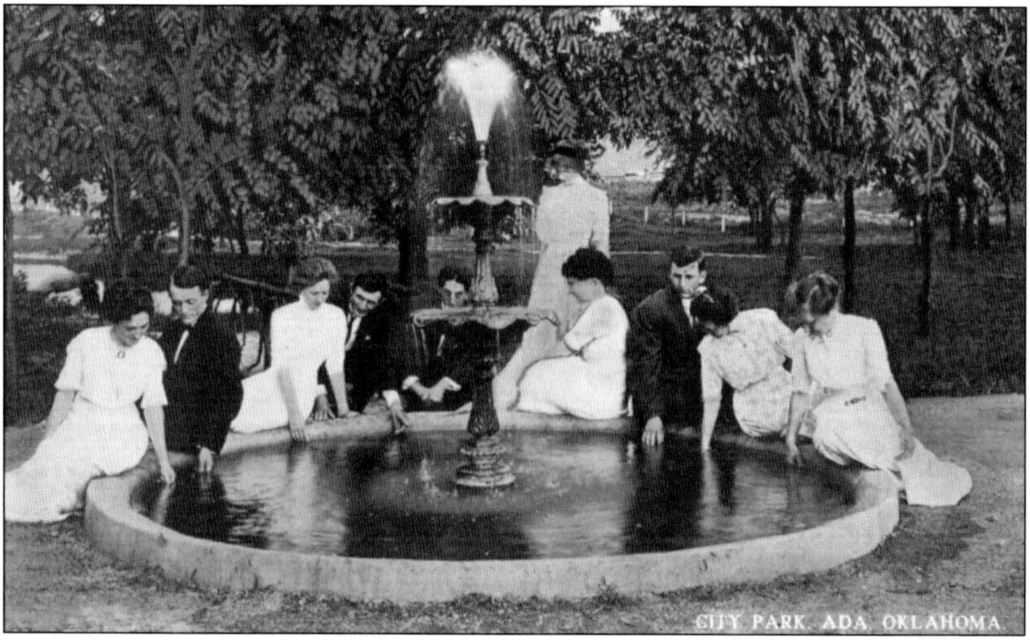

This city park fountain was a good place to meet friends, wash your hands, and look pretty while doing it. The ladies' clothing is the height of fashion for the times. Modesty was in full bloom. (Courtesy of Gary Haney.)

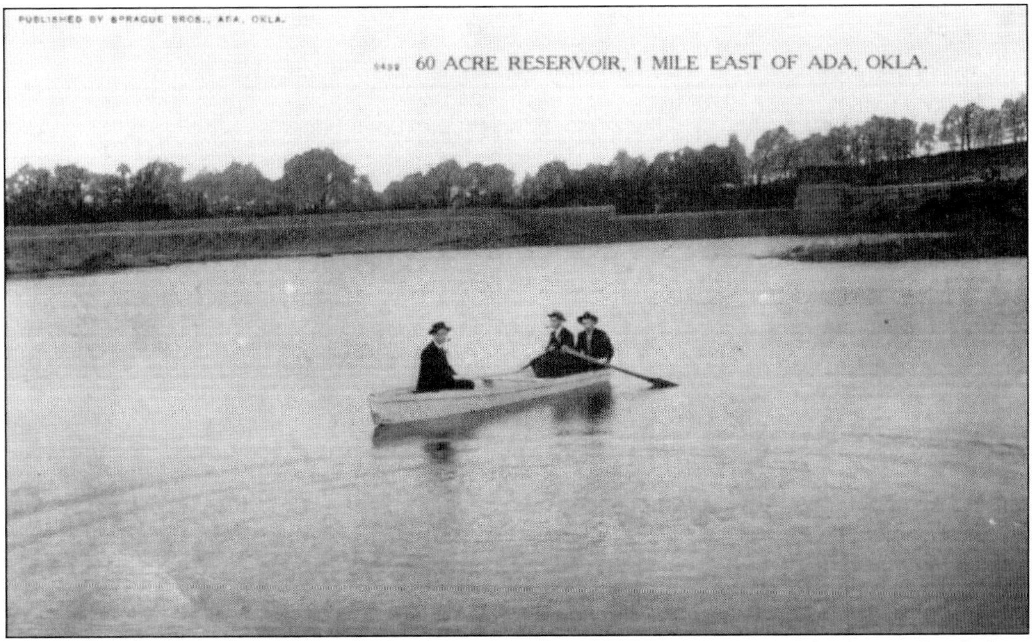

Wintersmith Lake put these three men's minds at ease. The lake helped supply the Portland Plant with water and, eventually, became a beautiful centerpiece for Wintersmith Park. (Courtesy of Gary Haney.)

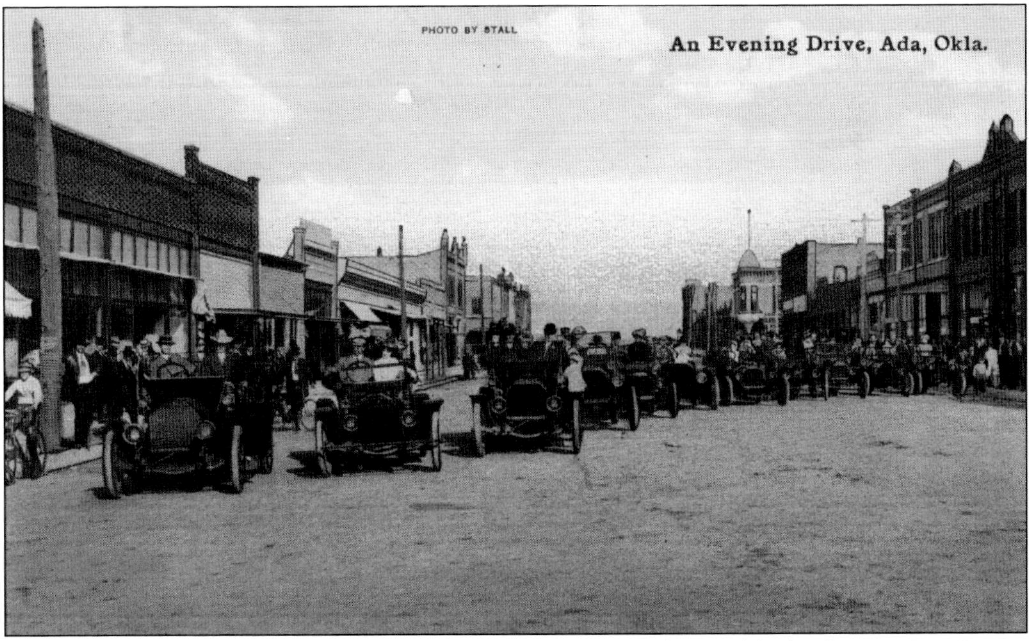

Staged for a photograph, drivers are in staggered order across the 100 block of West Main Street. The turret of the bank is on Broadway Avenue and Main Street. (Courtesy of Gary Haney.)

Located 12 Miles South of Ada in the Chimney Top Mountains

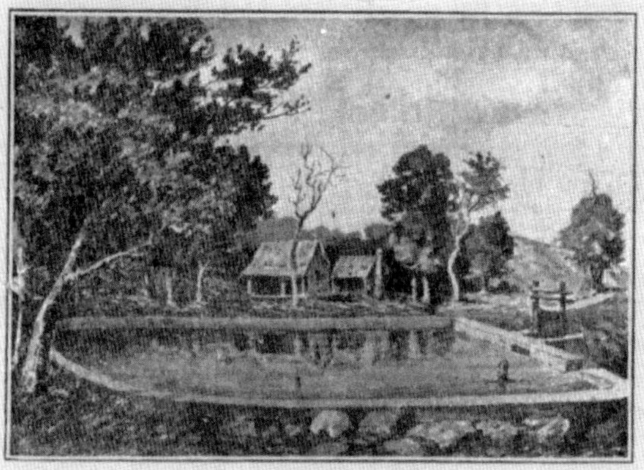

Famous Byrd's Mill Spring. Capacity, 6,100,000 Gallons per Day.

ADA, OKLA., MAY 1ST, 1912

We now have our New Machinery in operation. HAVING ONE OF THE LARGE PLANTS OF OKLAHOMA, we will have a large surplus of Ice. If, for any reason, you are short, phone, wire or write. We have the M., K. & T. and Frisco tracks into our plant, and prompt switching service to the Oklahoma Central Railway.

The only Ice in Oklahoma made from absolutely pure spring water. Retain this card for reference. You may need us befor the summer is over.

Yours truly, ADA ICE AND COLD STORAGE CO.

This is the Ada Ice and Storage Company outside of town. Ice was an important item in the early days. The pool shown here became a popular swimming spot; the water was fresh and very cold. A tower and a concession were added later. (Courtesy of Gary Haney.)

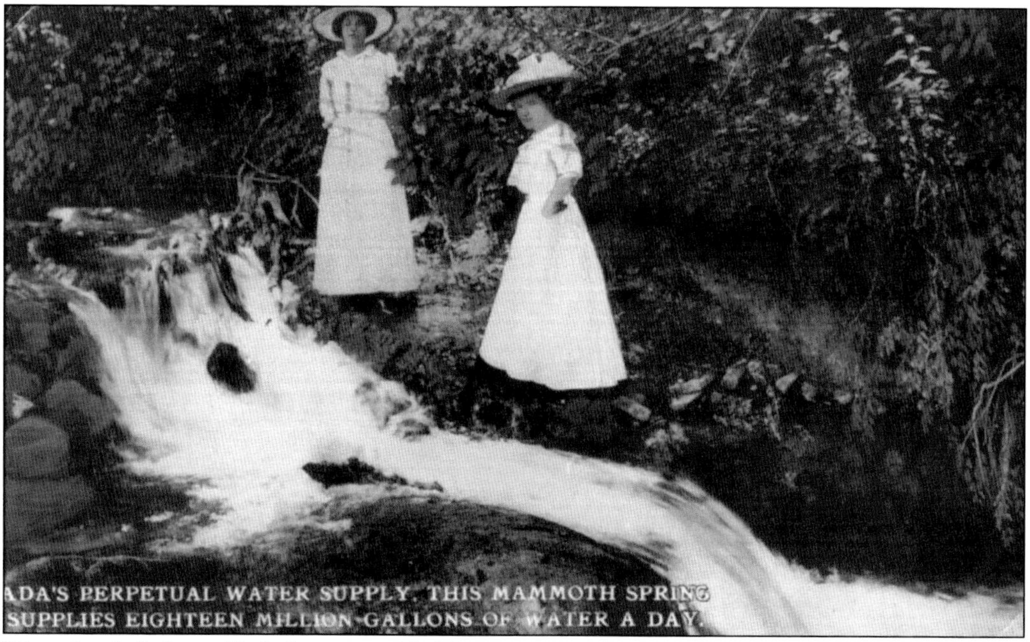

These lovely fashionable ladies were added for interest in this picture of a waterfall at the perpetual spring of Byrd's Mill. Hats were very popular back then. (Courtesy of Gary Haney.)

Three

Boom

The exodus of the Bloody Bucket bunch was a welcome catalyst for Ada's future growth. The cotton boom finally wore down the land, which made way for the oil boom. Oil was discovered a few miles south of Ada in Fittstown, and rigs were set up all over the area.

The hotels in Ada were kept full of businessmen. The Aldridge Hotel was luxurious for its time and included a well-attended coffee shop. Many a deal was sealed in this agreeable atmosphere. The Harris Hotel was also kept busy with people in Ada for the second largest rodeo in America. The Ada Rodeo drew people from all over, celebrities included.

When Julia Smith became rich from the oil boom in Fittstown, she moved to Ada and bought the Harris and added an extra floor and a fancy neon sign. It was renamed the Julianna Hotel and sat on the corner of Main and Rennie Streets. It later became a hazard and was torn down and turned into what is now a beautiful corner park.

Several famous baseball players called Ada their home. Politics and the music industry owe Ada for nurturing some of their best contributors. Vaudeville started at the McSwain Theater, which has become a draw for special musical events.

Homes and churches filled the empty spaces in the lives of Adans. Ada is known for its religious leadership. As a clean, well-kept town, it became the seat of Pontotoc County and is known for overcoming many trials set against its survival.

It has become the headquarters of the Chickasaw Nation and has prospered because of it. East Central Normal School became the highly respected East Central University.

Many industries became viable in Ada. The "Spit and Whittle Tree" still stands on West Main Street, making shade year after year for observers who sit and correct the world in the traditional, home-town way.

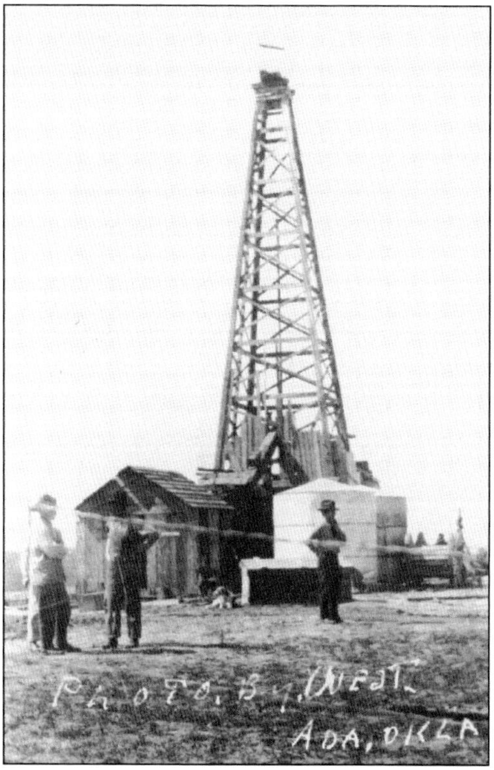

This is one of the many oil rigs that surrounded Ada during the oil boom. Four men take a break, as a friendly dog checks out the perimeter. (Courtesy Gary Haney.)

The dam at the man-made lake helped keep the cement plant going. It is now a fenced walkway for joggers and the curious and a safe place to set off the Fourth of July fireworks display every year. (Courtesy of Gary Haney.)

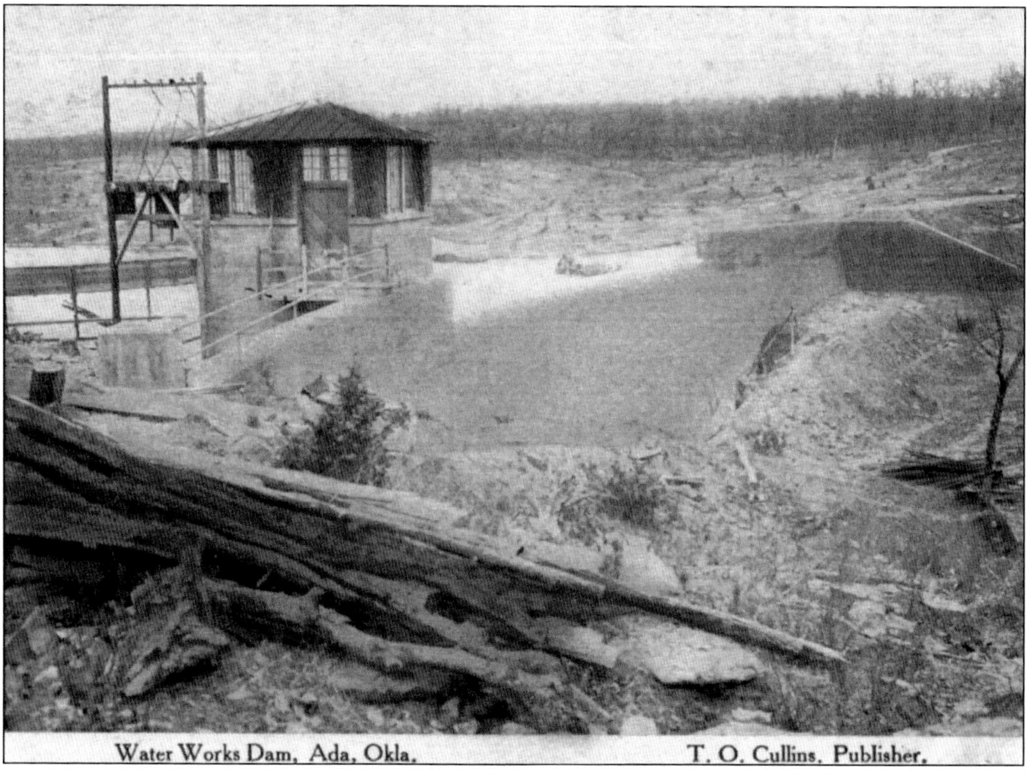

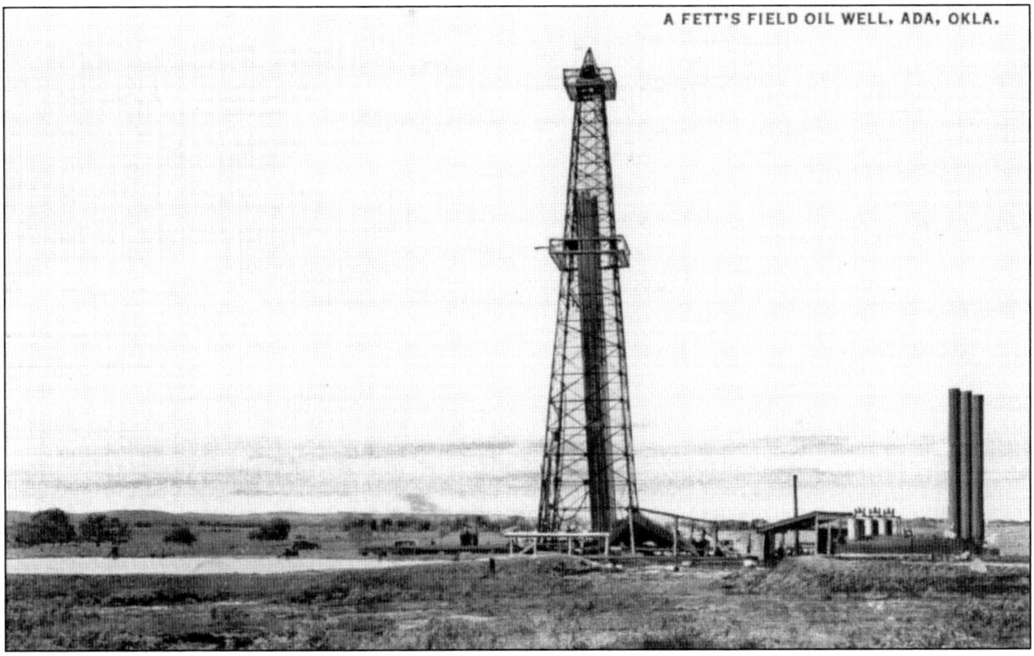

These sights became common around Ada. At Fitts Field, it was just part of the scenery. (Courtesy of Gary Haney.)

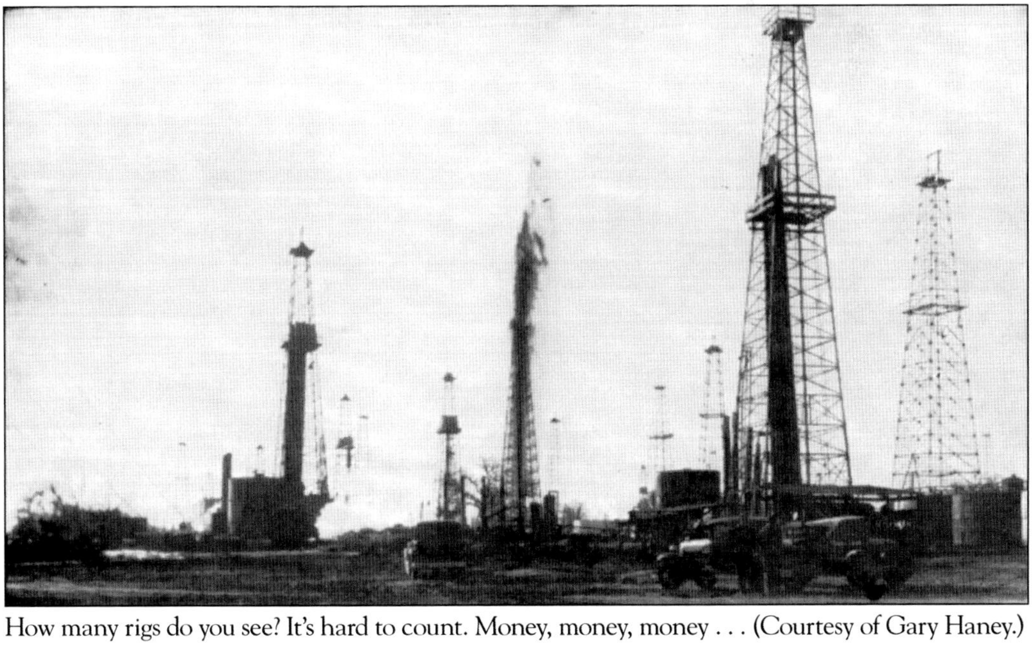

How many rigs do you see? It's hard to count. Money, money, money . . . (Courtesy of Gary Haney.)

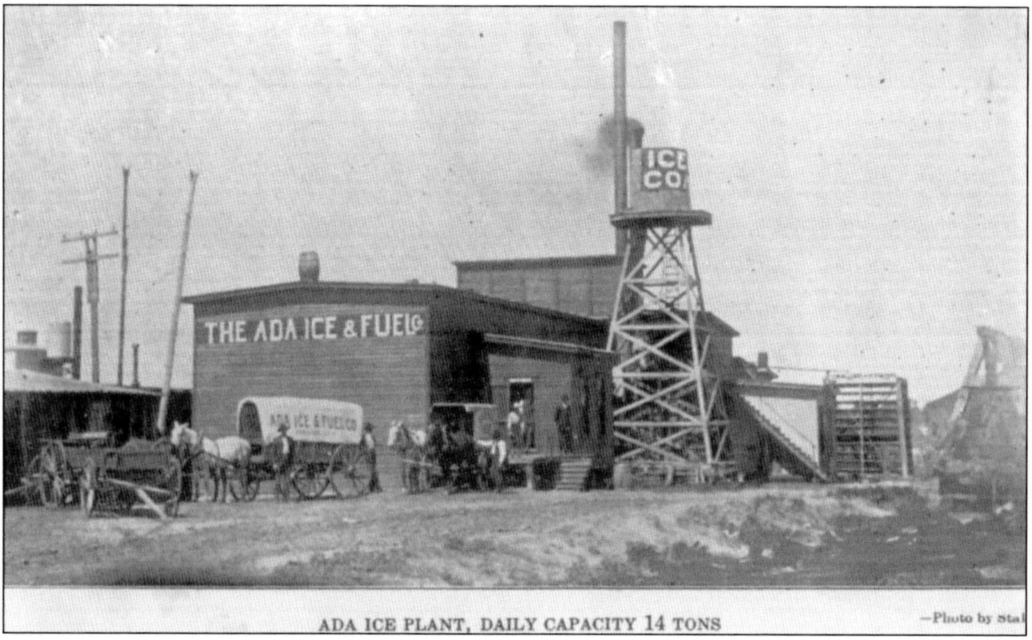

The city of Ada put in its own ice plant. The daily capacity was 14 tons of ice, which is a lot of ice for any town. (Courtesy of Gary Haney.)

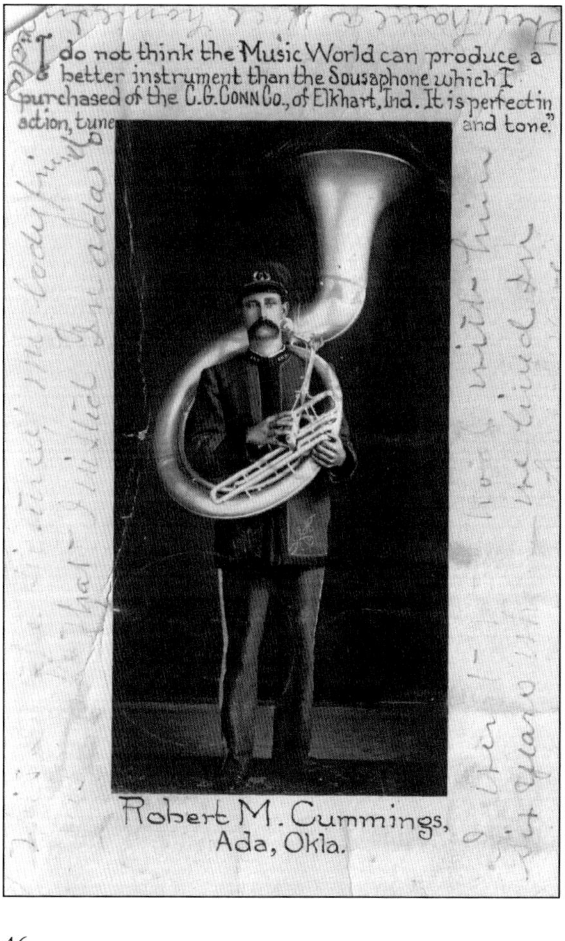

Shown here wearing his band uniform, Robert Cummings was a sousaphone player. The instrument looks amazingly like a tuba. Cummings wrote his proud opinion of its classic sound around the picture. (Courtesy of Gary Haney.)

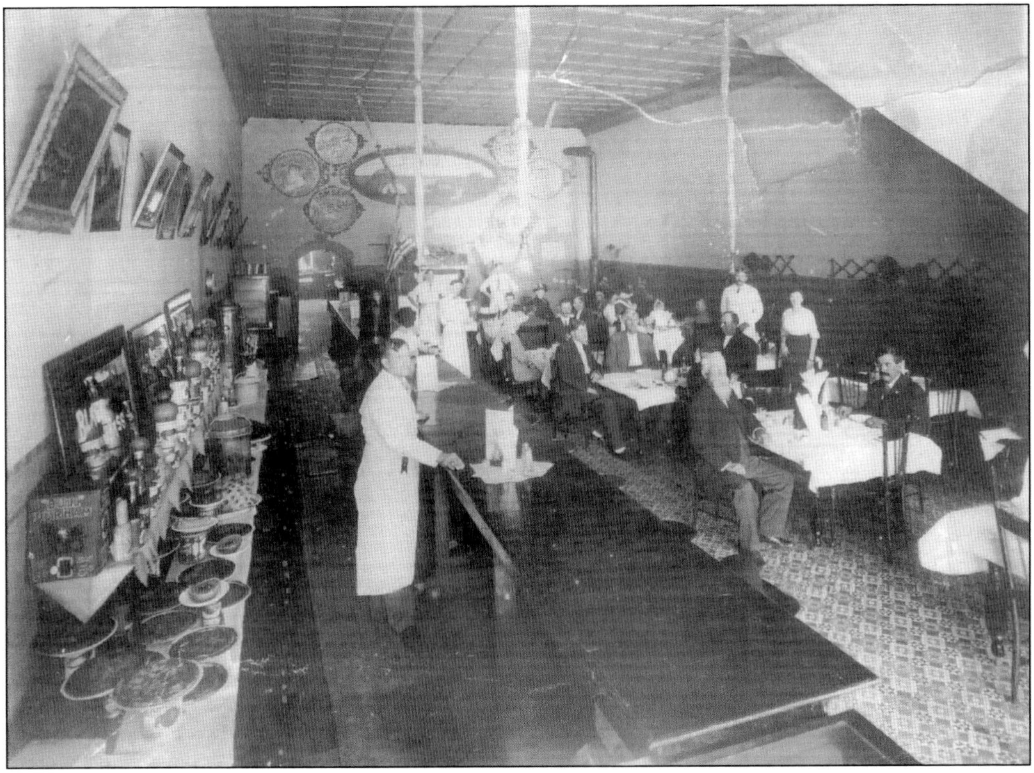

In this picture, Gov. William Byrd sits in a public cafe while eating a meal. He is in the middle of the crowd, with the beard. (Courtesy of Alberta Blackburn.)

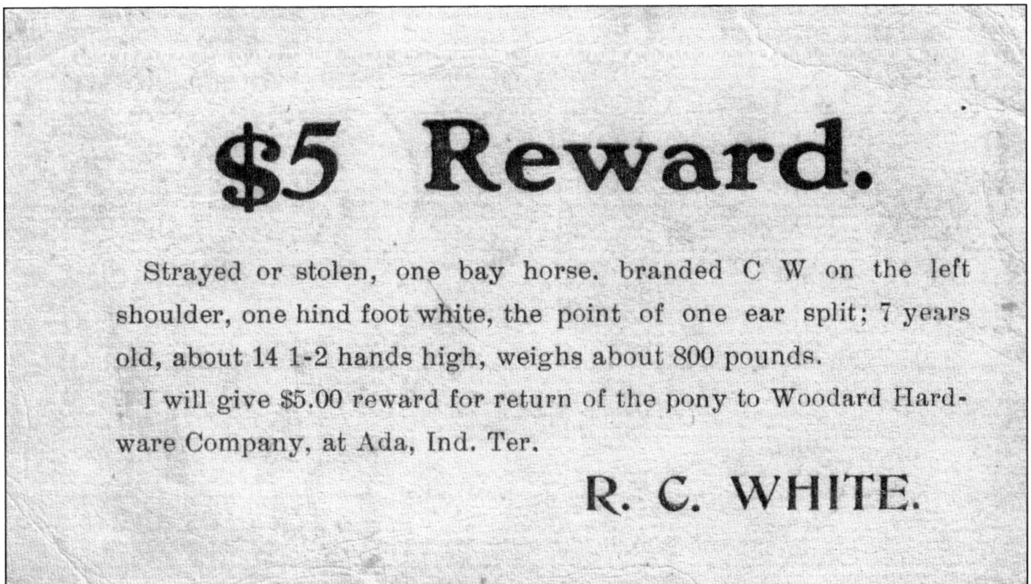

$5 Reward.

Strayed or stolen, one bay horse, branded C W on the left shoulder, one hind foot white, the point of one ear split; 7 years old, about 14 1-2 hands high, weighs about 800 pounds.

I will give $5.00 reward for return of the pony to Woodard Hardware Company, at Ada, Ind. Ter.

R. C. WHITE.

This stolen horse was well inventoried by its owner. The reward of $5 was a lot of money then. Horse thieves were hung at that time. (Courtesy of Gary Haney.)

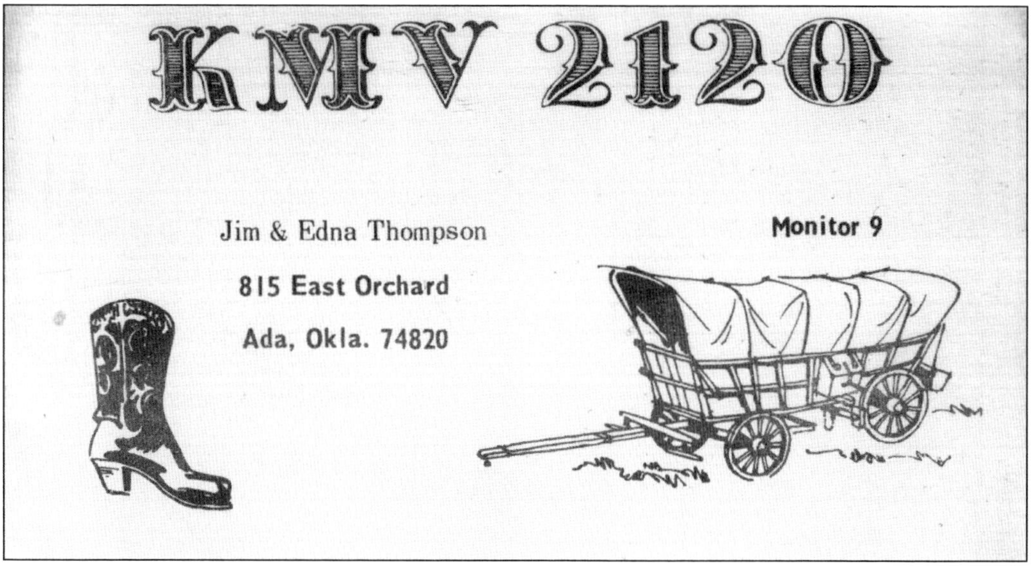

Jim and Edna Thompson held down monitor 9 at home. It looks like they were into the west from their art. There were several ham radio sets in local homes, for better contact with others outside the Ada area. (Courtesy of Gary Haney.)

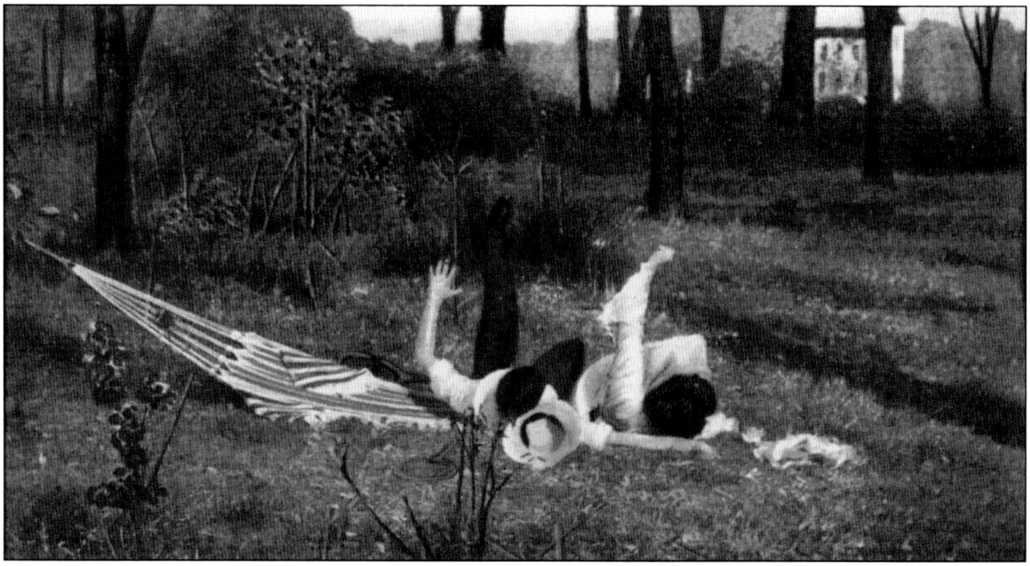
In the summer, there is nothing like a broken hammock to bring a couple together. Time spent outside is also a popular way to waste away a summer. (Courtesy of Gary Haney.)

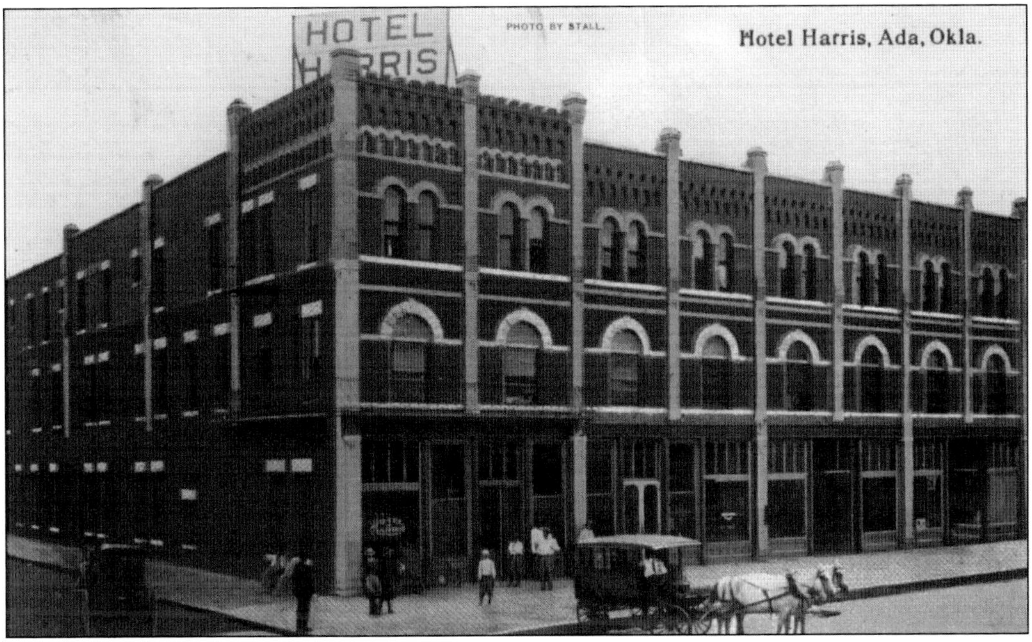

The Harris Hotel was a very busy place, sitting on the corner of Constant and Main Streets. It was luxurious for the time and was seldom empty. Later it was bought, upgraded, and remodeled as the Juliana Hotel. (Courtesy of Gary Haney.)

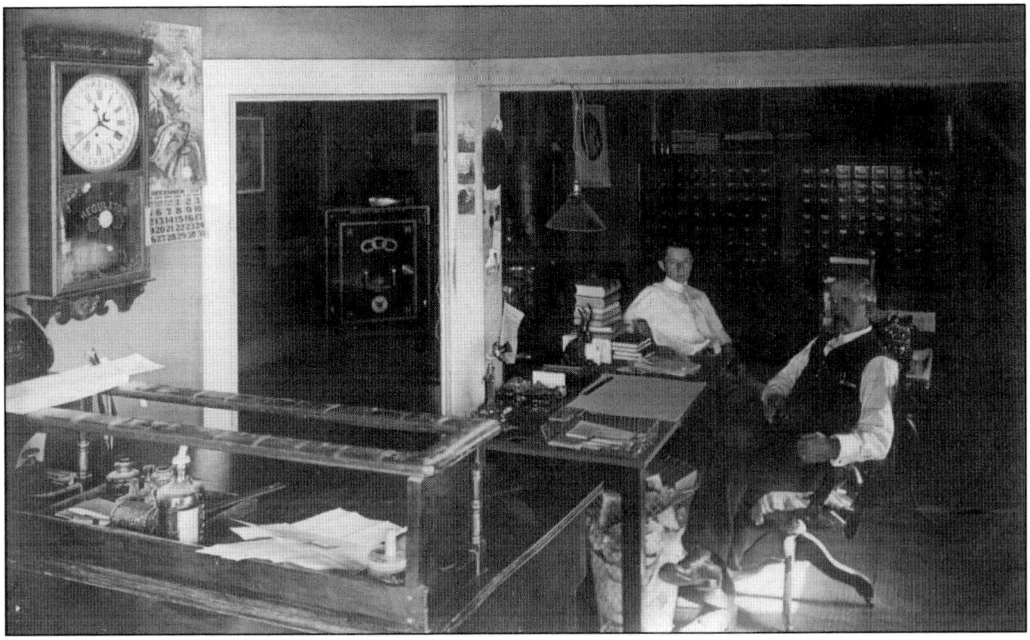

The patrons and help in the lobby of the Harris Hotel are at attention. The workers are alert and ready for business. (Courtesy of Gary Haney.)

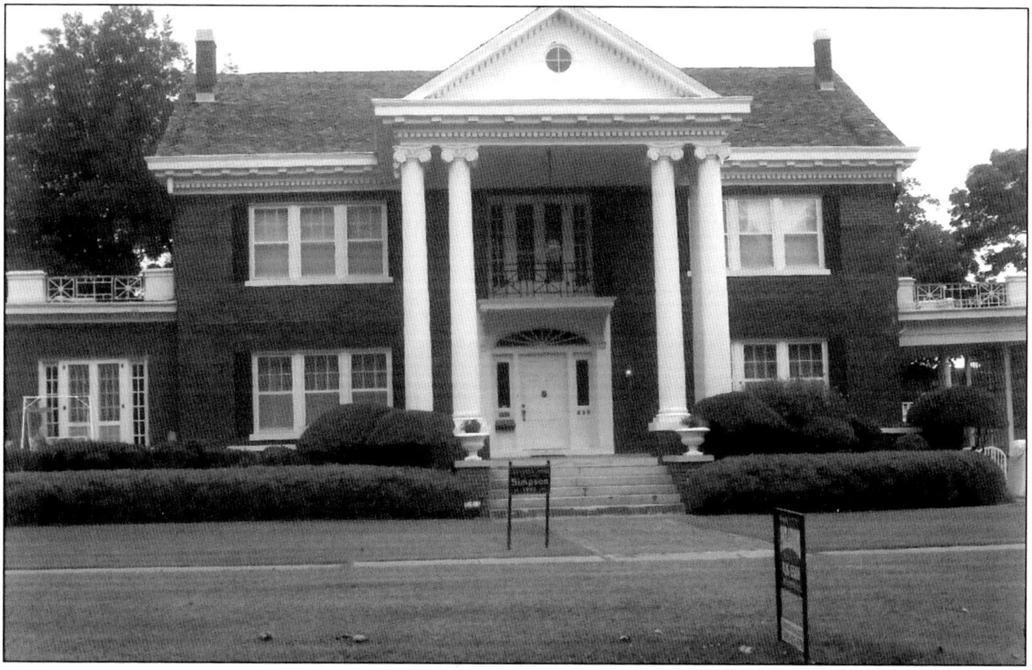

This art gallery on the southwest corner of Main and Townsend Streets was once a bank. It now displays original art by local talent. (Author's collection.)

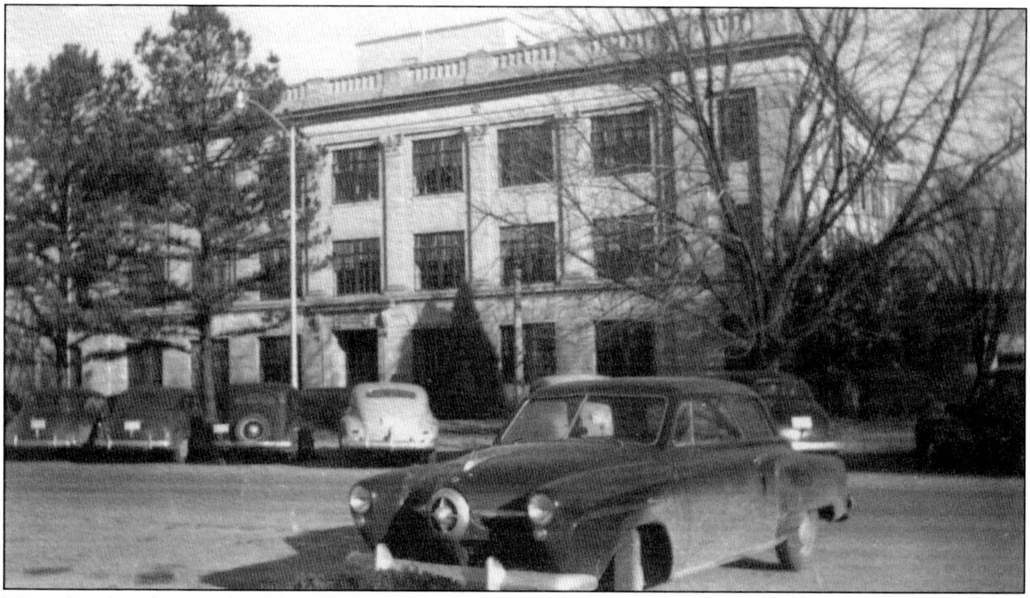

This Studebaker looks like all it needs is a propeller. Low in the front and the back, it sits forebodingly, without the benefit of a bath, and guards the courthouse across the street on Thirteenth Street. (Courtesy of Gary Haney.)

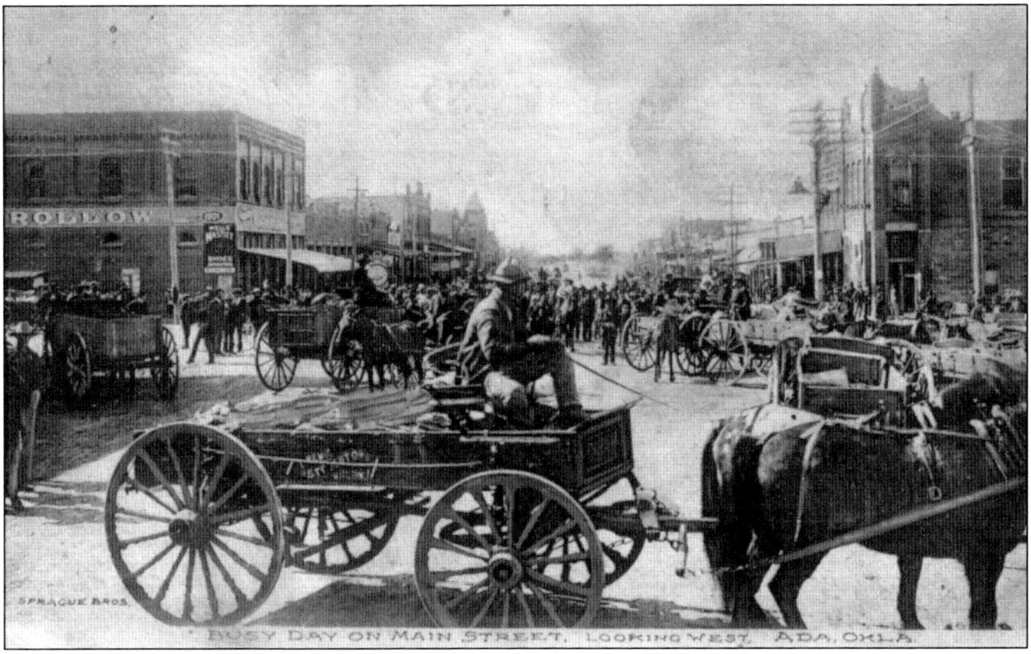

Rollows and First National Bank were the northeast and southeast corners of Main Street and Broadway Avenue. (Courtesy of Gary Haney.)

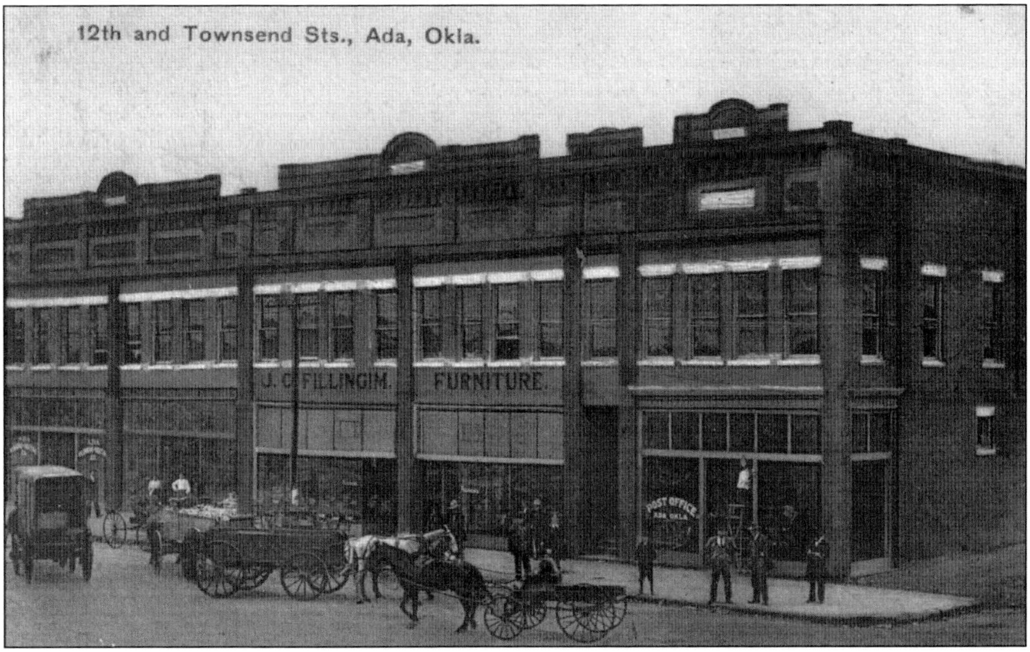

Fullingham Furniture and surrounding businesses sat where the Citizens Bank is now located. The bank's drive-through is on the very corner of Twelfth and Townsend Streets, next to the Main Bank. The Main Fire Station is on the west end of the block, across from the Aldridge Hotel. (Courtesy of Gary Haney.)

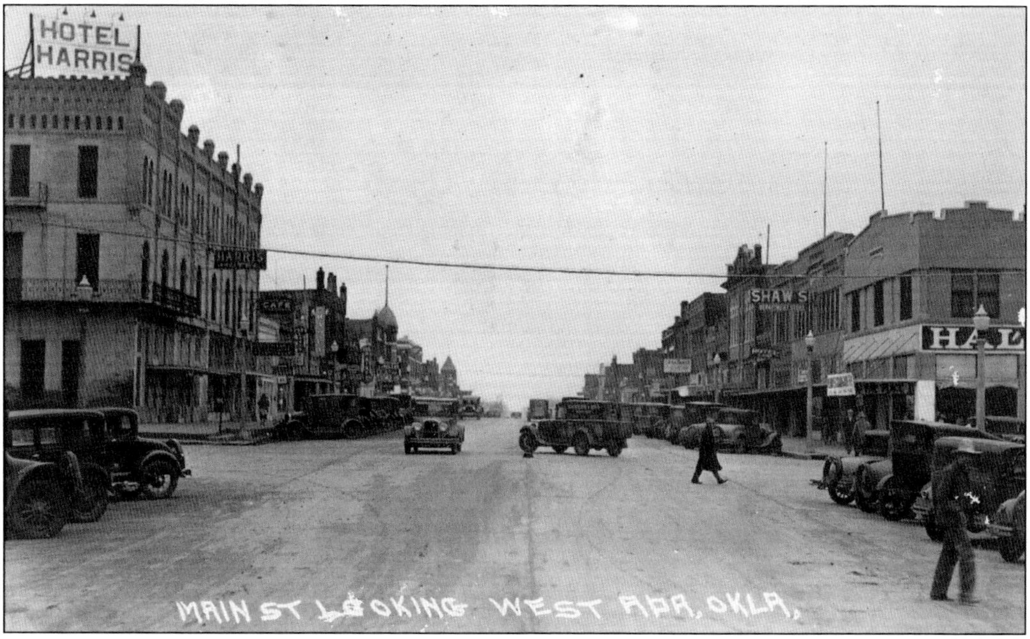

The Hotel Harris really shines in this shot of Main Street. Looking west, this corner was only three blocks east of "The Bloody Bucket," later called "Tough Block" in the 1950s. The block was a well-known hideout for killers and criminals. (Courtesy of Gary Haney.)

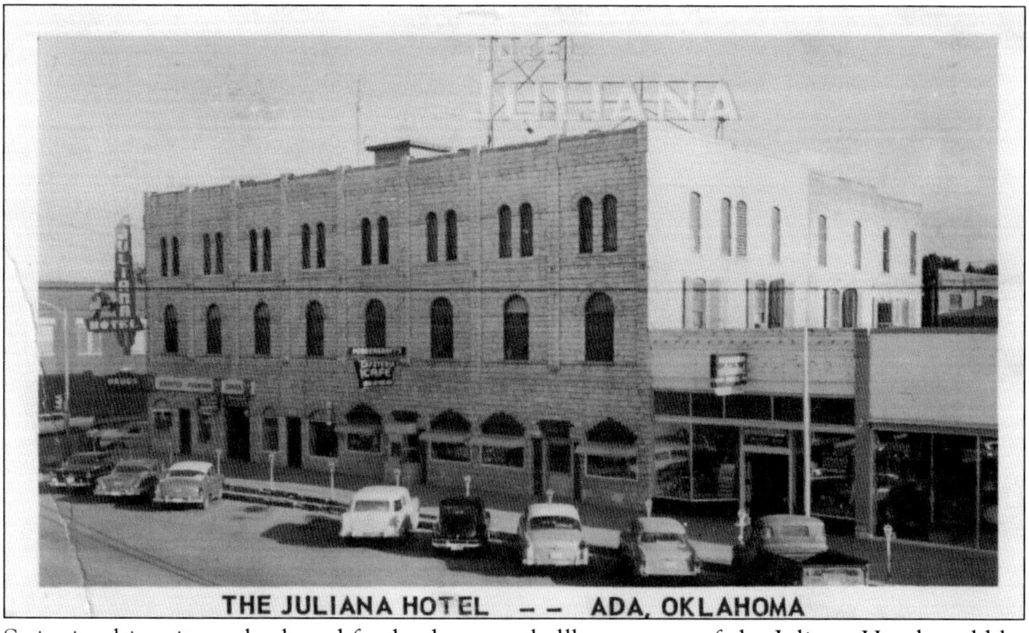

Swinging his suitcase back and forth, the neon bellboy on top of the Juliana Hotel could be seen from blocks away. In its later years, the top floor became notorious for its friendly but questionable activities. Rumor had it that female companionship was only a stairwell away. (Courtesy of Gary Haney.)

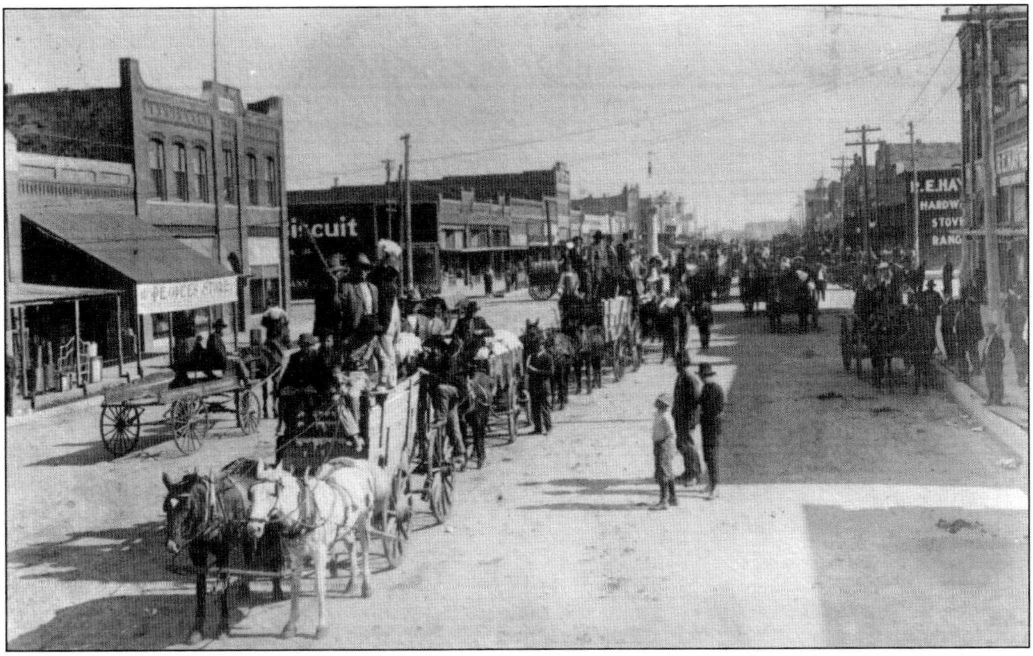

This looks like a wagon train, but these wagons are just going home after a day of stocking up on supplies. (Courtesy of Gary Haney.)

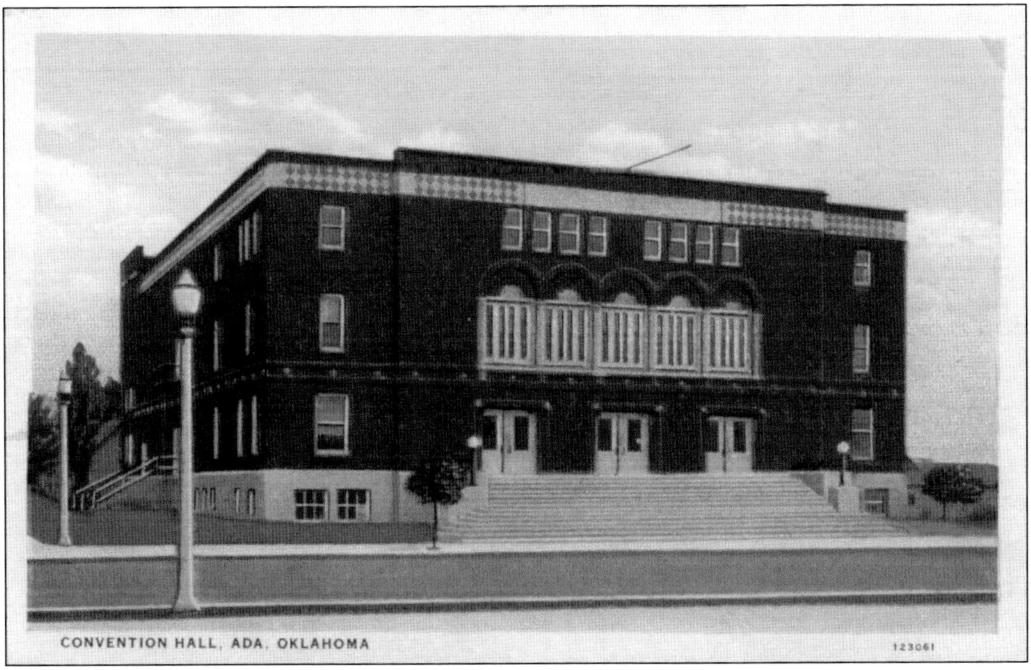

The Convention Hall was on the corner of Townsend and Thirteenth Streets. The Ada Police Station was in the basement, and eventually a youth center was on the first floor. It had a jukebox with rock and roll music and many other activities for teenagers to enjoy. Torn down, its site is now the Ada Police Station, which still stands across from the courthouse. (Courtesy of Gary Haney.)

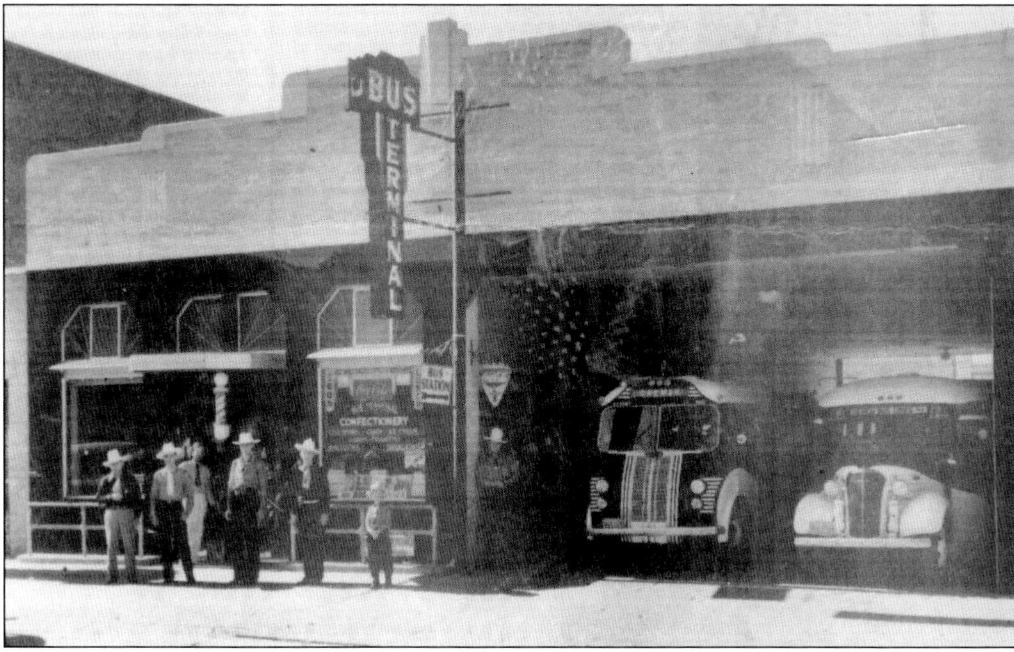

Located on Twelfth Street in the middle of the 100 block, the bus terminal and Denco Bus Line was across from the Aldridge Hotel. The men are, from left to right, Ross West, Raymond Cox, unidentified, Bud Sprinkler, unidentified, and Burt Cox. It is now a parking lot for the post office, the library, and the Aldridge Hotel and coffee shop. (Courtesy of Gary Haney.)

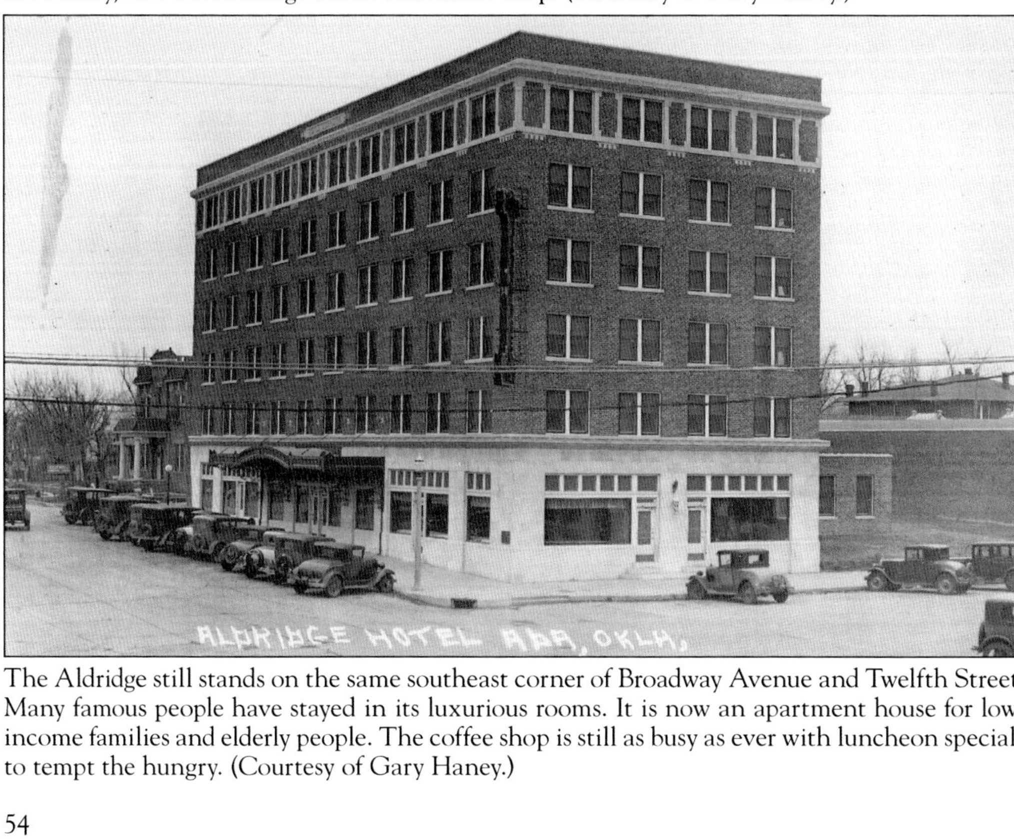

The Aldridge still stands on the same southeast corner of Broadway Avenue and Twelfth Street. Many famous people have stayed in its luxurious rooms. It is now an apartment house for low-income families and elderly people. The coffee shop is still as busy as ever with luncheon specials to tempt the hungry. (Courtesy of Gary Haney.)

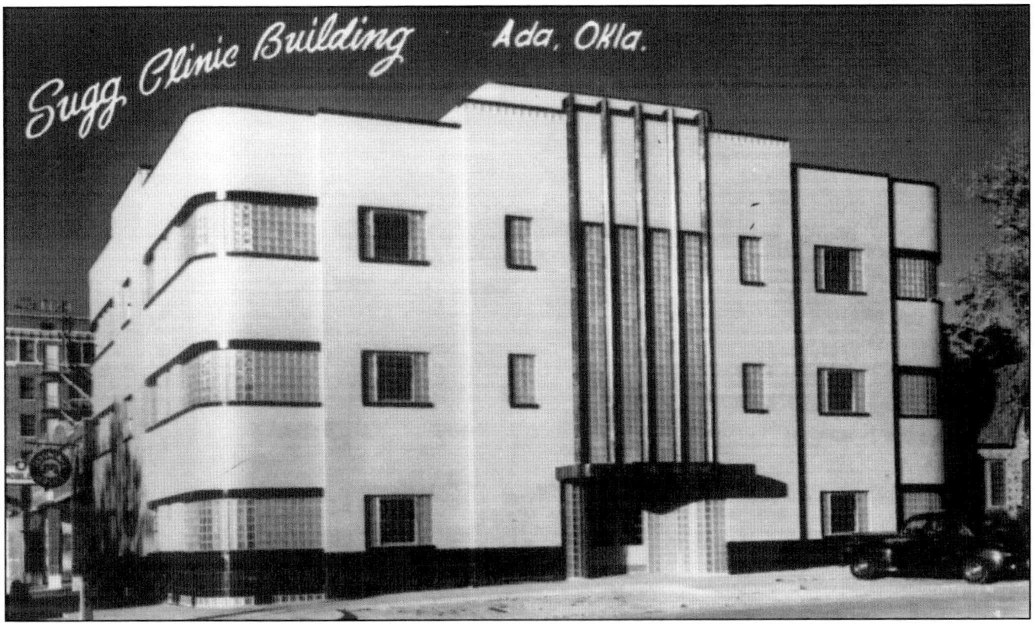

The Sugg, sometimes referred to as the "Little Mayo," was one of the first of its kind. Located on the northeast corner of Thirteenth Street and Broadway Avenue, it housed offices for doctors, a lab, and a small pharmacy. Constructed of limestone and marble, the building still stands behind the Aldridge Building. (Courtesy of Gary Haney.)

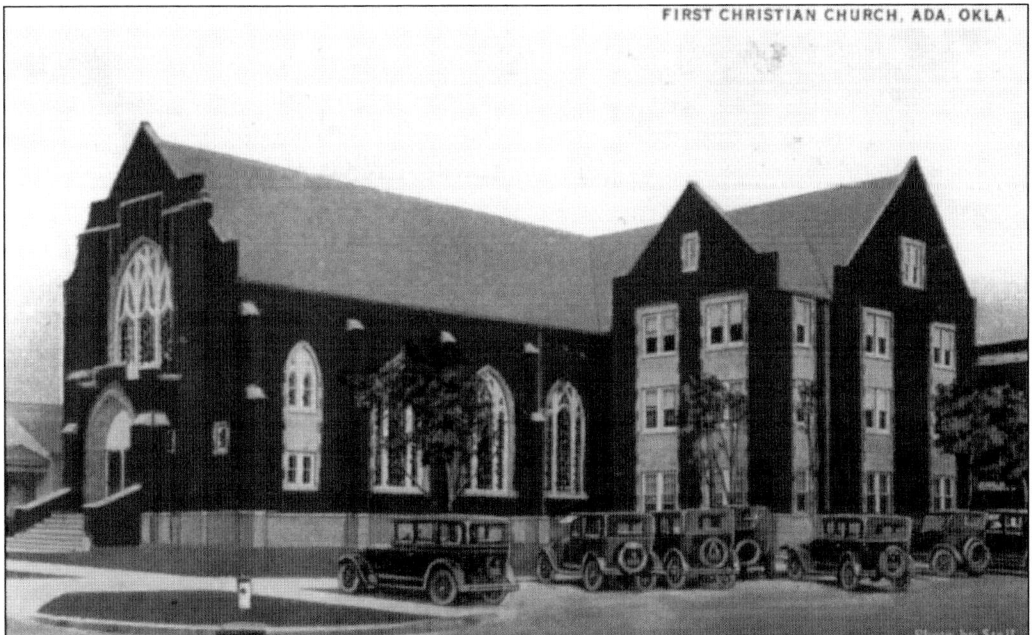

The following appeared in a bulletin in 1901: "The ladies of the Christian Church will give an entertainment at Barringer's new store building on East Main Street on the evening of September 6. An 'Old Maid's Convention' will hold the boards, and those who attend may expect something rich, rare, and racy. It should be well patronized, as the proceeds will be appropriated to the building of a Christian Church at this place." (Courtesy of Gary Haney.)

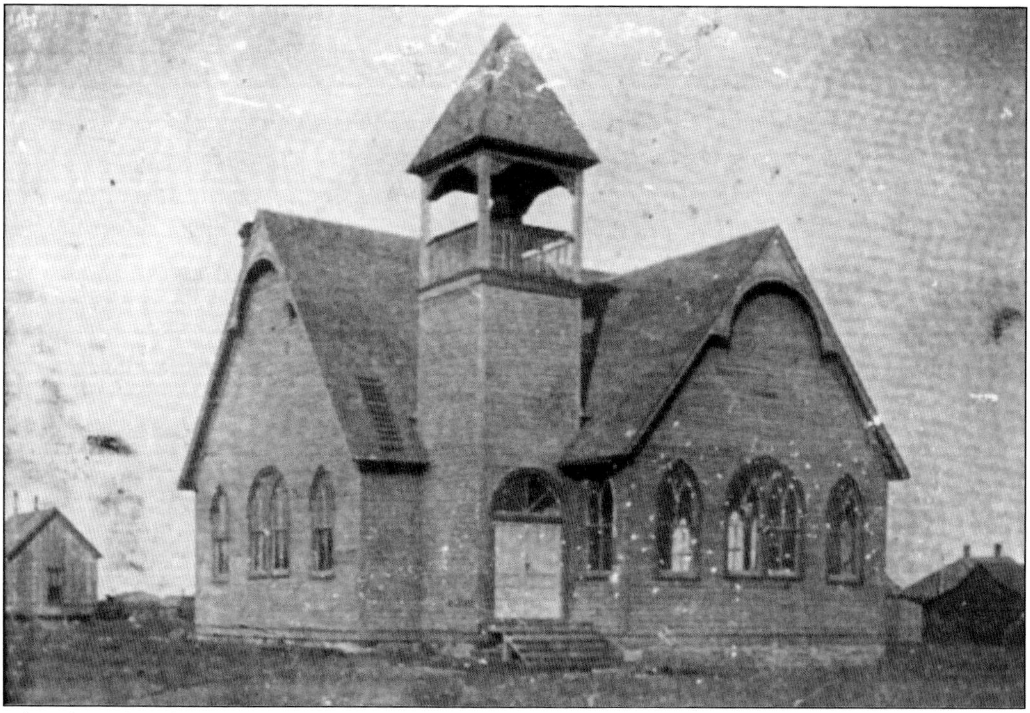

Churches played a very important role in Ada's growth. It has been said that the minister of First Baptist Church ruled the town. C. C. Morris battled Sunday movies, drinking, and dancing, and was a very strong influence in Ada. (Courtesy of Bud Throne.)

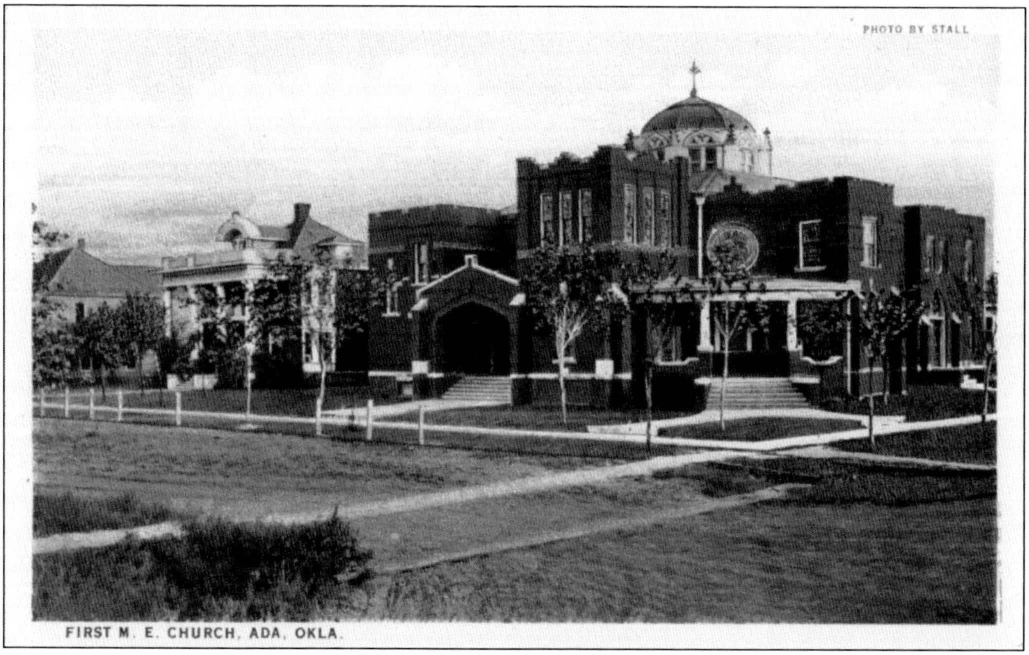

Both the Methodist and the Baptist churches had humble beginnings in Ada, but at present they are two of the most beautiful churches in Ada. Located side by side on Broadway Avenue, they are very impressive buildings. (Courtesy of Gary Haney.)

Until it was taken over by Vision Bank in 2005, the First National Bank had been an inhabitant of the southeast corner of Main Street and Broadway Avenue since 1901. The corner turret became a clock, which still works. (Courtesy of Alberta Blackburn.)

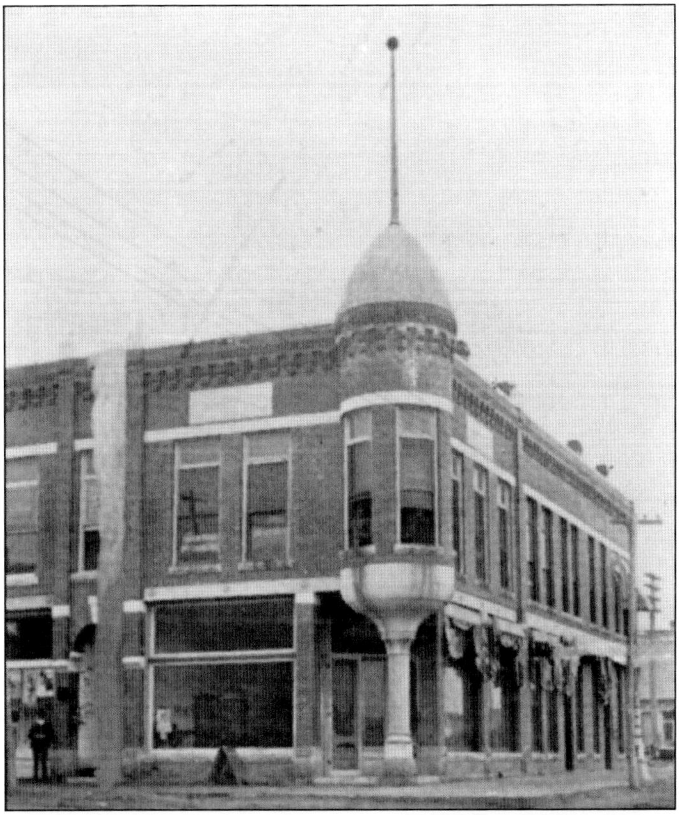

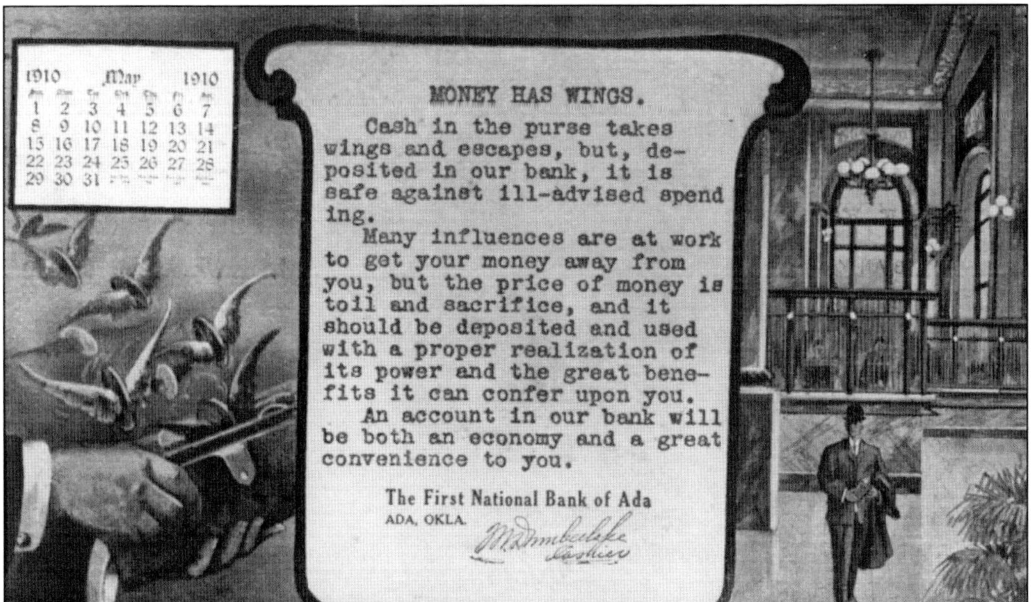

In 1910, the First National Bank advised people to be frugal in their spending and warned against ill-advised spending. This card shows money flying out of a wallet, as well as an affluent man leaving a luxurious bank lobby while holding a savings book. (Courtesy of Gary Haney.)

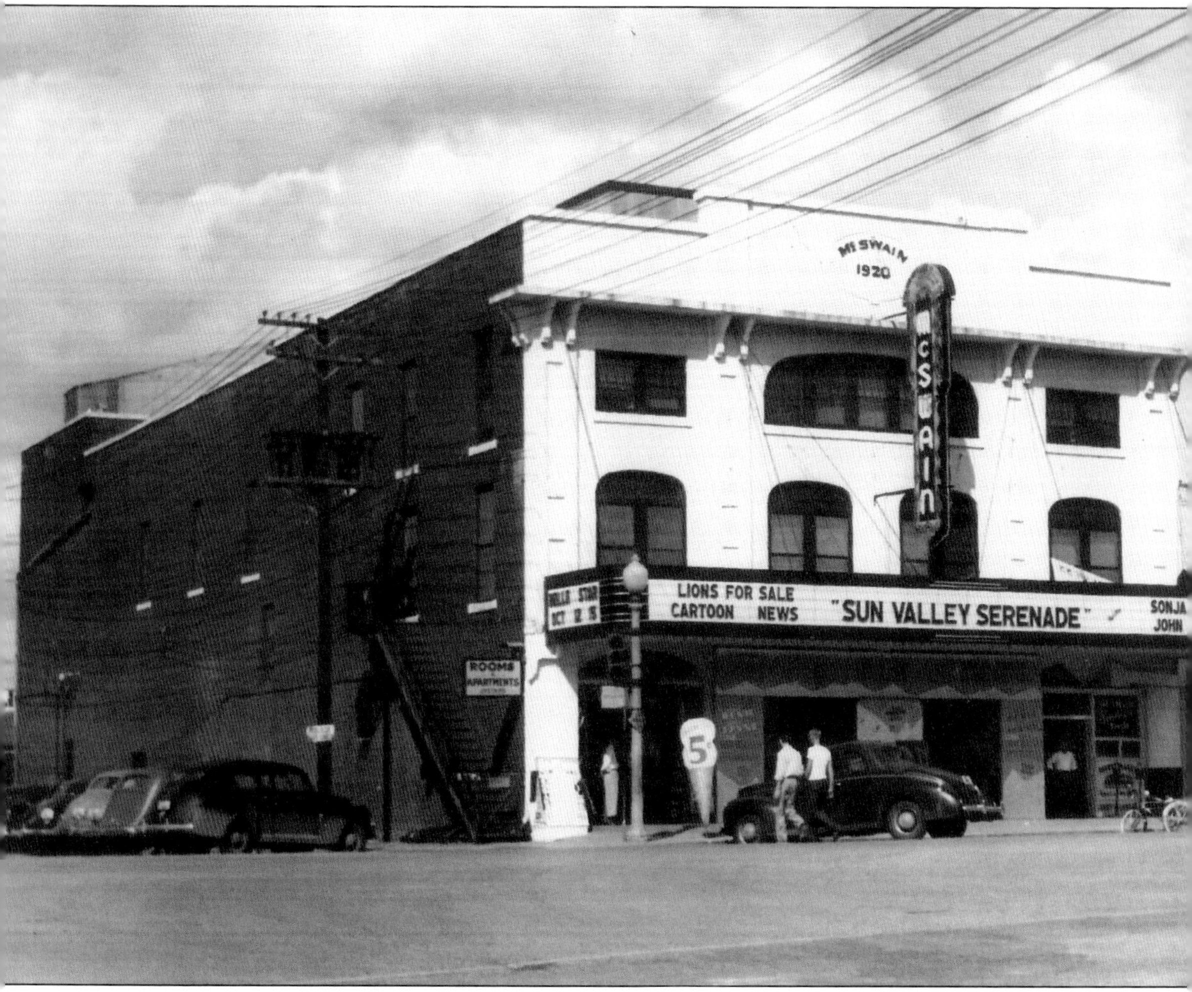

At one time, people could rent rooms and apartments above the McSwain Theater. For only 10¢, patrons could watch the news, a cartoon, and a movie; however, concessions were not available at that time. A staircase that led up to a segregated balcony was located on the right just as one entered the doors. The street in front of the theater was used as a place to be dropped off or as a place to park bicycles. In later years, a new, large, and extraordinarily bright marquee covered the front. It has since been completely renovated back to its original look. Currently, it offers live entertainment that rivals the Branson. (Courtesy of Bud Throne.)

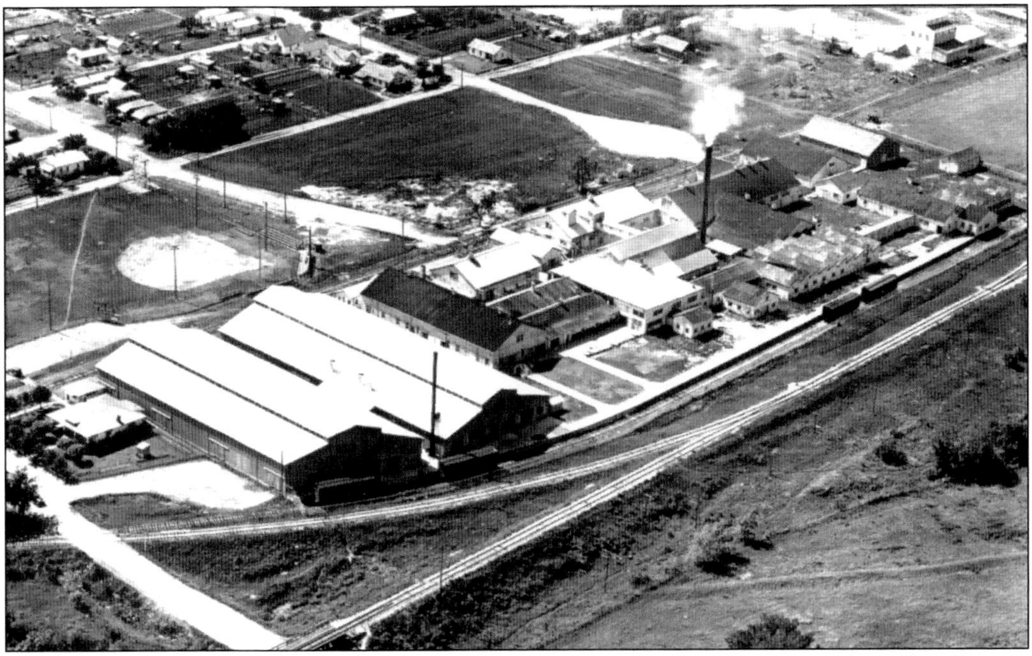

This is an aerial view of the Hazel-Atlas Glass Works in its heyday. Located on East Fourth Street then, it is now on Arlington Boulevard. Hazel-Atlas produced glass caskets at one time. (Courtesy of Gary Haney.)

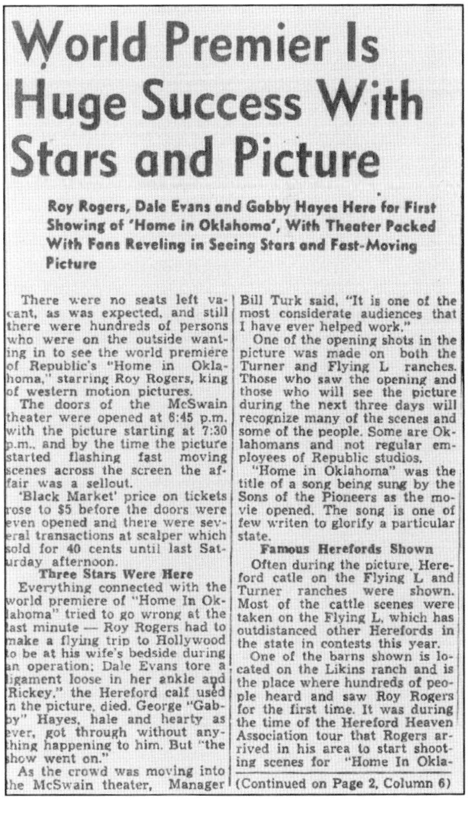

World Premier Is Huge Success With Stars and Picture

Roy Rogers, Dale Evans and Gabby Hayes Here for First Showing of 'Home in Oklahoma', With Theater Packed With Fans Reveling in Seeing Stars and Fast-Moving Picture

There were no seats left vacant, as was expected, and still there were hundreds of persons who were on the outside wanting in to see the world premiere of Republic's "Home in Oklahoma," starring Roy Rogers, king of western motion pictures.

The doors of the McSwain theater were opened at 6:45 p.m. with the picture starting at 7:30 p.m., and by the time the picture started flashing fast moving scenes across the screen the affair was a sellout.

'Black Market' price on tickets rose to $5 before the doors were even opened and there were several transactions at scalper which sold for 40 cents until last Saturday afternoon.

Three Stars Were Here

Everything connected with the world premiere of "Home In Oklahoma" tried to go wrong at the last minute — Roy Rogers had to make a flying trip to Hollywood to be at his wife's bedside during an operation; Dale Evans tore a ligament loose in her ankle and "Rickey," the Hereford calf used in the picture, died. George "Gabby" Hayes, hale and hearty as ever, got through without anything happening to him. But "the show went on."

As the crowd was moving into the McSwain theater, Manager Bill Turk said, "It is one of the most considerate audiences that I have ever helped work."

One of the opening shots in the picture was made on both the Turner and Flying L ranches. Those who saw the opening and those who will see the picture during the next three days will recognize many of the scenes and some of the people. Some are Oklahomans and not regular employees of Republic studios.

"Home in Oklahoma" was the title of a song being sung by the Sons of the Pioneers as the movie opened. The song is one of few writen to glorify a particular state.

Famous Herefords Shown

Often during the picture, Hereford catle on the Flying L and Turner ranches were shown. Most of the cattle scenes were taken on the Flying L, which has outdistanced other Herefords in the state in contests this year.

One of the barns shown is located on the Likins ranch and is the place where hundreds of people heard and saw Roy Rogers for the first time. It was during the time of the Hereford Heaven Association tour that Rogers arrived in his area to start shooting scenes for "Home In Okla-

(Continued on Page 2, Column 6)

Western movies were once very popular. Roy Rogers and his gal, Dale Evans, along with Roy's sidekick, George "Gabby" Hayes, were huge stars. In 1946, they came to a special showing of *Home in Oklahoma* at the McSwain Theater. Dale had broken her leg falling from her horse Buttermilk and was on crutches. (Courtesy of Alberta Blackburn.)

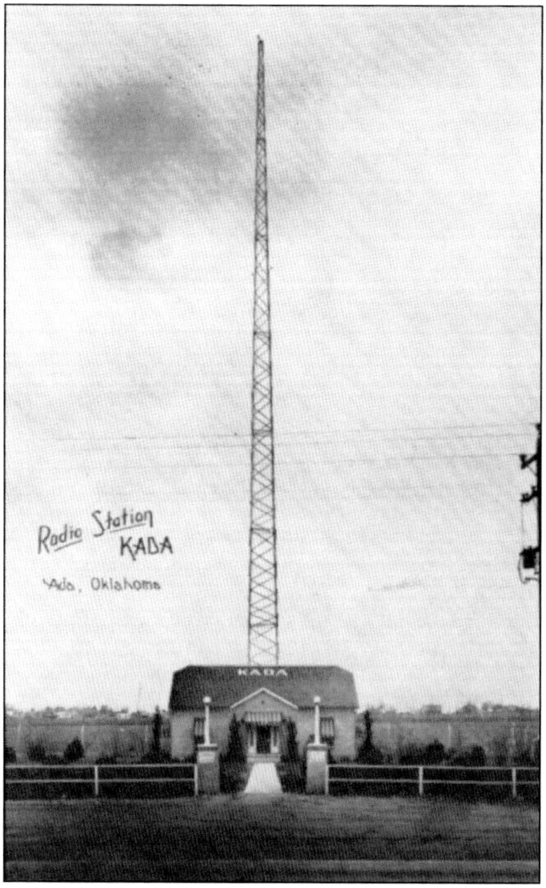

The Chickasaw Nation not only controls the popular radio station KADA, which is the original station, but also KYKC, KXFC, and KTLS. These other stations currently operate out of the North Hills Center, while the original station is being renovated, and once the renovations are completed, all types of music will be included under one roof. (Courtesy of Gary Haney.)

The Holiday Motel on Cradduck Road was built in 1969 by Melvin Chilcoat and Weldon Killian. It was bought, and the restaurant at far left was named after Conway Twitty. It has since been renamed the Village Inn and Club. It had a small swimming pool in front of the office. Sue Clark, an office employee for 16 years, said that it was closed because of the locals' disregard of the safety rules. (Courtesy of Gary Haney.)

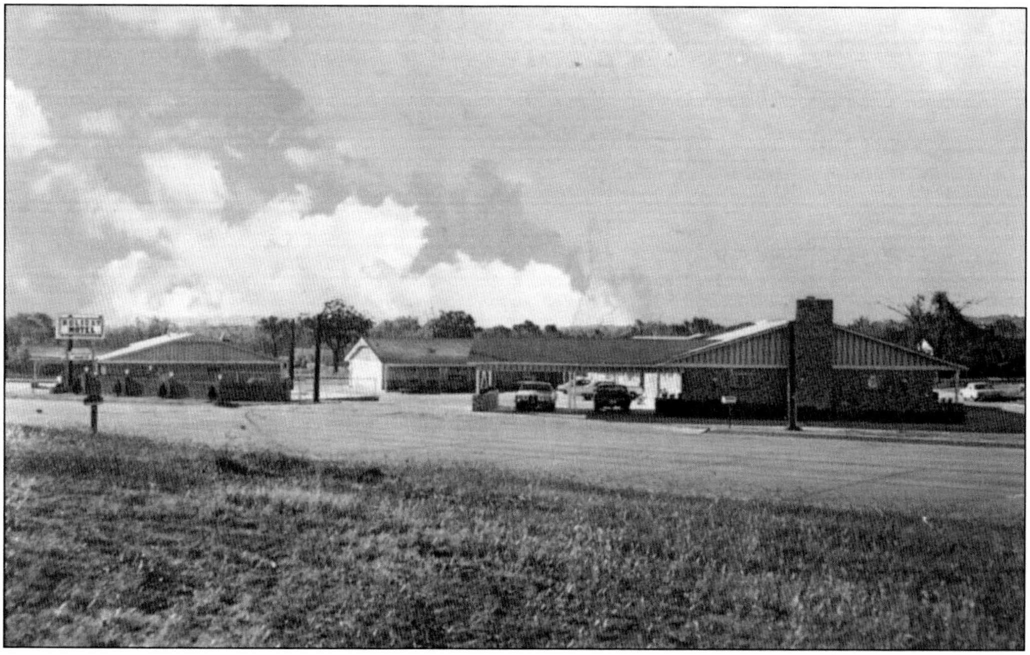

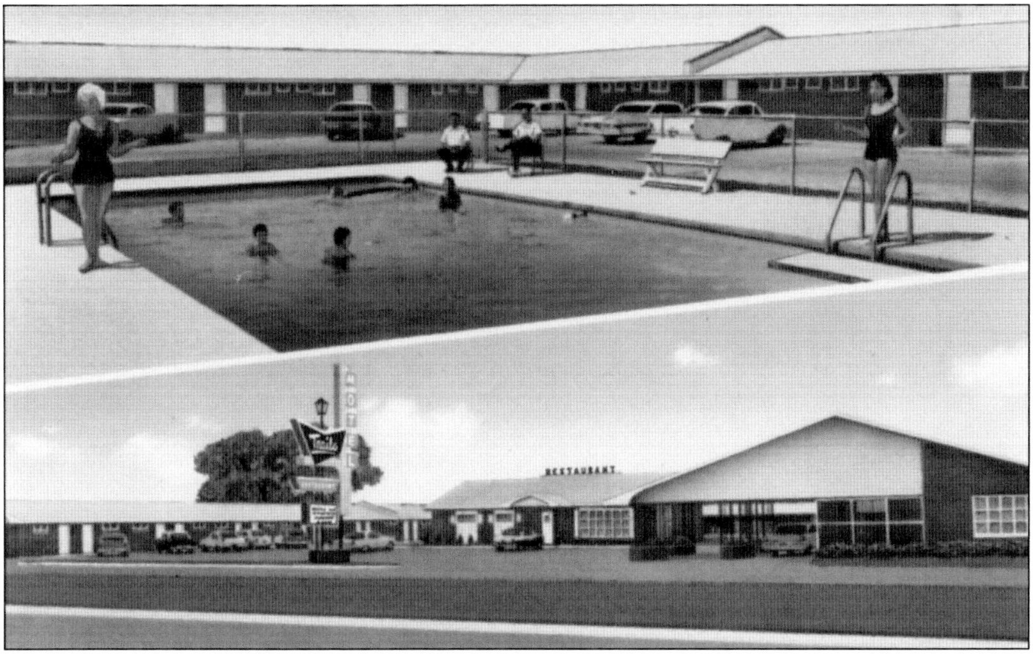

Here is the Trails Motel. This motel held the honor of being the first motel in Ada to have a swimming pool. The pool was fairly large and was located behind the motel's restaurant. (Courtesy of Gary Haney.)

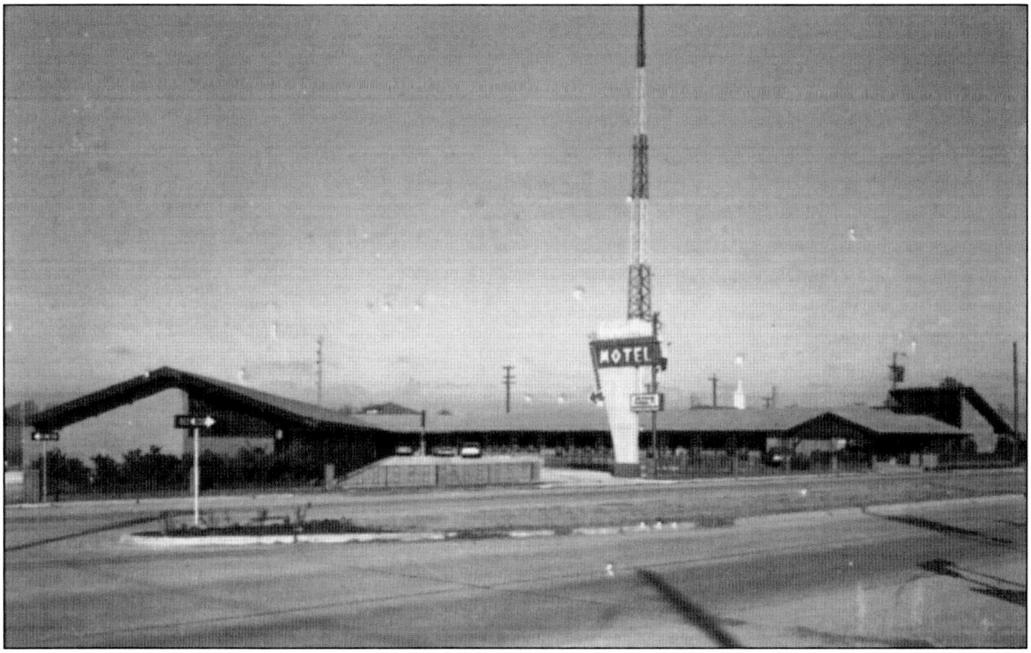

Indian Hills Motel on Broadway Avenue was built very close to the original Ada Rodeo grounds. It was one of the first luxury motels in the Ada area. (Courtesy of Gary Haney.)

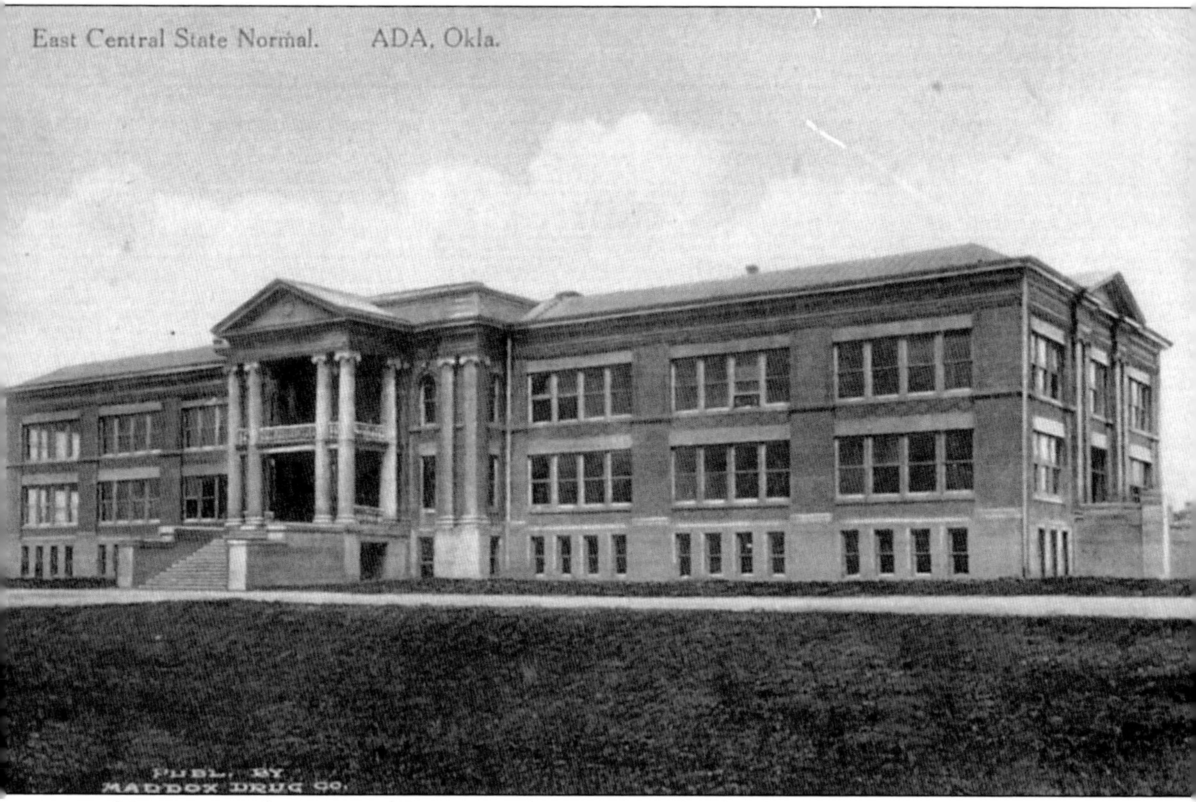

Here is an early picture of East Central State Normal School, which later became East Central University. ECU's campus now occupies the entire east end of Ada. (Courtesy of Gary Haney.)

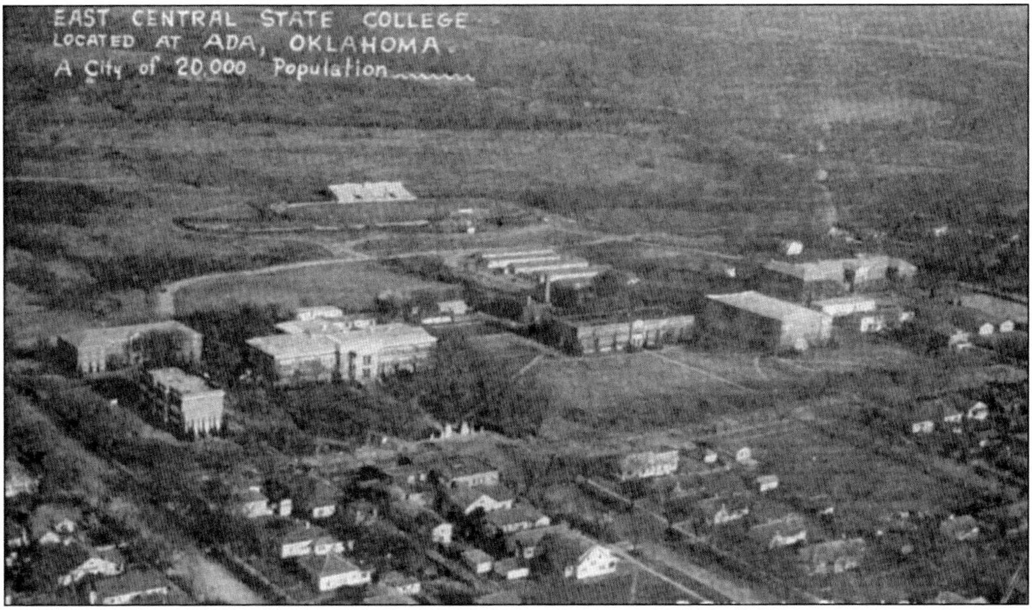

East Central Normal became a state college before becoming a university. The gateposts at the entrance on East Main were dedicated to the soldiers of World War I. (Courtesy of Gary Haney.)

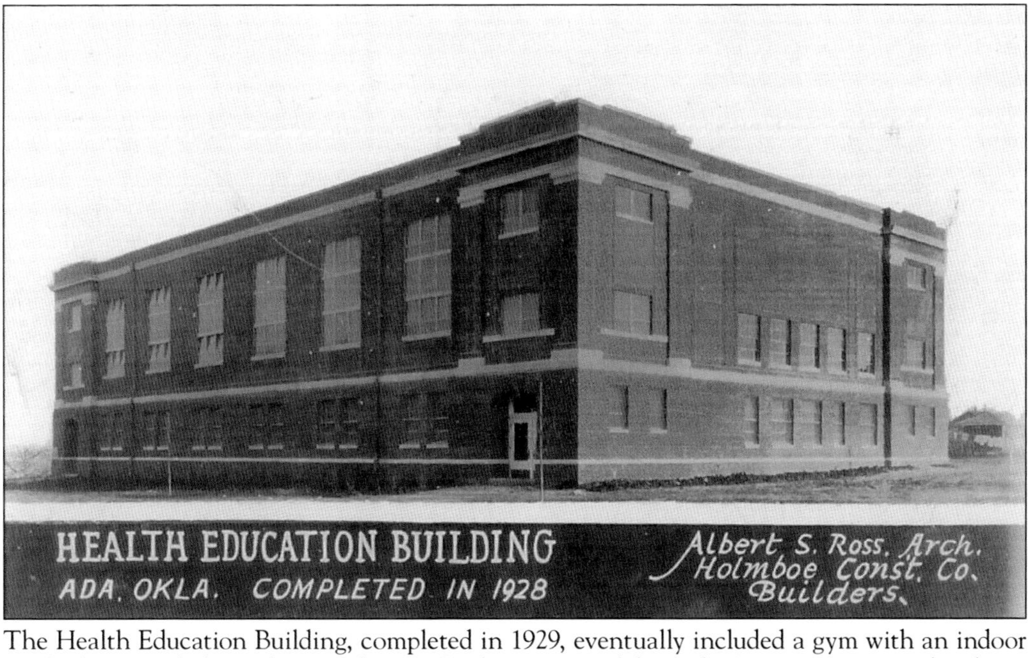

The Health Education Building, completed in 1929, eventually included a gym with an indoor track that was dedicated to Mickey McBride, a successful coach. Since a new gym has been constructed on Stadium Road, the old gym in the Health Education Building is mainly used for intramural sports. (Courtesy of Gary Haney.)

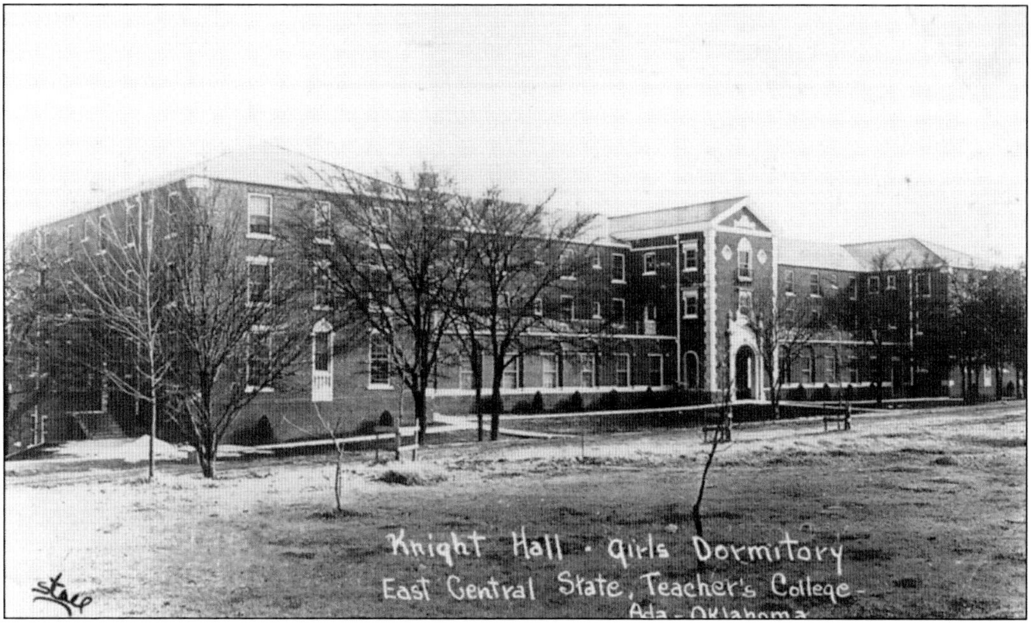

The girls' dormitory was built behind the McBride Gym and Health Facility. Still East Central Teacher's College, it had a lot of female students. (Courtesy of Gary Haney.)

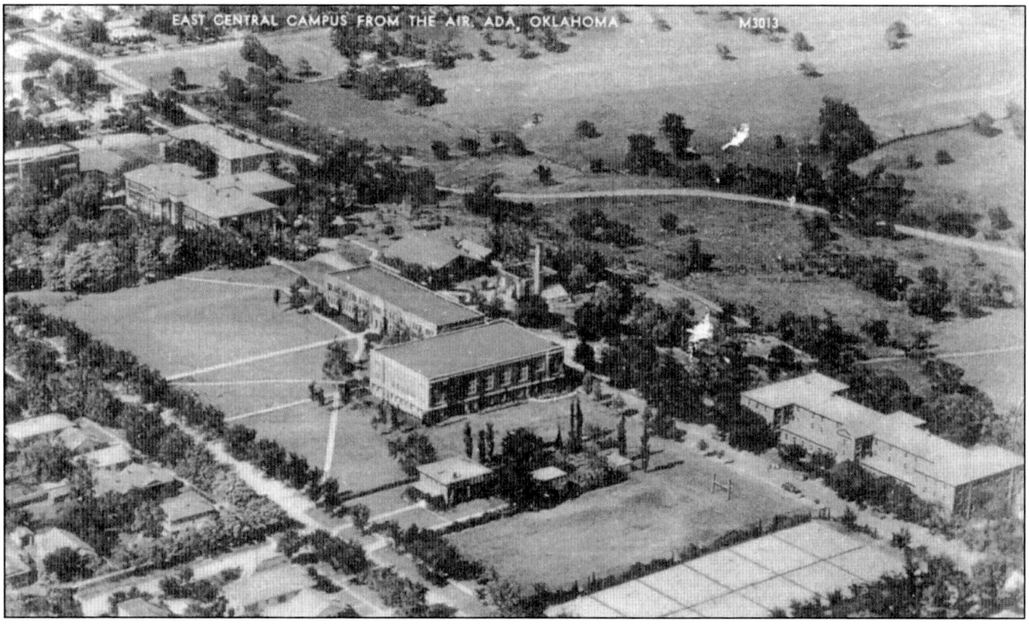

This 1950s aerial picture shows how Ada has grown. Behind the football field, there was very little, but today neighborhoods are located there. The university's campus begins at the gatepost entrance. The campus has expanded one city block west and has a new area dedicated to the arts at the end of East Main. (Courtesy of Gary Haney.)

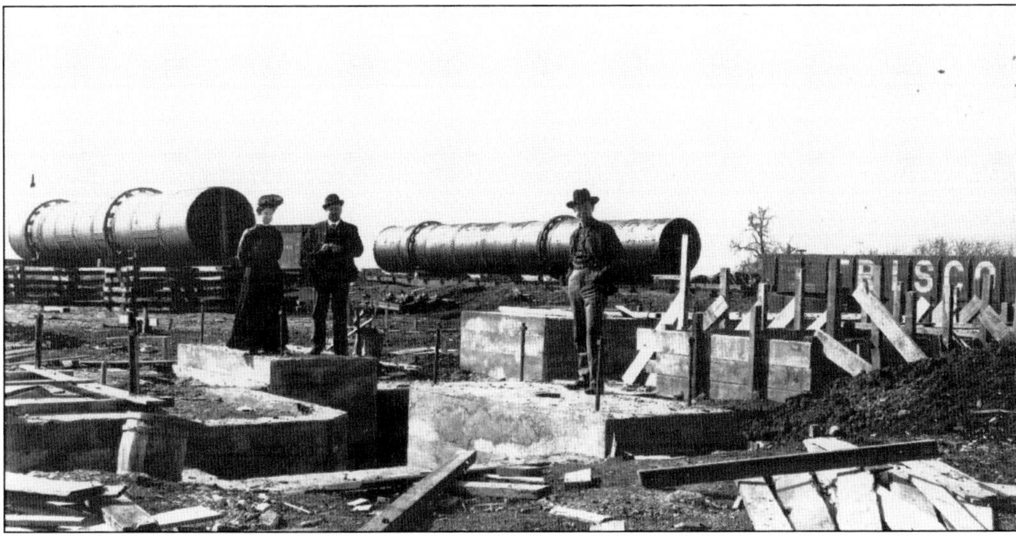

Curious visitors look at the beginnings of the Portland Cement plant. Judging by their clothing and demeanor, they were not there to work. (Courtesy of Gary Hancy.)

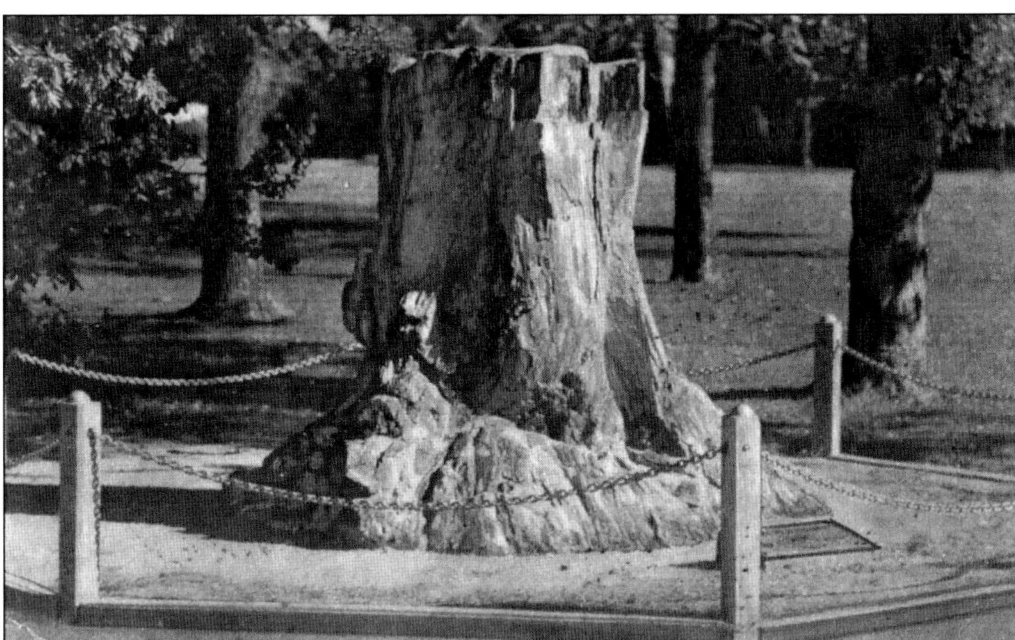

This giant, petrified Devonian tree was assembled and dedicated to well-known geologist David White. John Fitts, local oil man, was essential to its arrival. The tree stump still greets people who enter the East Central University gate. (Courtesy of Gary Haney.)

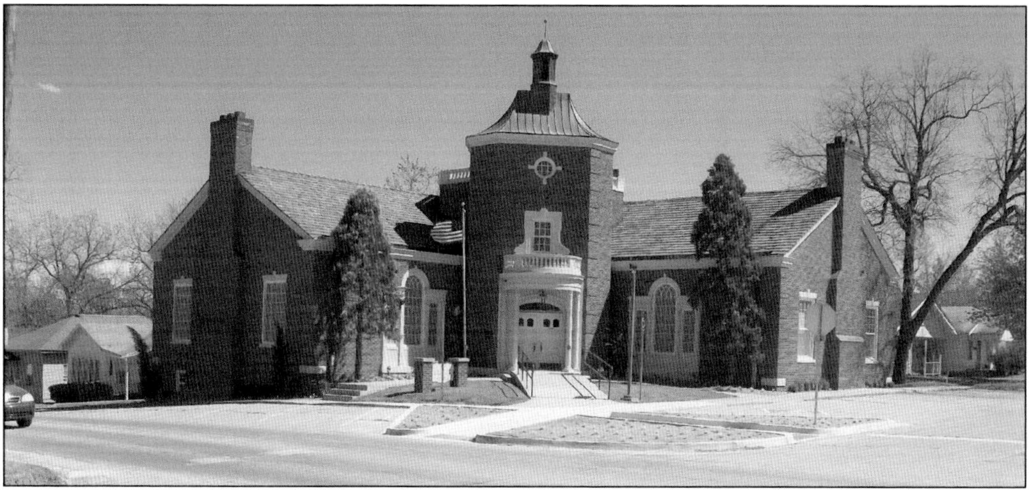

The Ada Public Library was built in 1939 in the Williamsburg style. It was designed by architect Albert Ross. The library moved to another location when the weight of all the books began to cause the foundation to fail. Since the mid-1980s, this beautiful building has been the Ada Arts and Heritage Center. It is a community building used for special events. (Author's collection.)

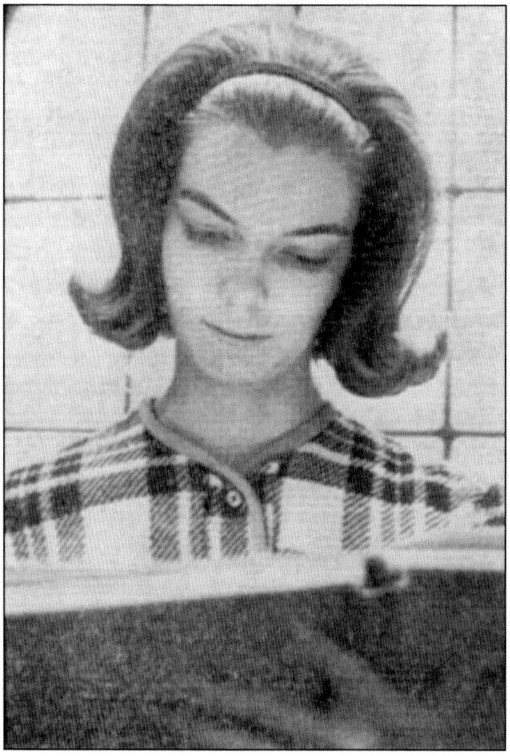

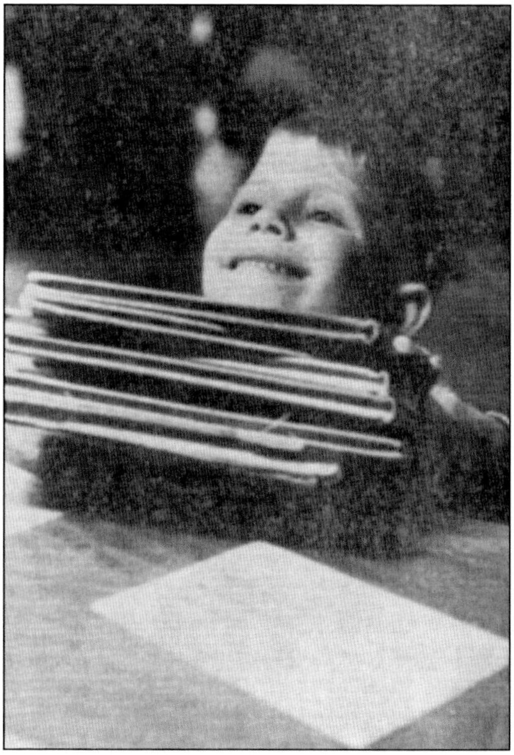

On the left, East Central student Judy Brawner studies in the original library. On the right, looking barely old enough to read, Fred Romine returns a stack of books to the checkout desk. The building had a special ambiance that never failed to impress young readers. (Both courtesy of Alberta Blackburn.)

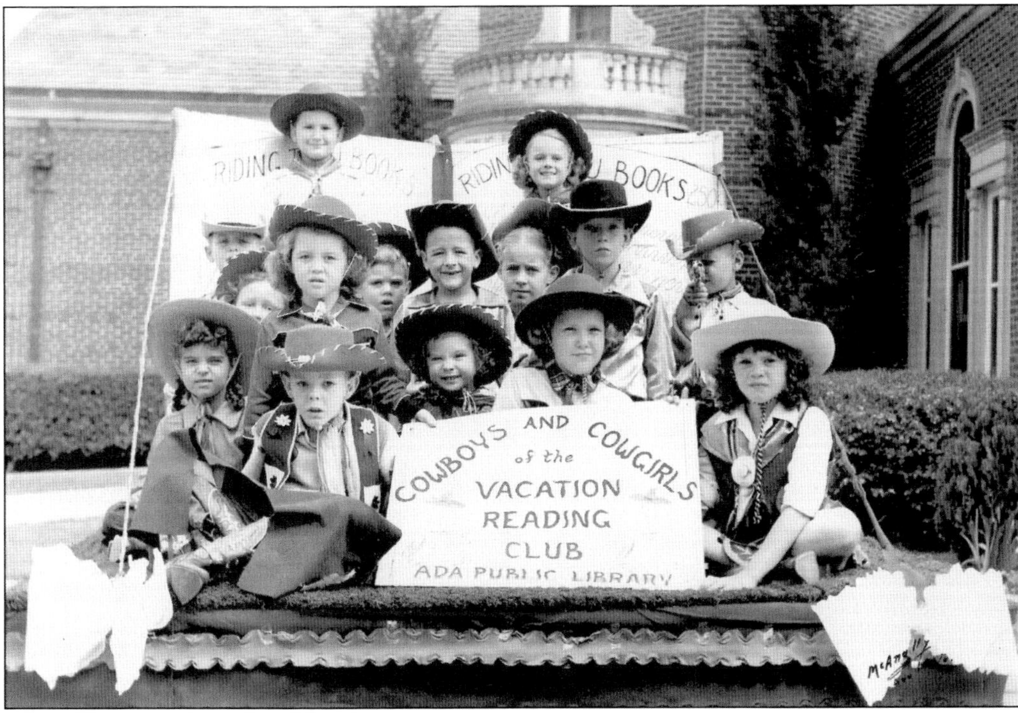

In 1949, children gather on a float in front of the public library to advertise their vacation-reading club. In the 1980s, the city moved the library to a new location at Twelfth and Rennie Streets. (Courtesy of Ada Public Library.)

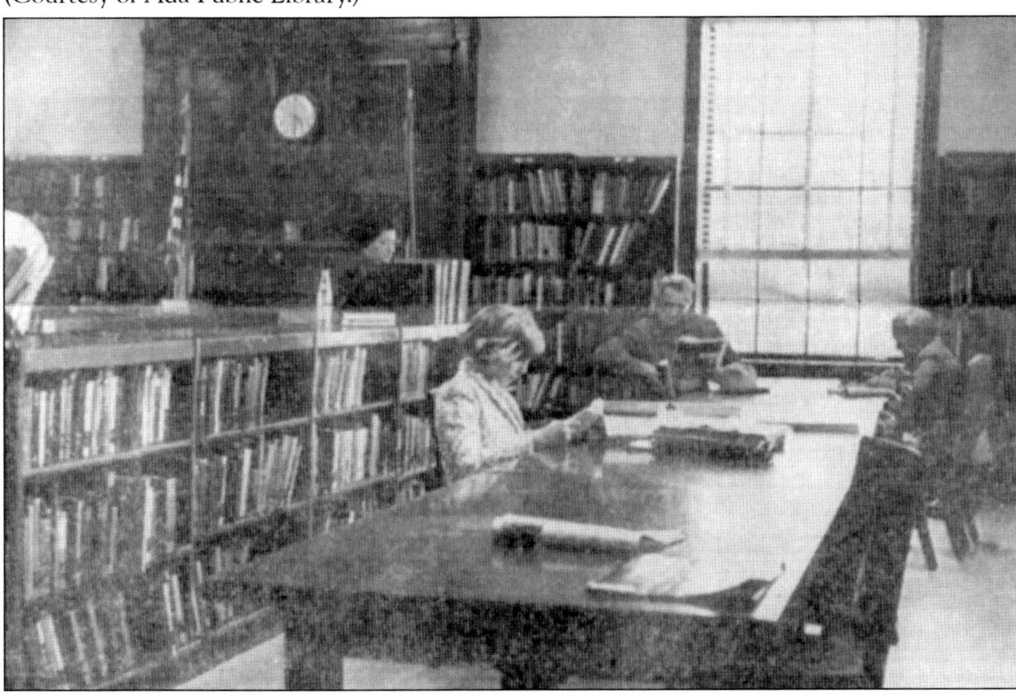

In the quiet of the old library, readers relax and enjoy the atmosphere in the west reading room. (Courtesy of Alberta Blackburn.)

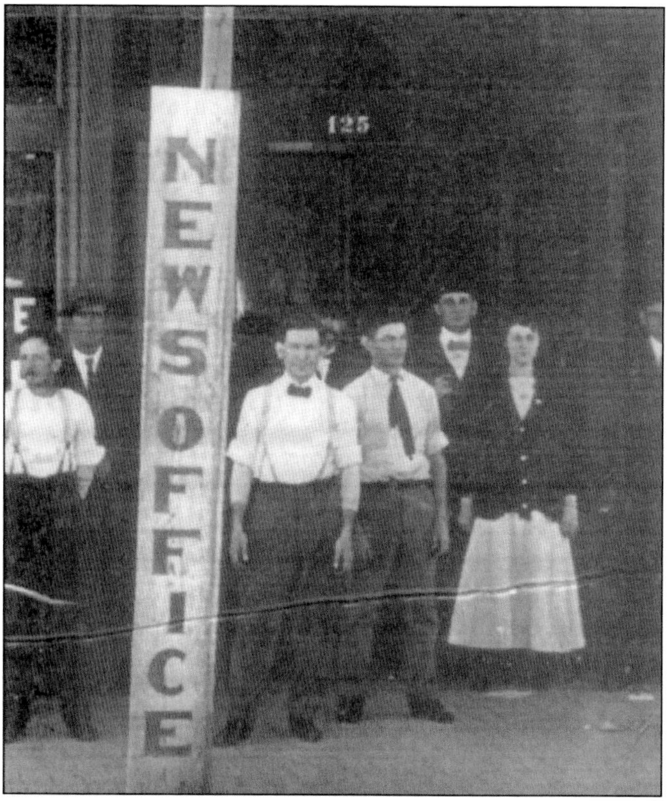

Employees of the *Ada News* proudly pose outside their building. (Courtesy of Alberta Blackburn.)

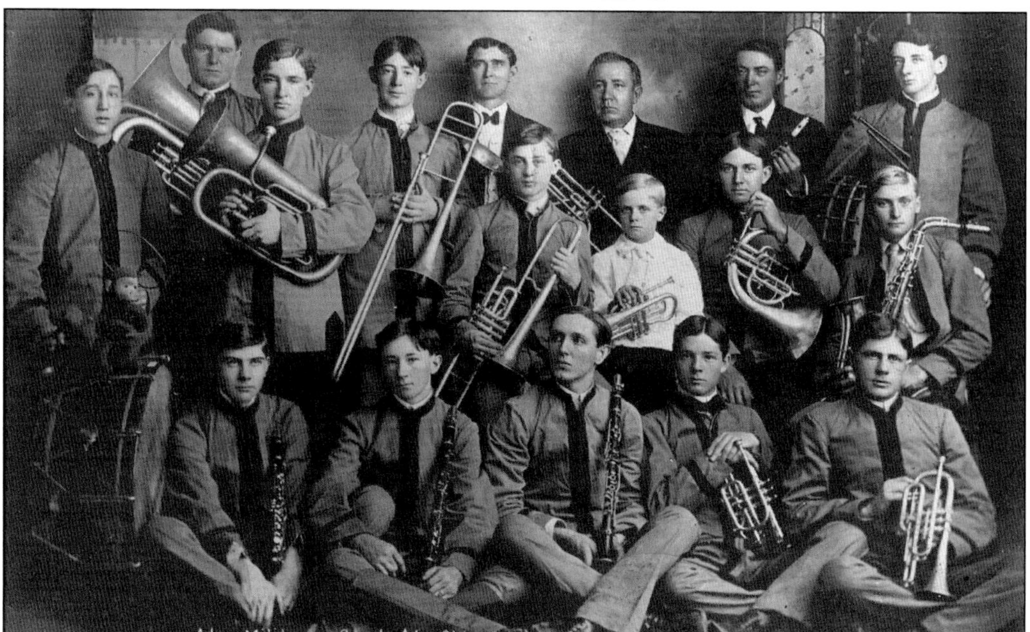

There isn't a harp in sight, but brass instruments were abundant. The drum was used to keep these men in time. The Ada Military Band was certainly composed of serious musicians. (Courtesy of Gary Haney.)

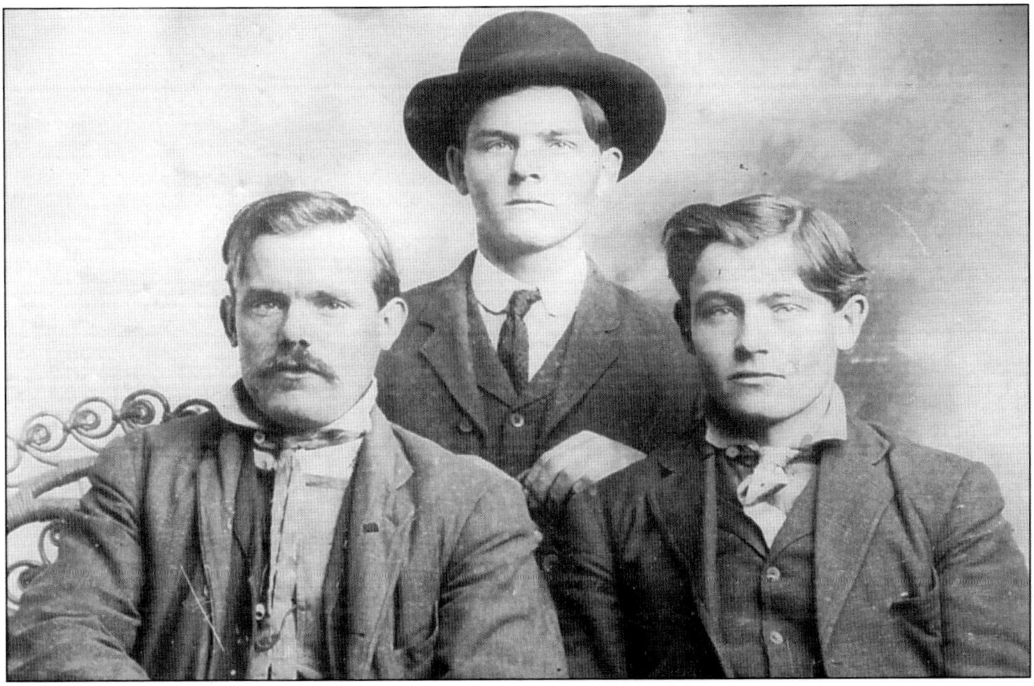

Three Campbell brothers, Samuel Dewitt, Marvin, and Monroe, are dressed for a trip to Ada. These local farmers wanted a picture to capture the moment while looking handsome and debonair. (Courtesy of Juanita Scott.)

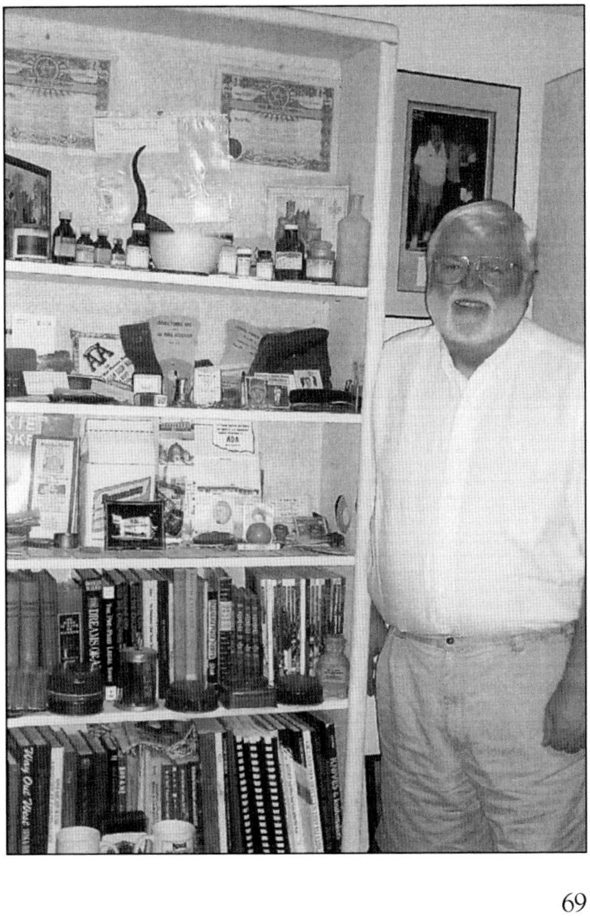

Gary Haney was a major contributor to this publication. Though he lives just outside of Ada, he has a passion for collecting historical items that pertain to the town. He has over 10,000 items in his collection. (Courtesy of Gary Haney.)

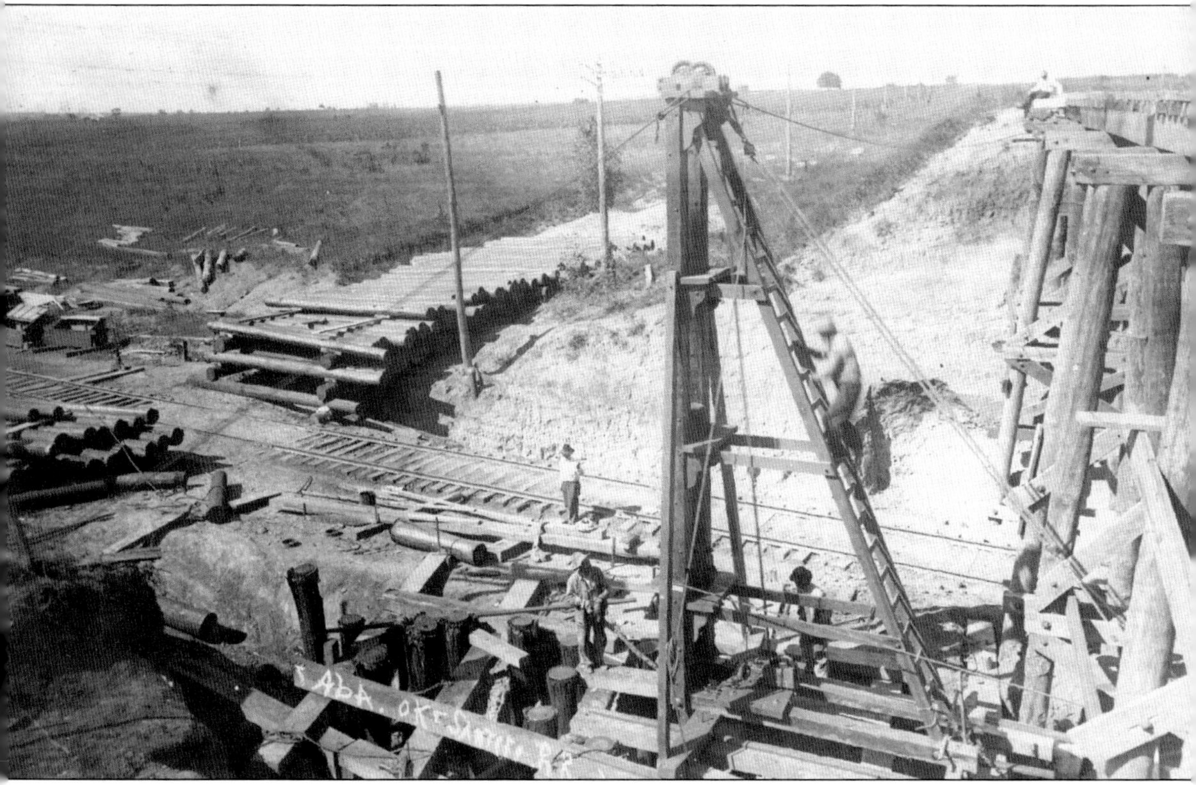

The trestle south of Ada was well built with wooden poles and iron. Walking across its open rail system became a local test of courage. (Courtesy of Gary Haney.)

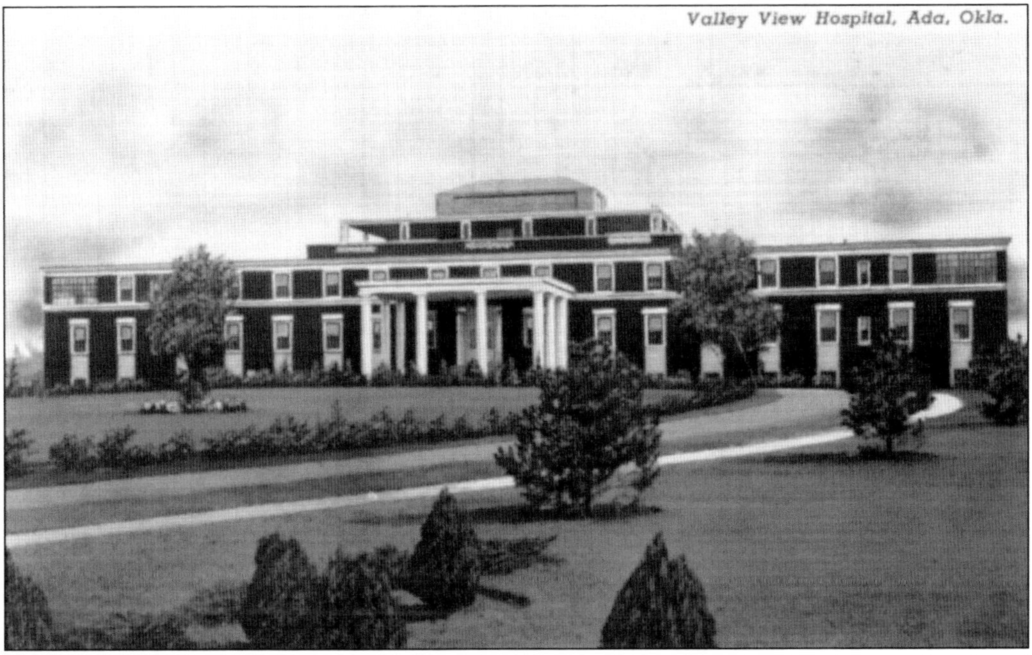

This is Ada's Valley View Hospital in its early days. It was an impressive building but was abandoned once the new hospital on Monte Vista Boulevard was built in 1986. The more modern facility continues to serve the Ada area with the latest medical technology. (Courtesy of Gary Haney.)

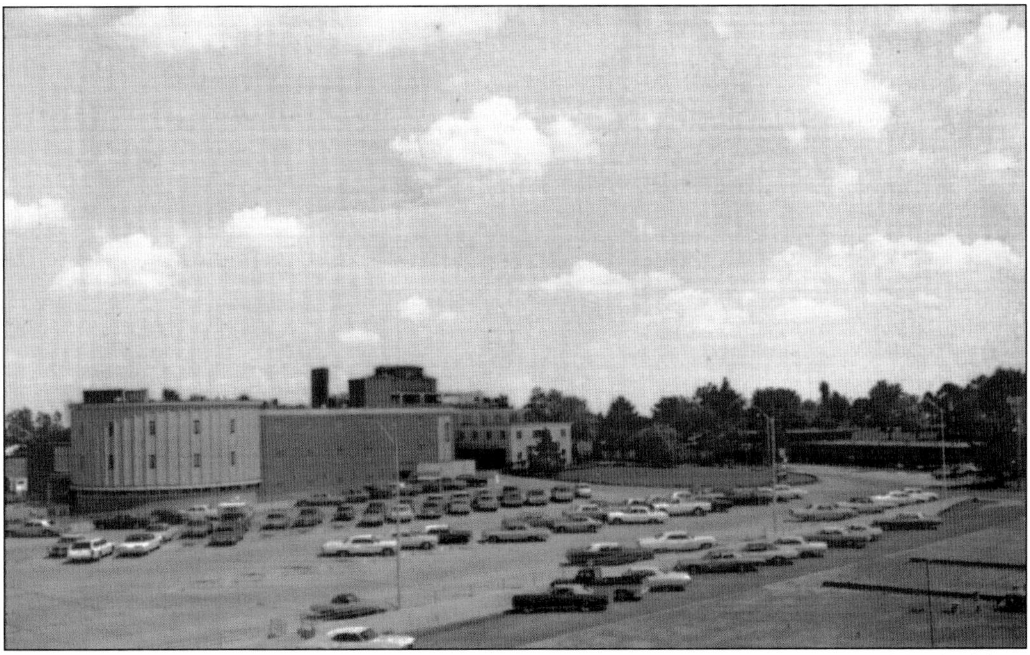

This is the old Valley View Hospital in the 1960s. At the time, the circular part of the building was the new obstetric ward. The old obstetric ward was a separate building to the north of the hospital. (Courtesy of Gary Haney.)

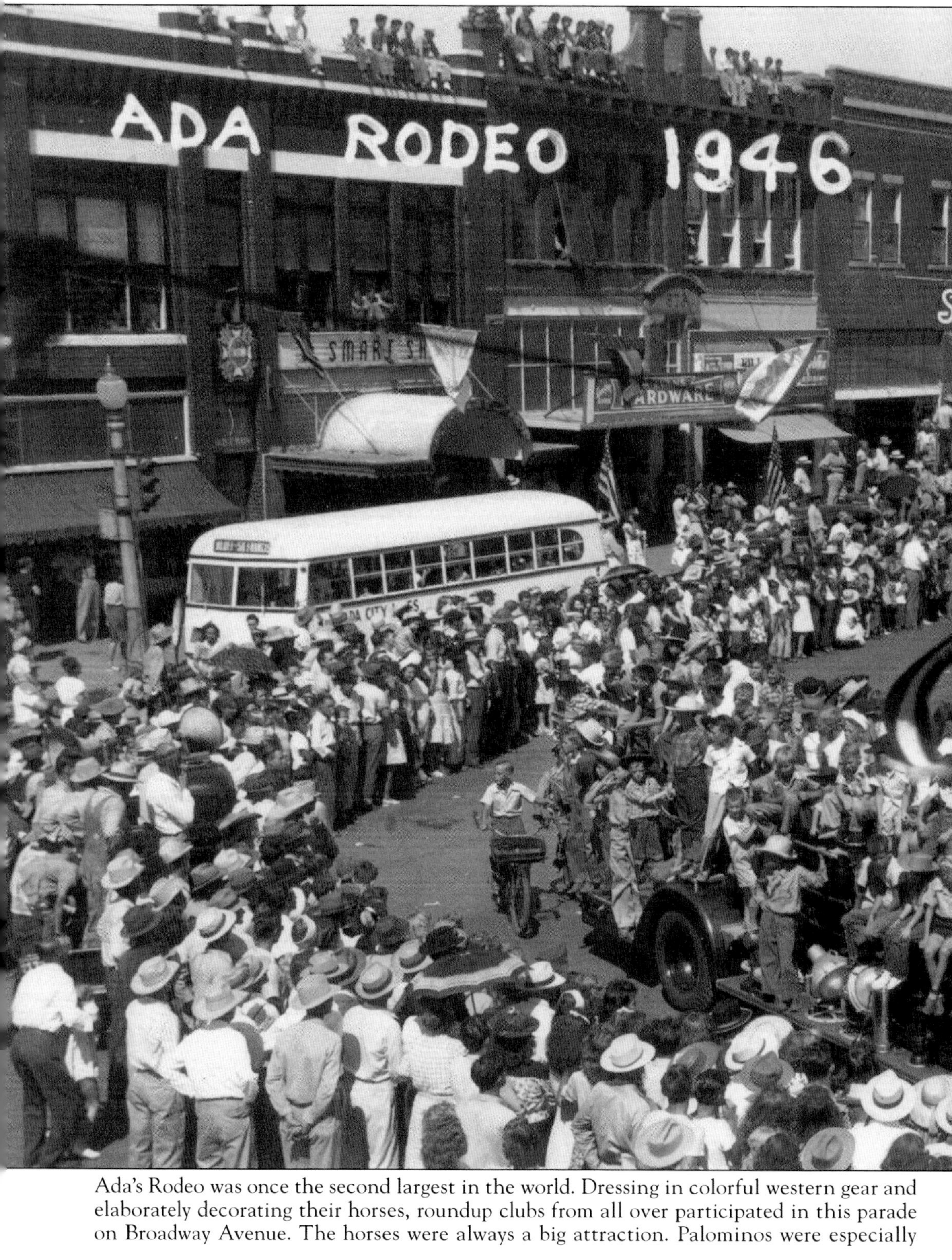

Ada's Rodeo was once the second largest in the world. Dressing in colorful western gear and elaborately decorating their horses, roundup clubs from all over participated in this parade on Broadway Avenue. The horses were always a big attraction. Palominos were especially

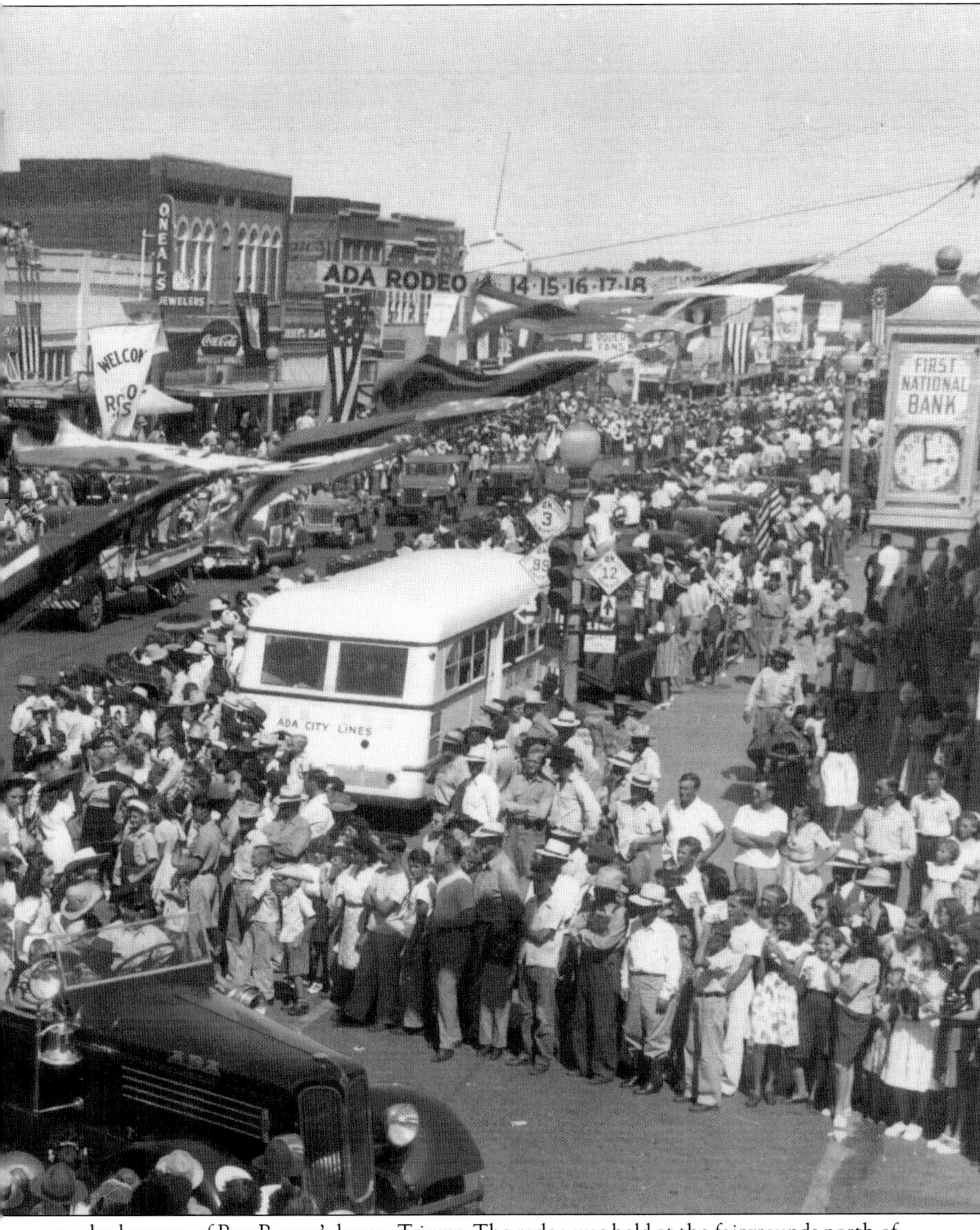

popular because of Roy Rogers's horse, Trigger. The rodeo was held at the fairgrounds north of Ada, which was also the home of the Ada Herefords Independents baseball team. (Courtesy of Gary Haney.)

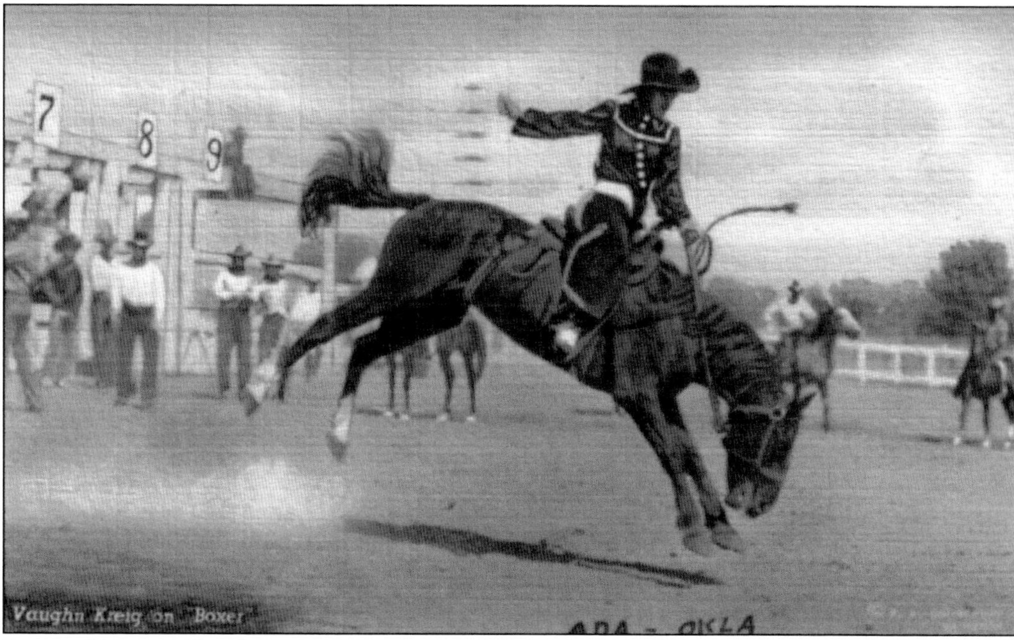

Pictured here is Vaughn Kreig on "Boxer." Women were allowed to ride in the rodeo under certain conditions; however, this was prohibited after Bonnie McCarroll died from an accident that occurred while riding her horse. (Courtesy of Gary Haney.)

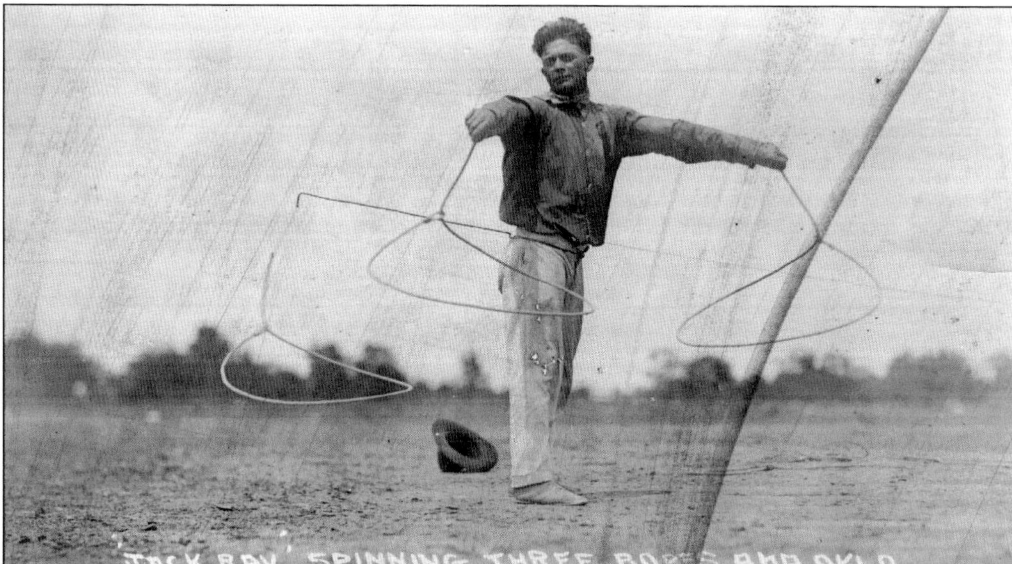

Jack Ray is spinning three lassos at once; one rope is being spun from a contraption around his waist. His attire is certainly not reminiscent of Roy Rogers, but Roy was never a good trick roper like Jack. (Courtesy of Gary Haney.)

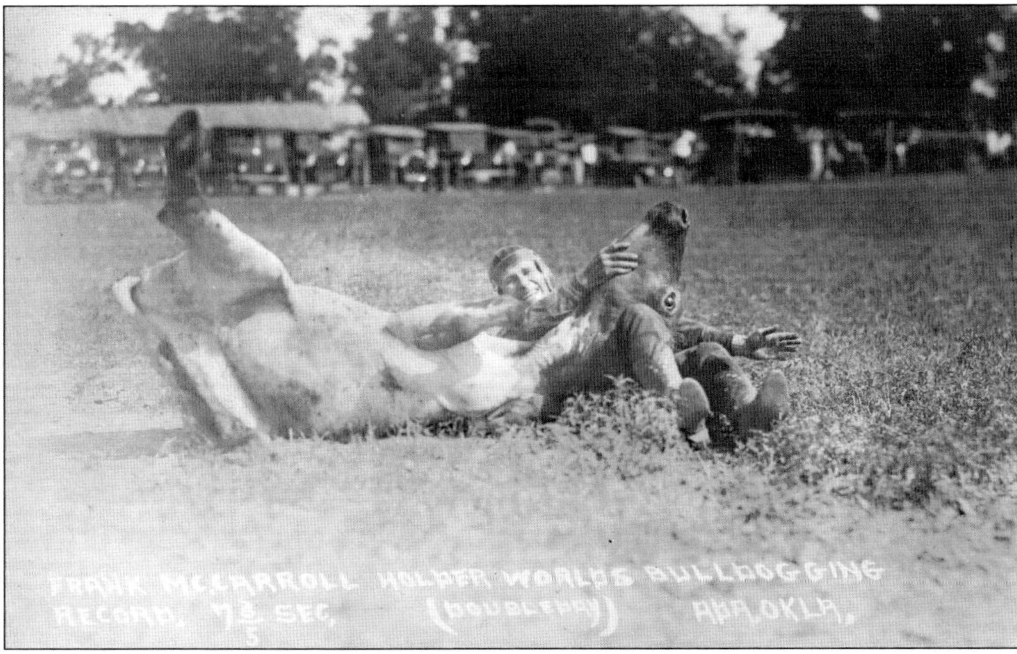

World champion bull dogger and the husband of Bonnie McCarroll, Frank Leo McCarroll shows off his specialty at the Ada rodeo. He set a bulldogging record of 7.35 seconds out of the gate. He seems pleased and even smiles for the camera. (Courtesy of Gary Haney.)

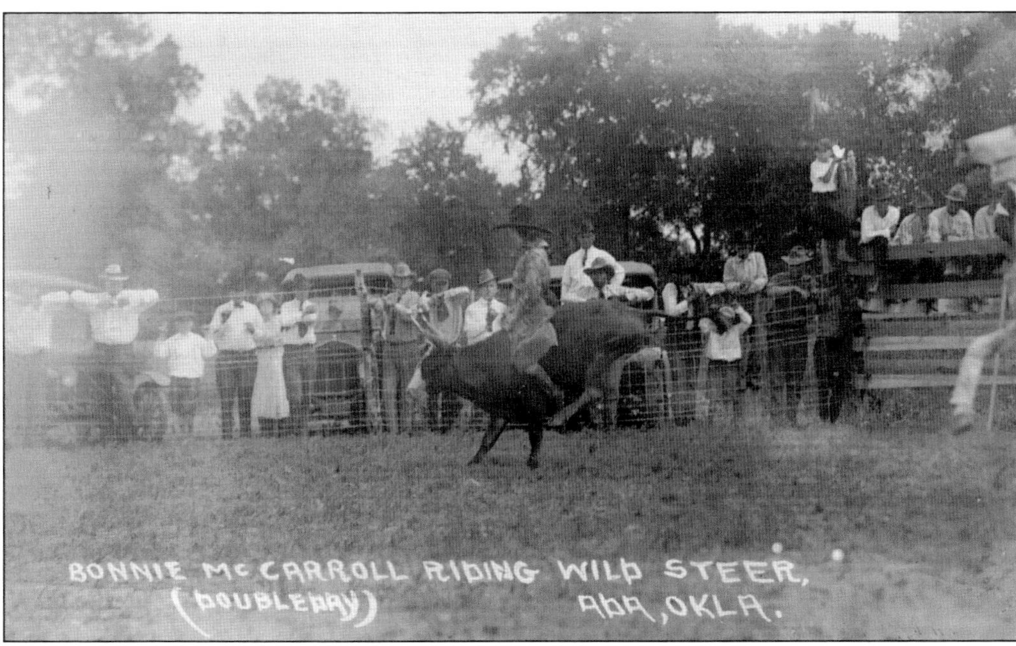

Bonnie McCarroll was one of the first women rodeo riders. She mainly rode broncos. She was killed when trappings on the horse she was riding caught her. Unbeknownst to her family, she rode her first bronco down a hill at her house. Rodeo fever wasn't exclusive to men, and bronco riding was Bonnie's passion. (Courtesy of Gary Haney.)

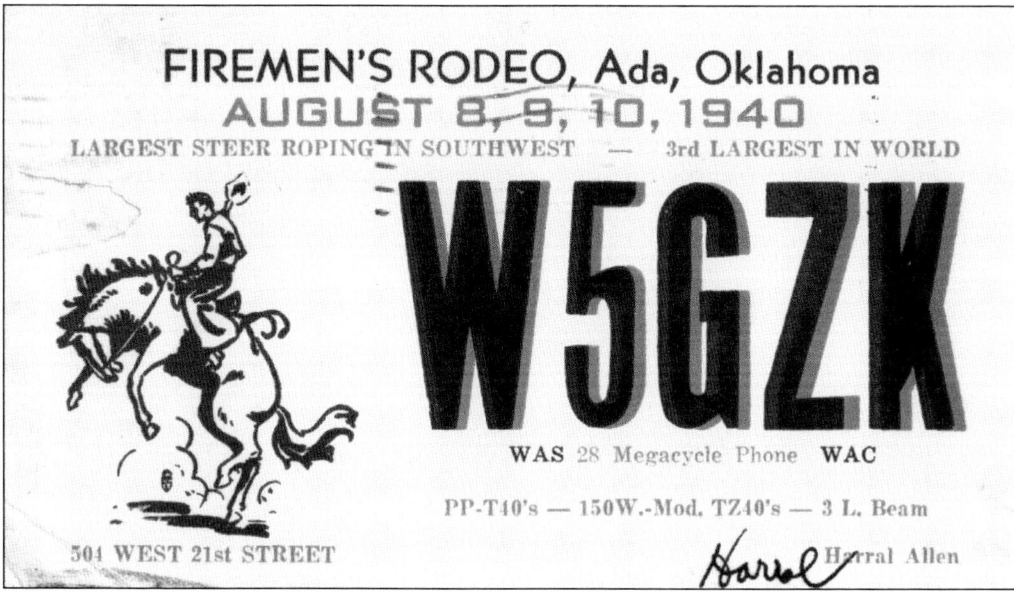

Cards advertising the Fireman's Rodeo were everywhere for cowboys and cowgirls to see. The rodeo featured the third largest steer roping in the southwest. This card is from a ham radio operator at 504 West Twenty-first Street. (Courtesy Gary Haney.)

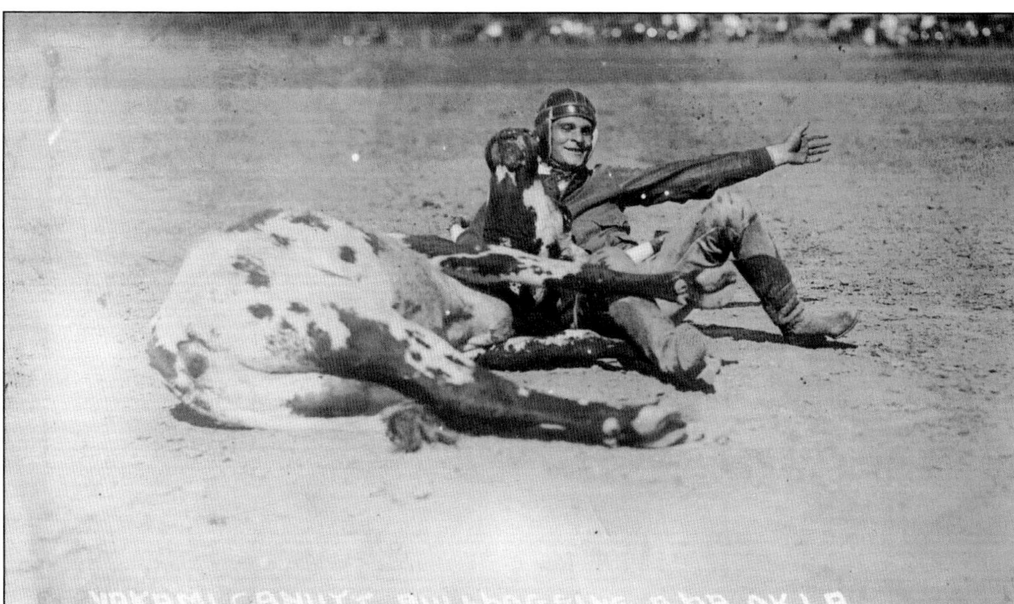

Yakami Canutt was a featured steer wrestler at the Ada Rodeo. He was also an acclaimed stuntman and an action director in other areas. This is a good picture of Yakami and his accomplishment that day. (Courtesy of Gary Haney.)

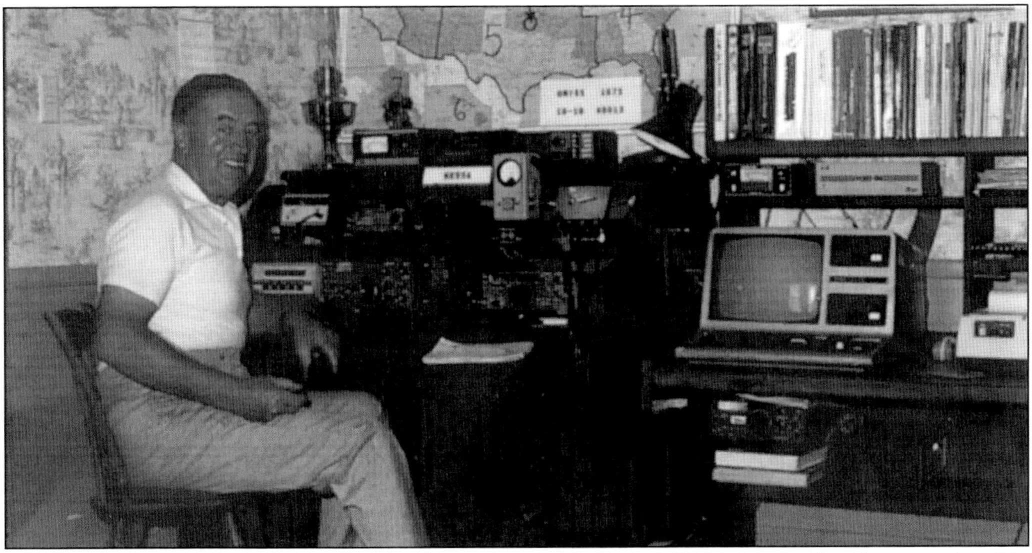

Here is another ham radio setup in Ada. Mr. Perry seems to be very proud of his comfortable home radio room. (Courtesy of Gary Haney.)

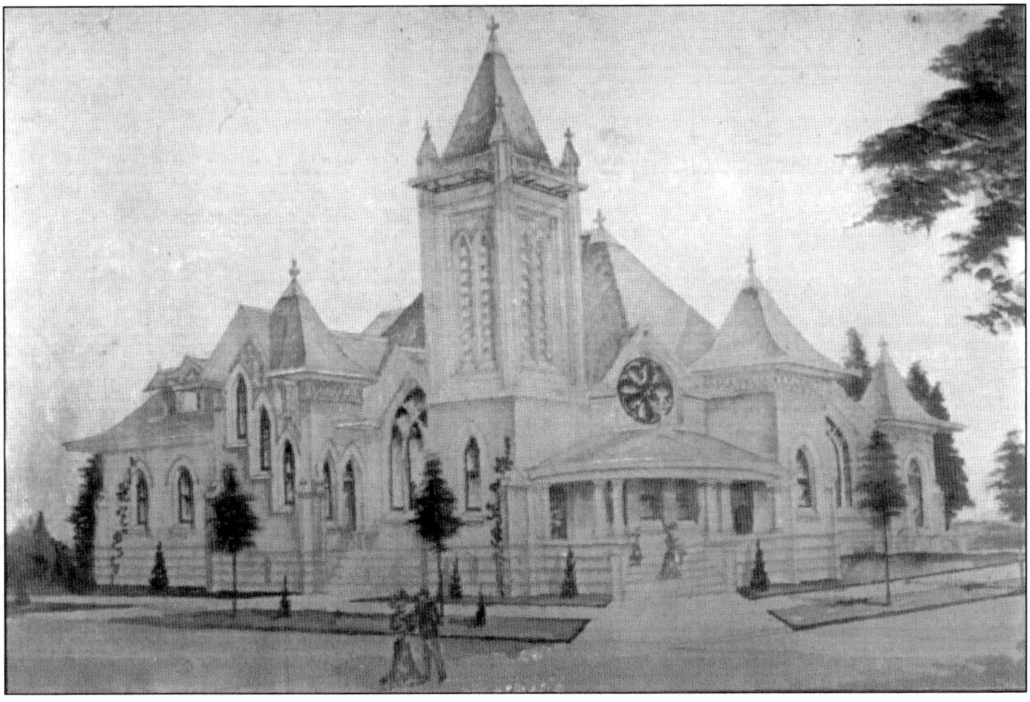

The First Methodist Church was unusual even back then. It is now one of the most impressive churches in Ada. The corner entrance and the dome made the building regal. Now stained-glass windows and arched walkways make the church a remarkable sight. (Courtesy of Gary Haney.)

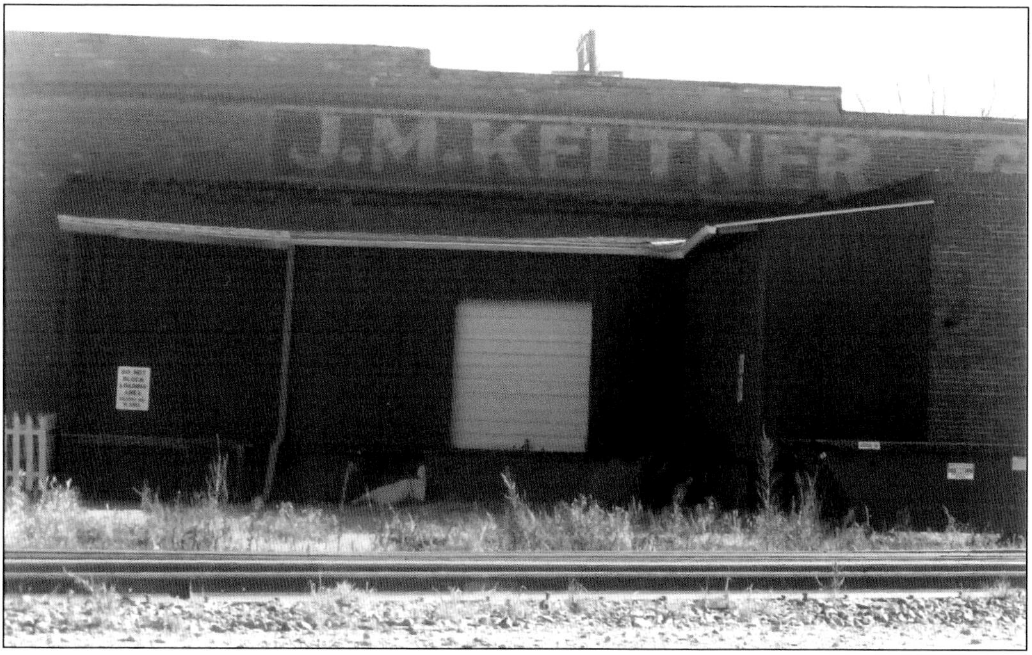

Here was where the stable stood that was used to hang the four men who murdered Bobbitt. The picket fence on the left surrounded the lynching monument and memorabilia. The J. M. Keltner Grocery and Produce Company went out of business, and the building seen here is gone because of a fire. The monuments will be replaced somewhere in the area. (Author's collection.)

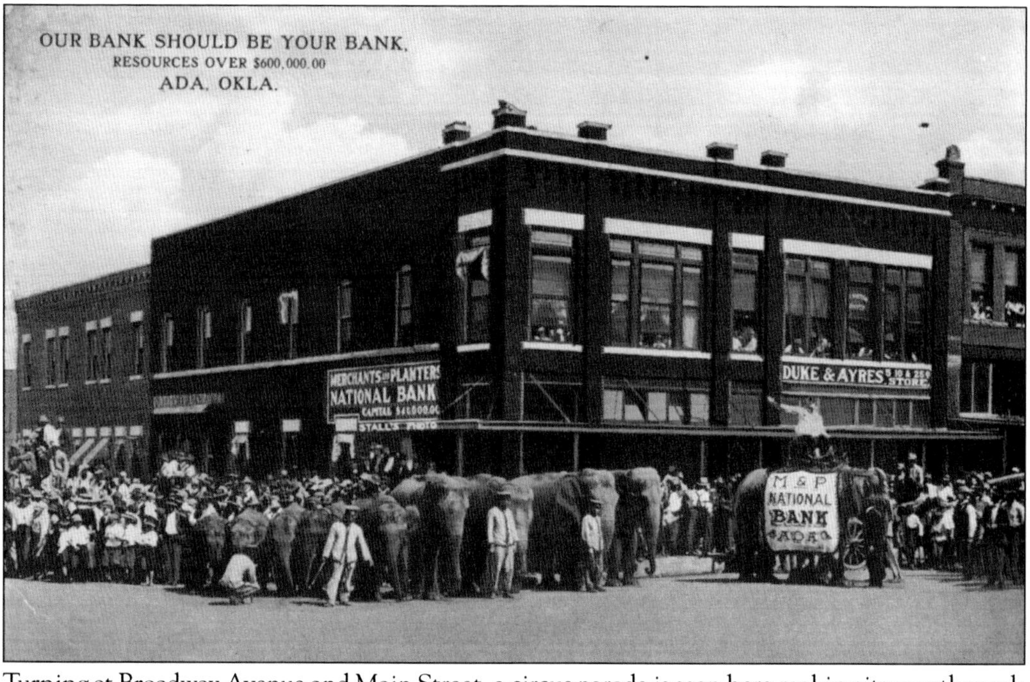

Turning at Broadway Avenue and Main Street, a circus parade is seen here making its way through town. The Diamond Shop is now in business on that corner. (Courtesy of Gary Haney.)

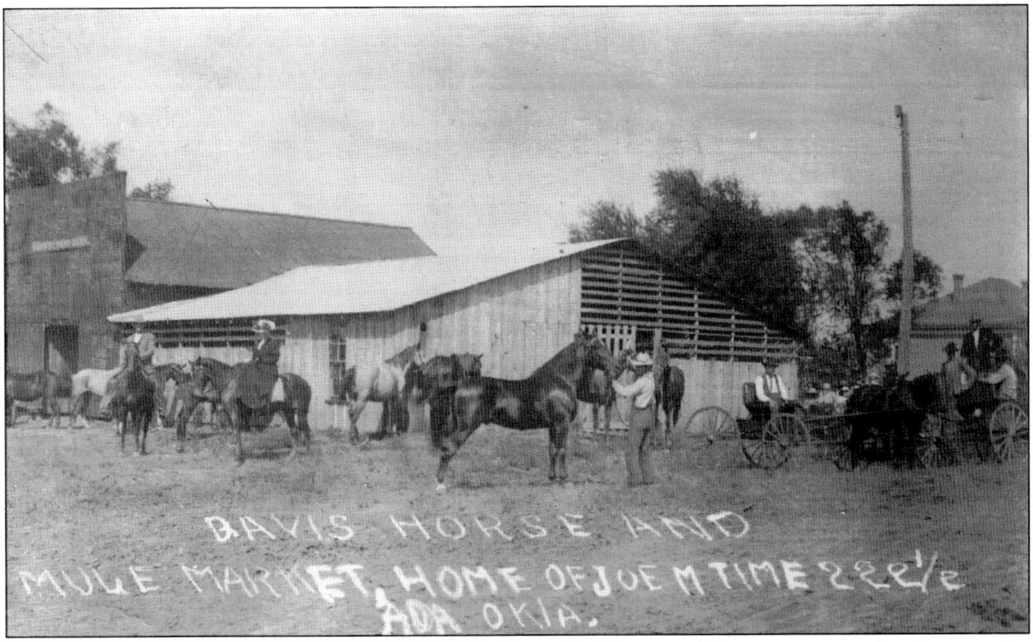

Out at the Davis Ranch, people stay busy working their horses. Horses were, and still are, a lot of work. (Courtesy of Gary Haney.)

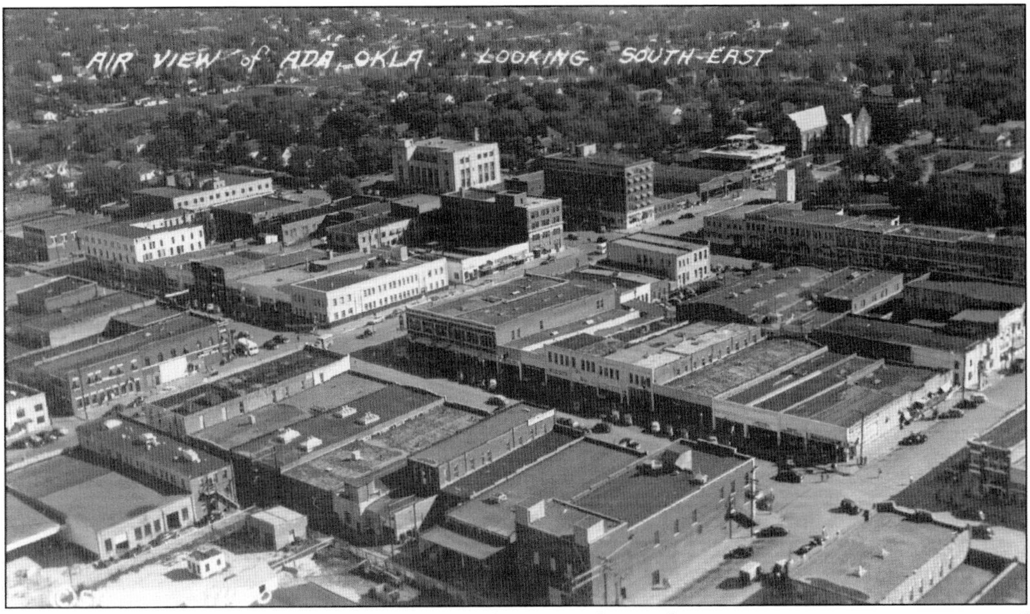

This is a bird's-eye view of town looking southeast. It shows the very important intersection of Broadway Avenue and Main Street. This is where Ada is separated into its east and west sides. The large white building in the middle is the First National Bank. (Courtesy of Gary Haney.)

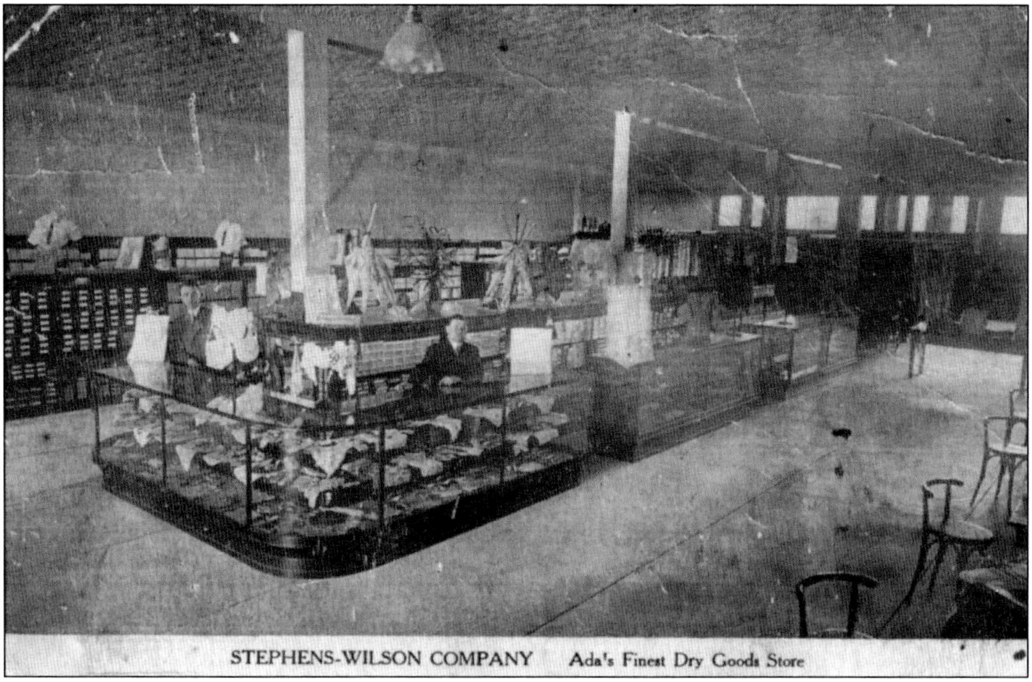

Stephens-Wilson Dry Goods store was a popular place to shop in Ada. Here Mr. Stephens and Mr. Wilson await the rush. (Courtesy of Gary Haney.)

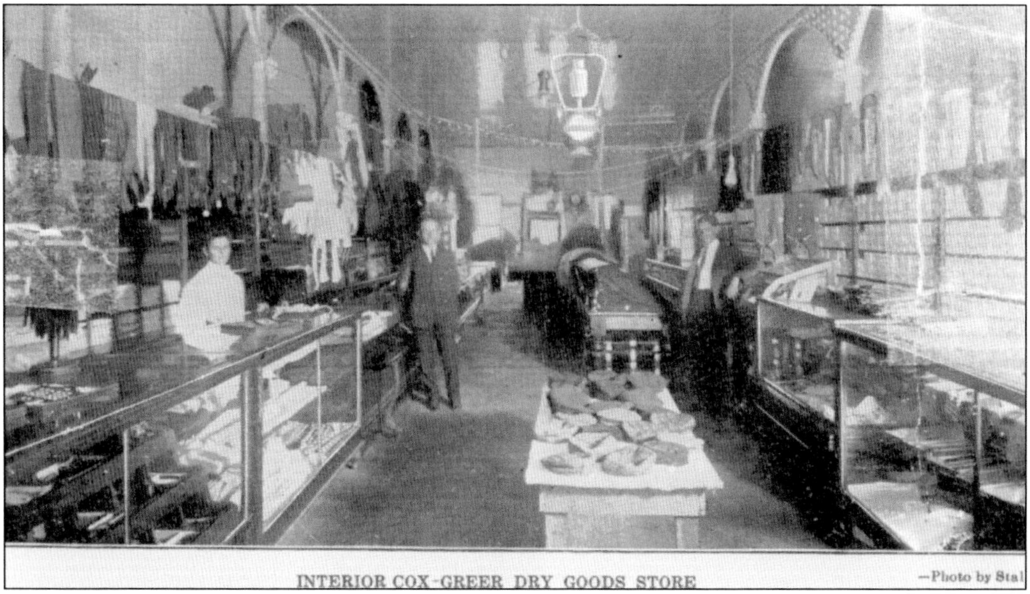

Evidently, Cox-Greer Dry Goods was ready for business. The light fixture, fancy for the time, showed the way for customers. (Courtesy of Gary Haney.)

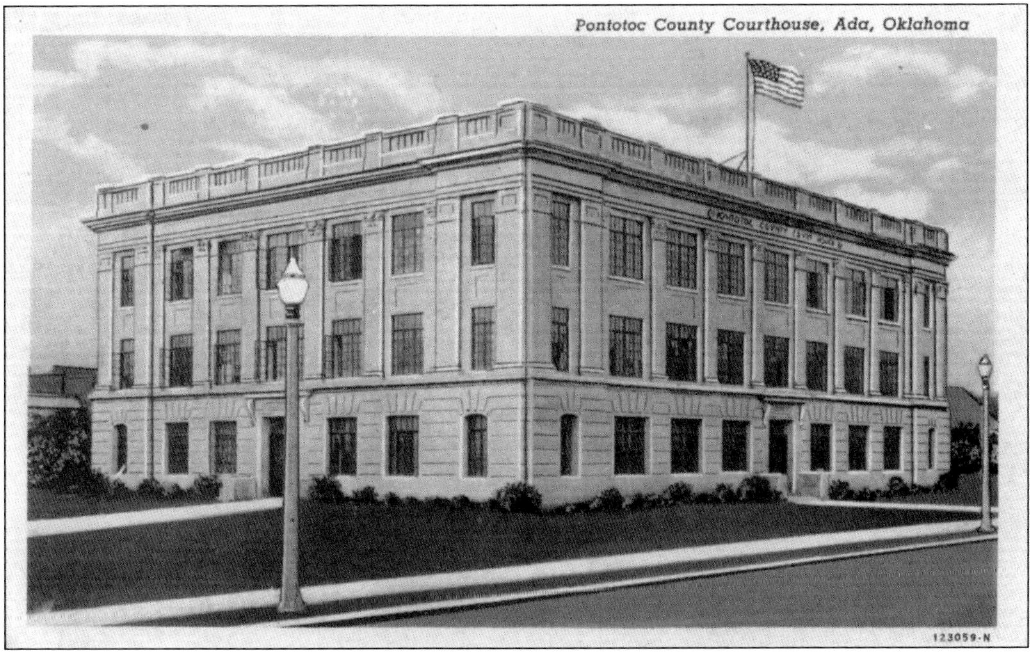

This Pontotoc County Courthouse architectural drawing looks much as the building does today. Made of marble and other rock, it was built to last. It now sits in the center of the whole block, surrounded by Broadway, Twelfth, Thirteenth, and Townsend Streets, just behind the Central Fire Station and Citizens Bank. (Courtesy of Gary Haney.)

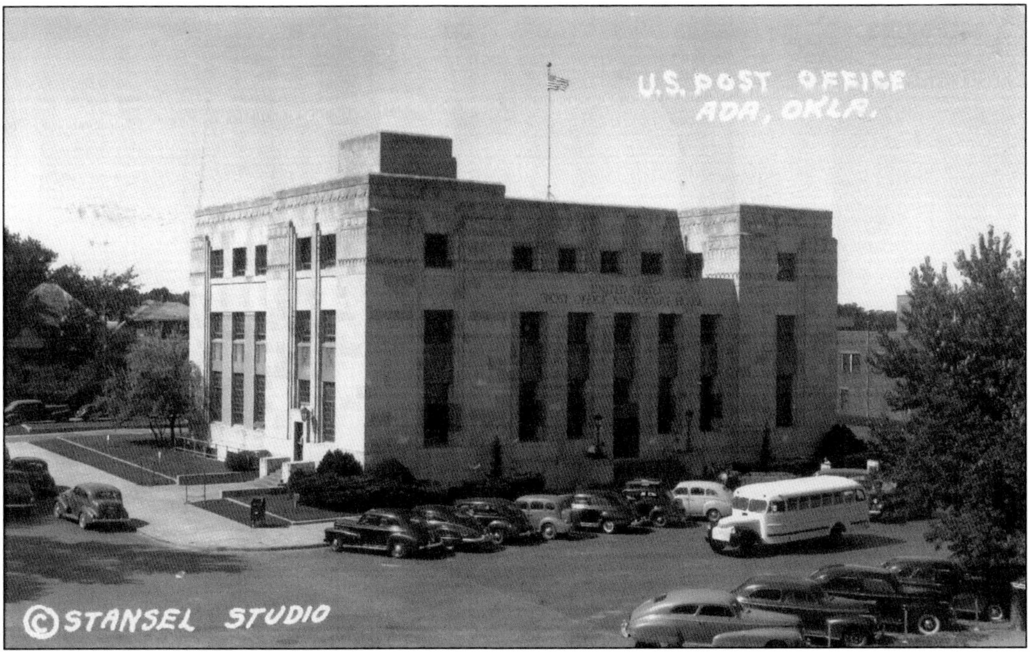

This is the post office in the 1940s. It finally found a permanent location at Twelfth and Rennie and has put up a formidable building to prove it. (Courtesy of Gary Haney.)

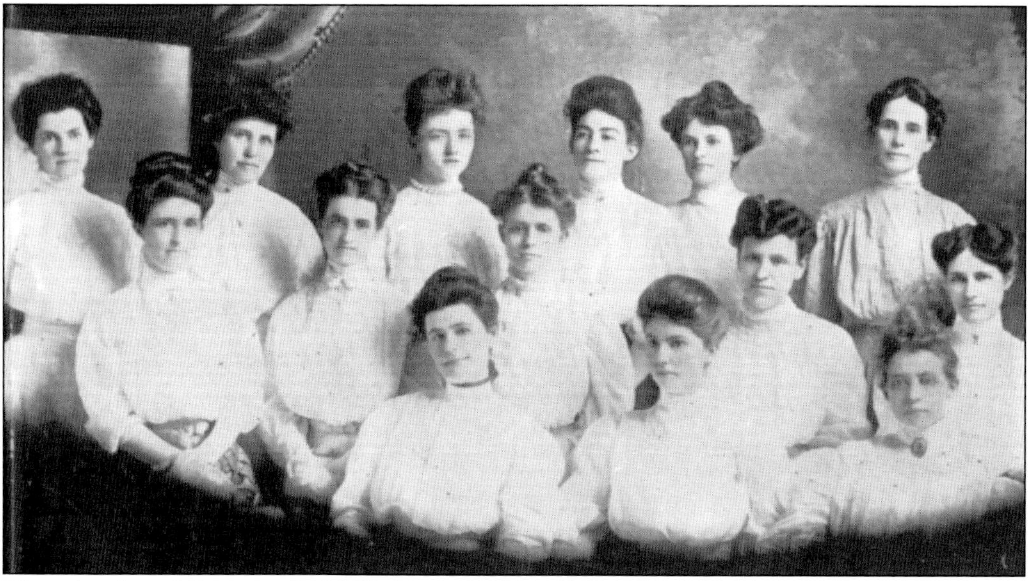

These lovely and distinguished ladies are members of the 20th-Century Club. Dressed in white, they took pride in themselves and their club. (Courtesy of Alberta Blackburn.)

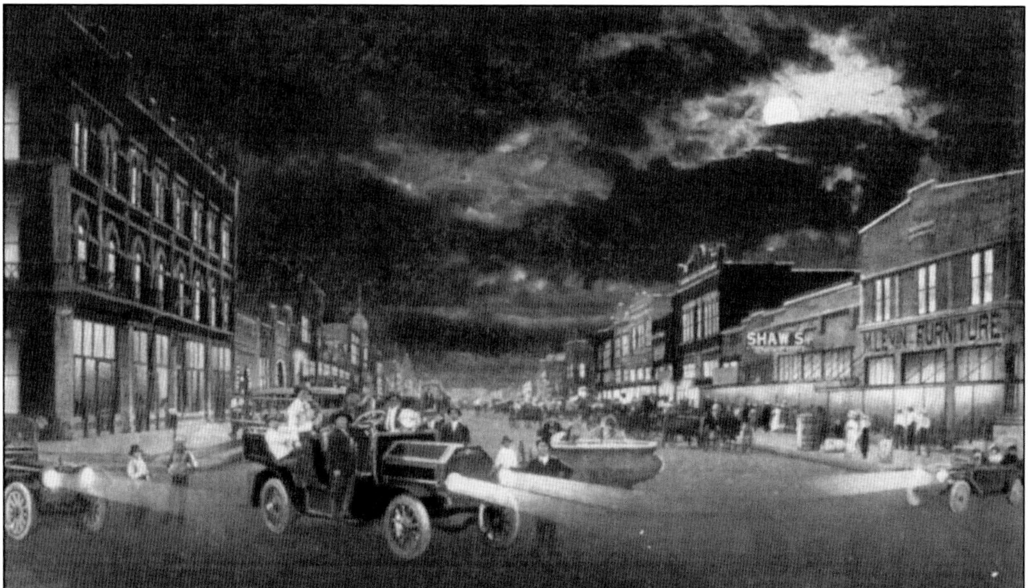

Pictured at nighttime, these people are by the fountain located near Main and Rennie Streets. The bank turret can be seen in the background, which is on the corner Broadway Avenue. This fountain has the inscription "Ada, not a lady, but a dandy place to live." The fountains are gone now. (Courtesy of Gary Haney.)

The American Building has been on the northeast corner of Main Street and Broadway Avenue for a long time. (Courtesy of Gary Haney.)

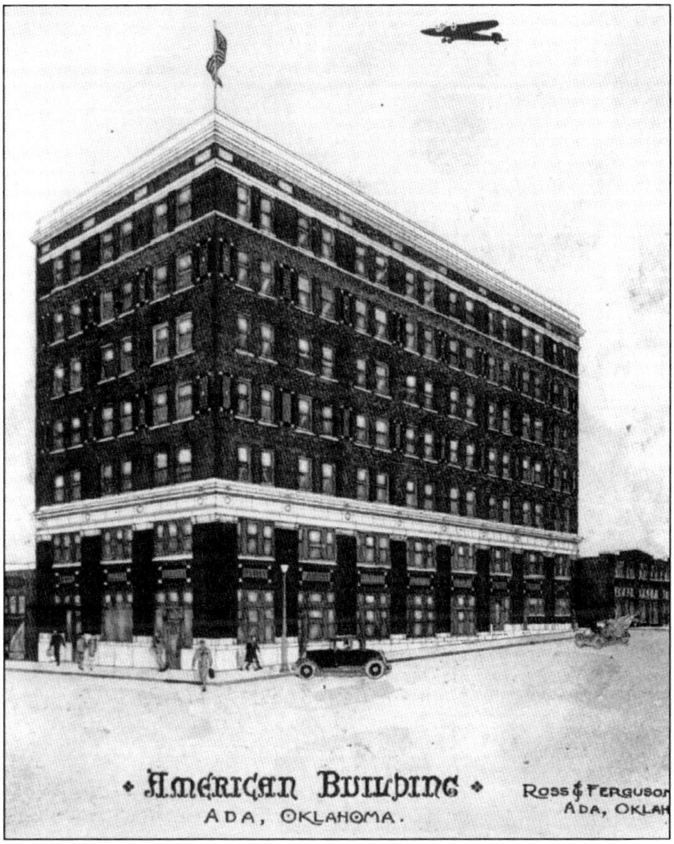

Here is a business card that belonged to photographer N. B. Stall. He used the image of a locomotive to draw the attention of potential customers. (Courtesy of Gary Haney.)

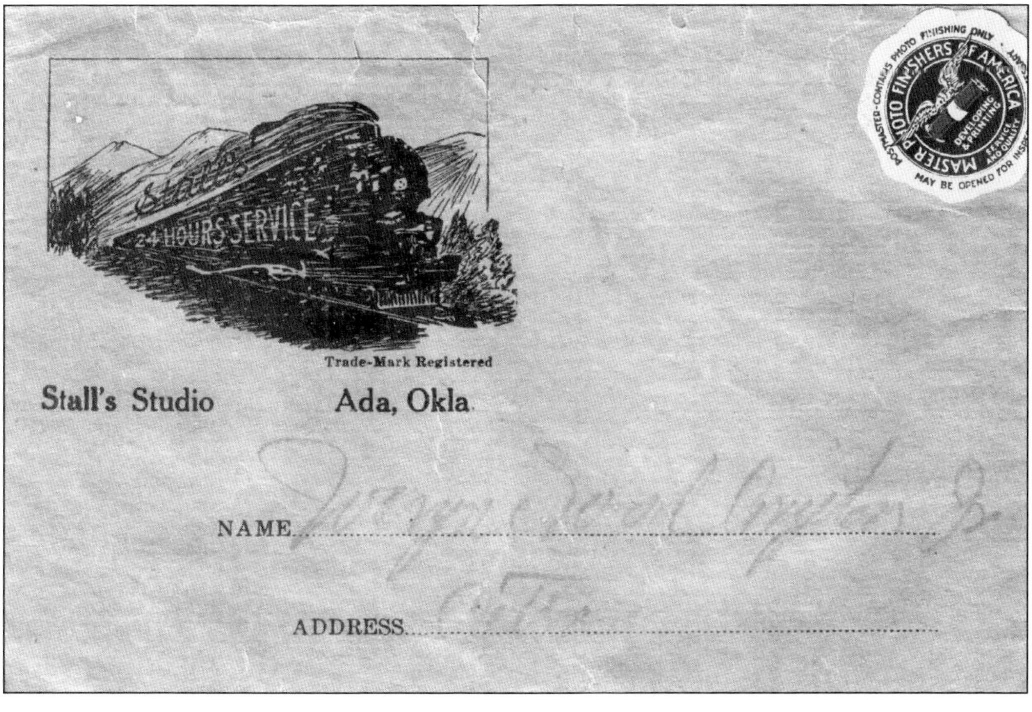

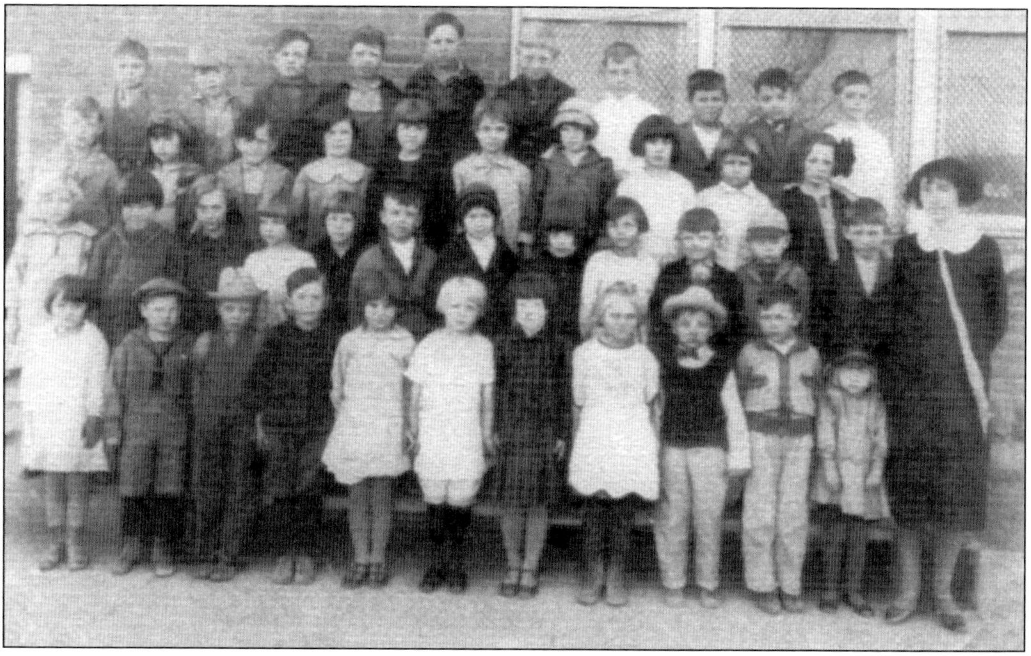

F. J. Wilbanks's vocal music club was very popular with young people. Here they are having their picture taken in front of Ada's second school building. Wilbanks must have been a good teacher to attract so many singers of varied ages. (Courtesy of Alberta Blackburn.)

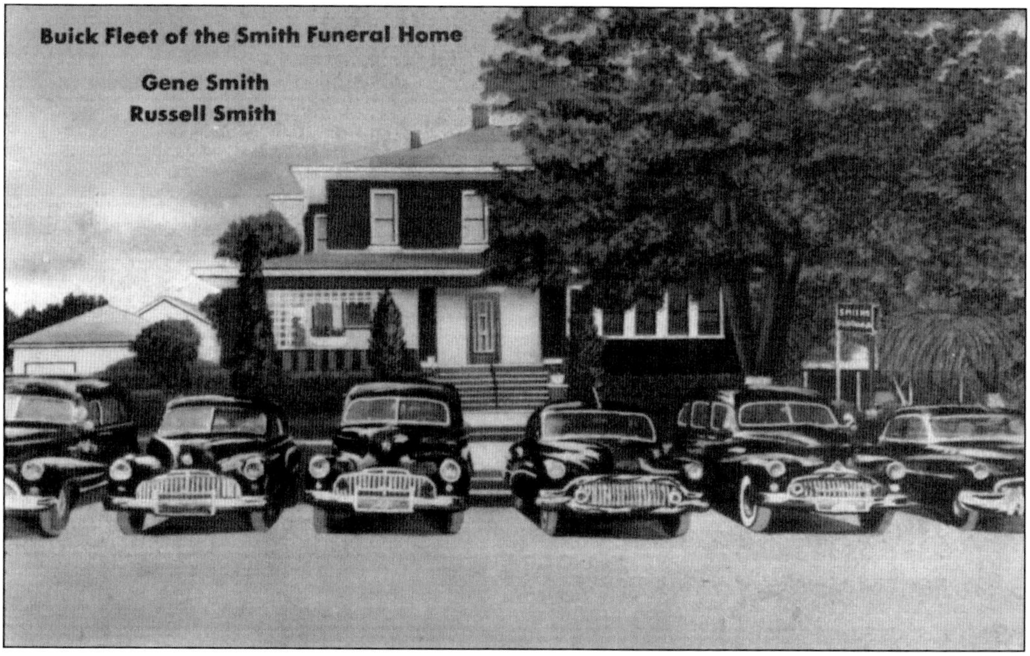

It's a pretty good guess that Smith's Funeral Home prefers Buicks for their business—the funeral home owned an entire fleet of them. (Courtesy of Gary Haney.)

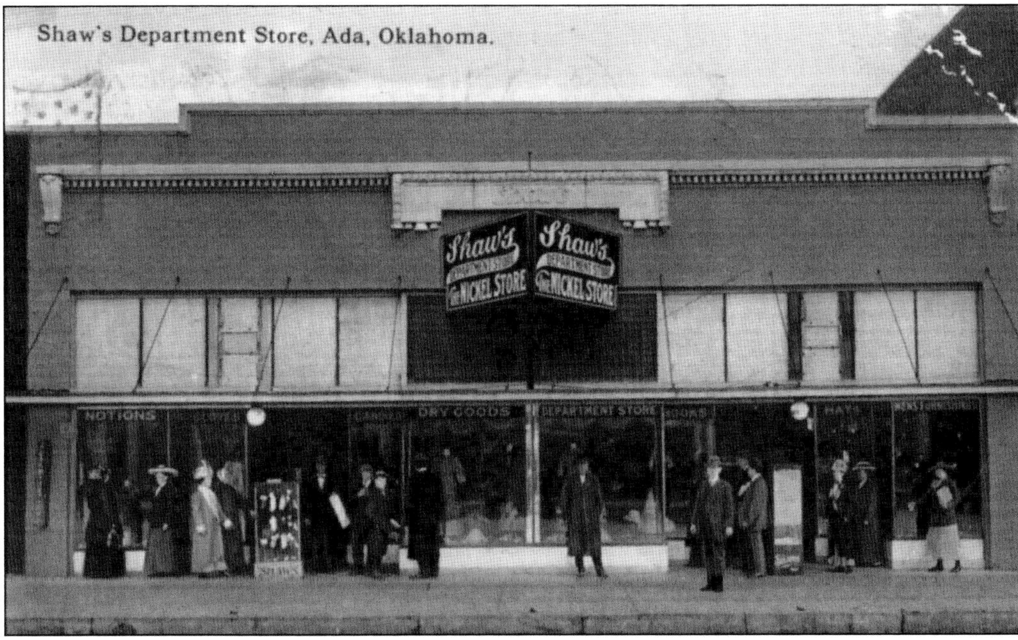

Shaw's Department and Nickel Store was one of the most popular stores in Ada. (Courtesy of Gary Haney.)

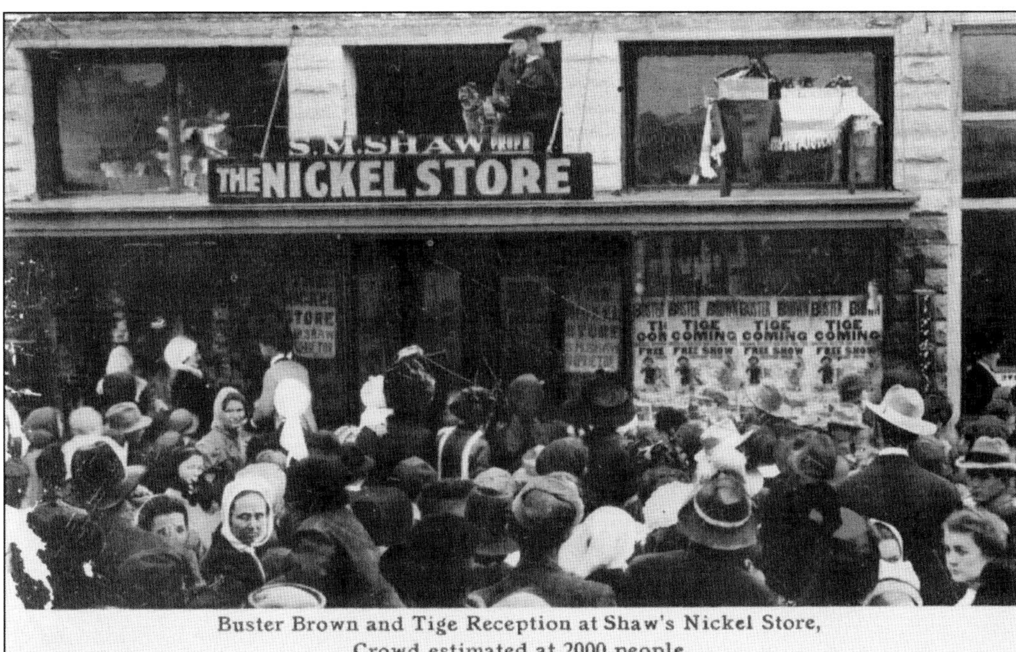

Tige the dog helped bring costumers to the Nickel Store. People gathered to hear the tag line for Buster Brown shoes recited: "Here's my dog Tige, he lives in a shoe. I'm Buster Brown. I live in there, too." (Courtesy Gary Haney.)

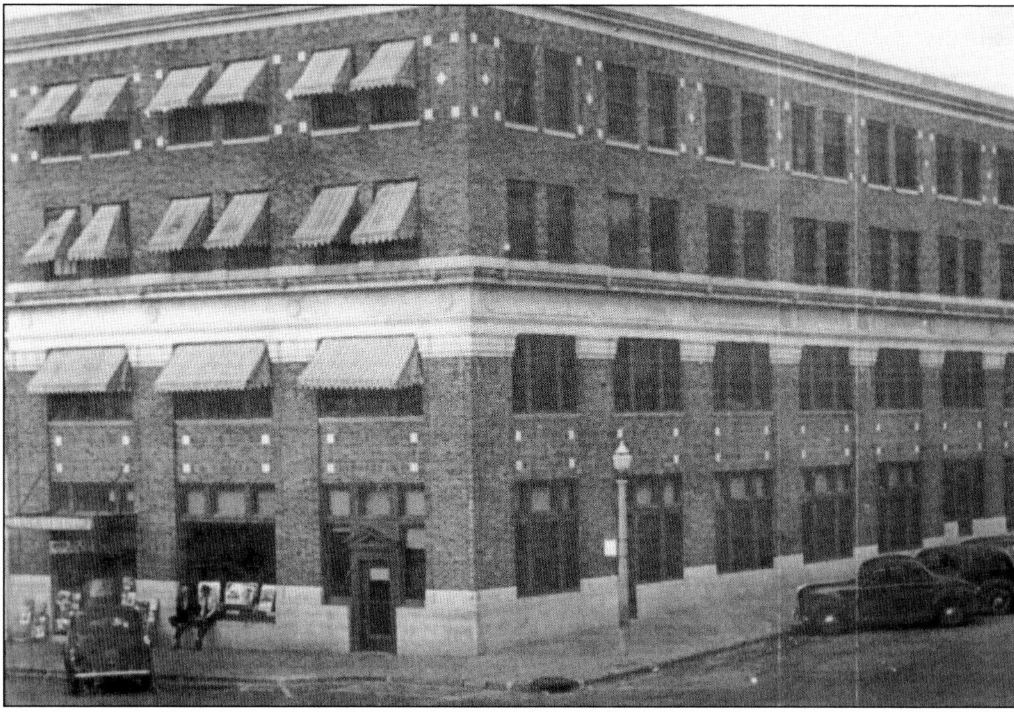

The American Building, which still stands, was called the Fleet Building at one time. It was on the prestigious corner of Broadway and Grande Avenues. (Courtesy of Alberta Blackburn.)

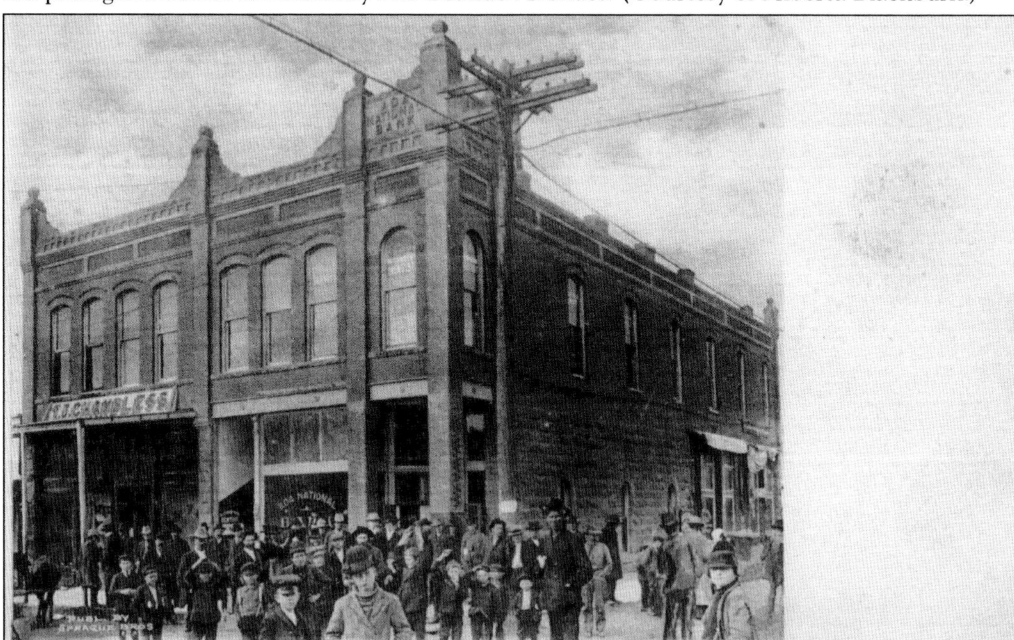

This scene is of the northwest corner of Main Street and Broadway Avenue. The Ada National Bank occupied this spot at one time. This building also housed the Leader Shoe Store, which was followed by Bryans Corner Drug and Coffee Shop. The H^{2}O church now occupies the popular corner. (Courtesy of Gary Haney.)

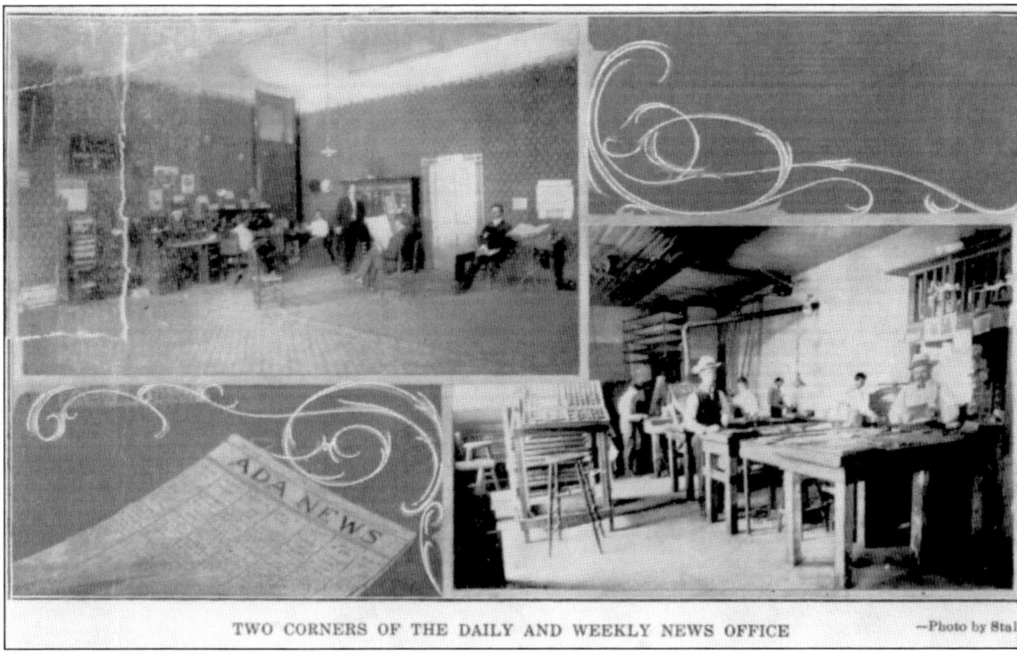

This postcard advertised two separate news services, weekly and daily. (Courtesy of Bud Throne.)

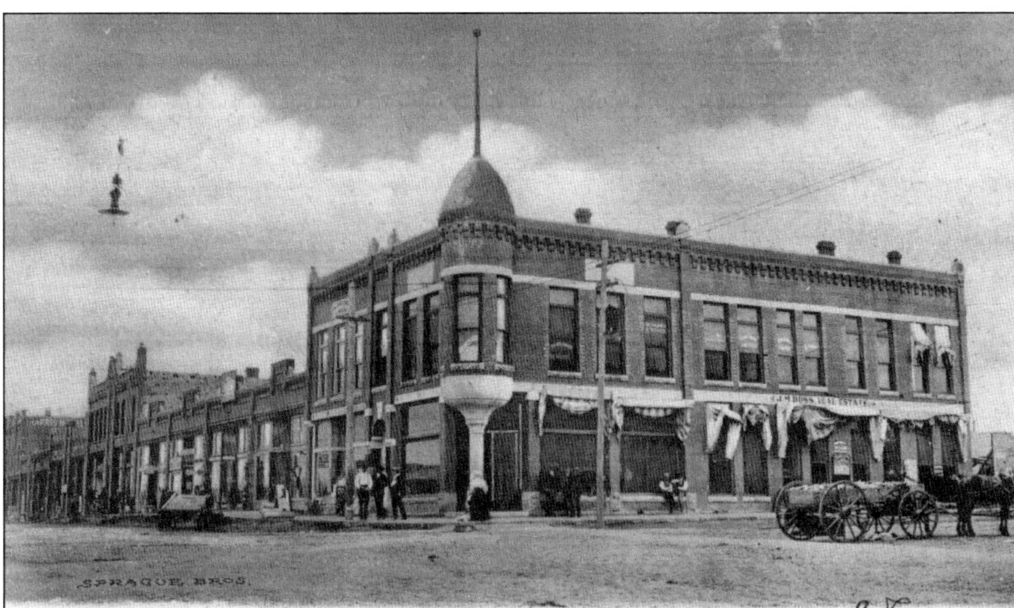

Notice the light in the intersection of Broadway Avenue and Main Street. People traveling in wagons really had to see well in order to know when to clop across the intersection without mishap. (Courtesy of Gary Haney.)

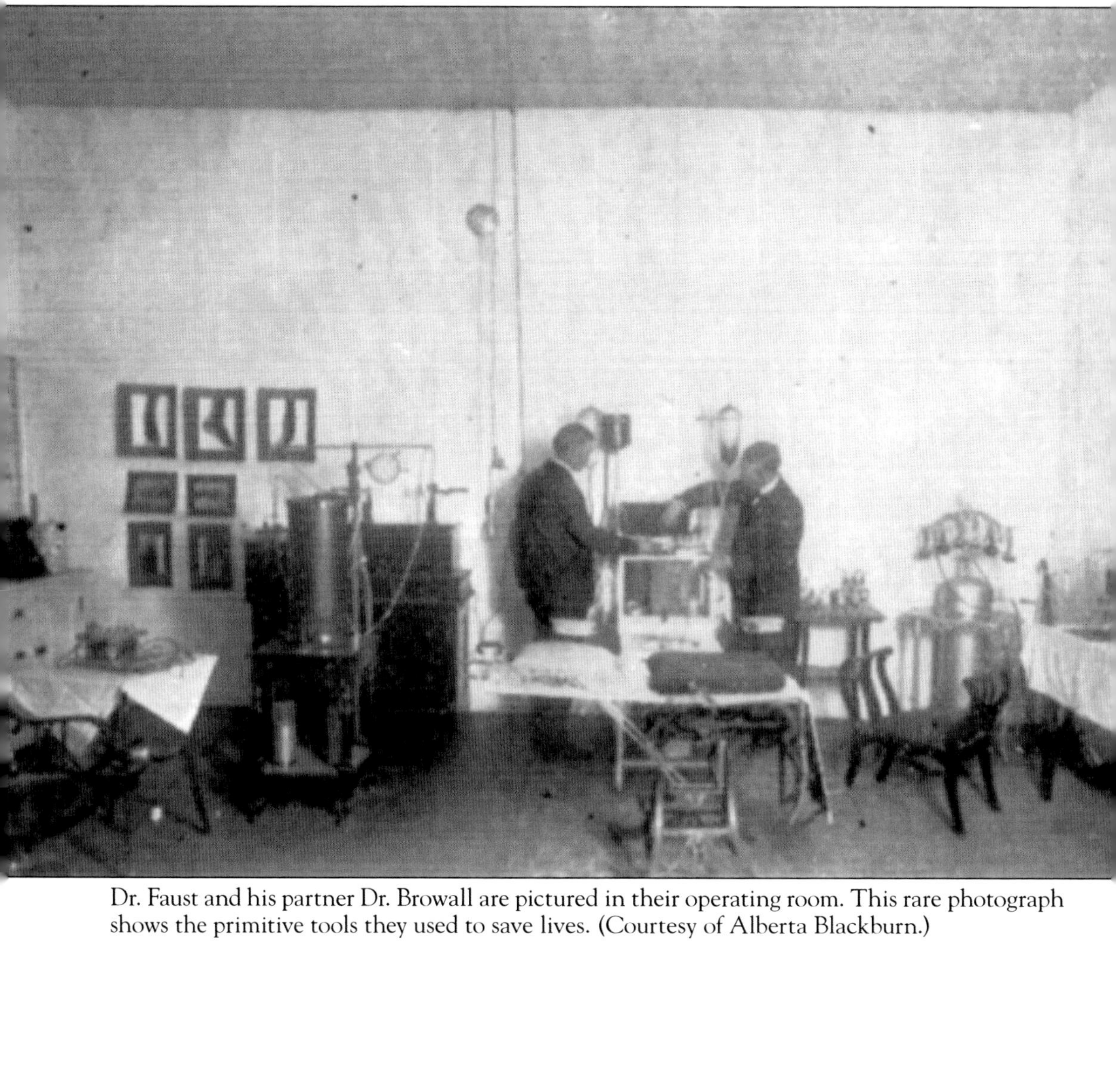

Dr. Faust and his partner Dr. Browall are pictured in their operating room. This rare photograph shows the primitive tools they used to save lives. (Courtesy of Alberta Blackburn.)

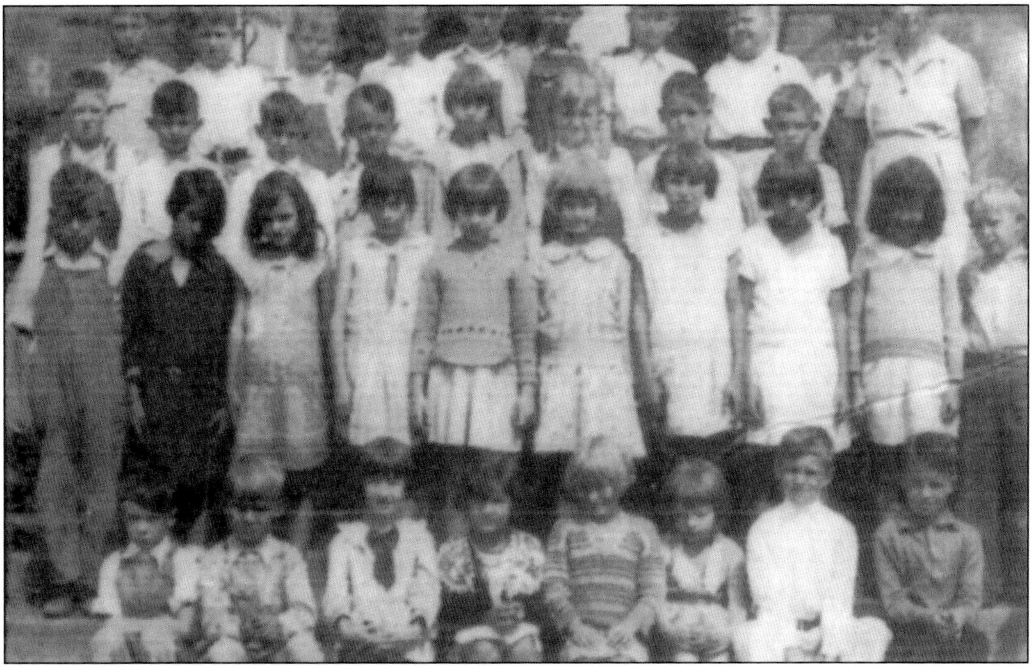

In the early 1920s, this third-grade class at Willard School posed on the school steps. It was a quiet class from the looks of it. Their teacher did a wonderful job lining them up—with hands in laps and arms at sides. (Courtesy of Alberta Blackburn.)

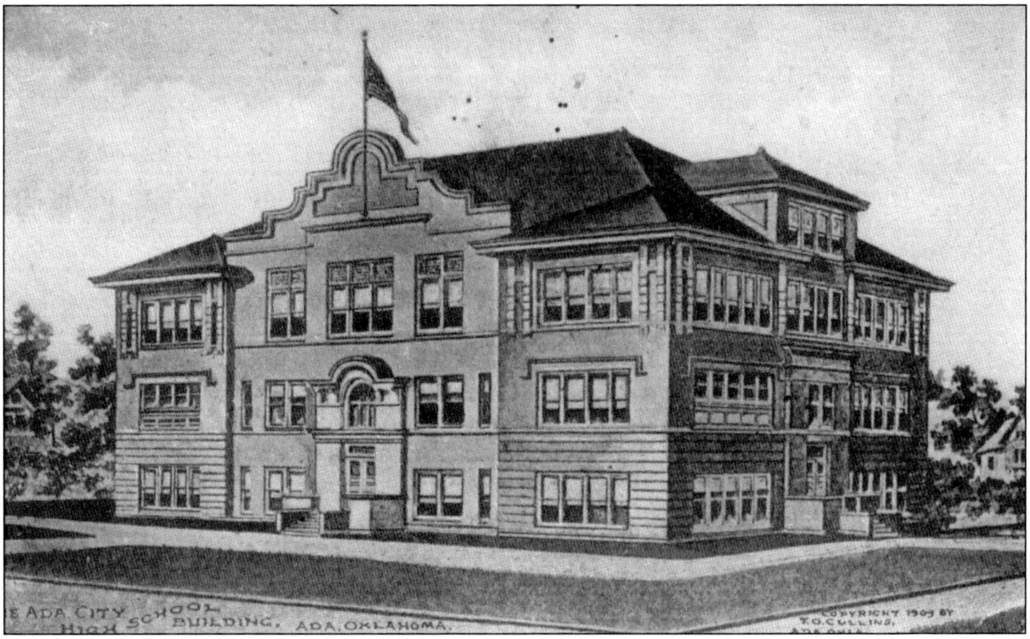

In 1909, the Ada City High School was drawn up for review. It was to be on East Eighteenth Street, which is in the middle of town. Being on the south side of town was convenient for most Ada students. A huge new high school was built later on the southeast side of town on what is now Stadium Drive, not far from the ECU's football stadium, which is shared with the high school. (Courtesy of Gray Haney.)

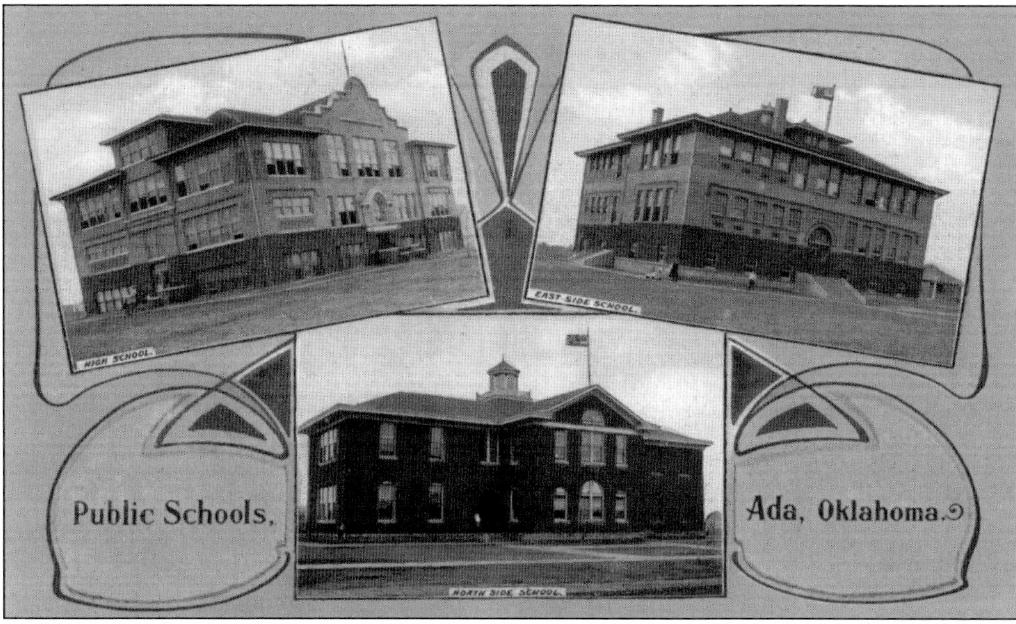

This postcard touts the public schools in Ada, which included its high school, the East Side School, and the North Side School. These schools were later renamed. (Courtesy of Gary Haney.)

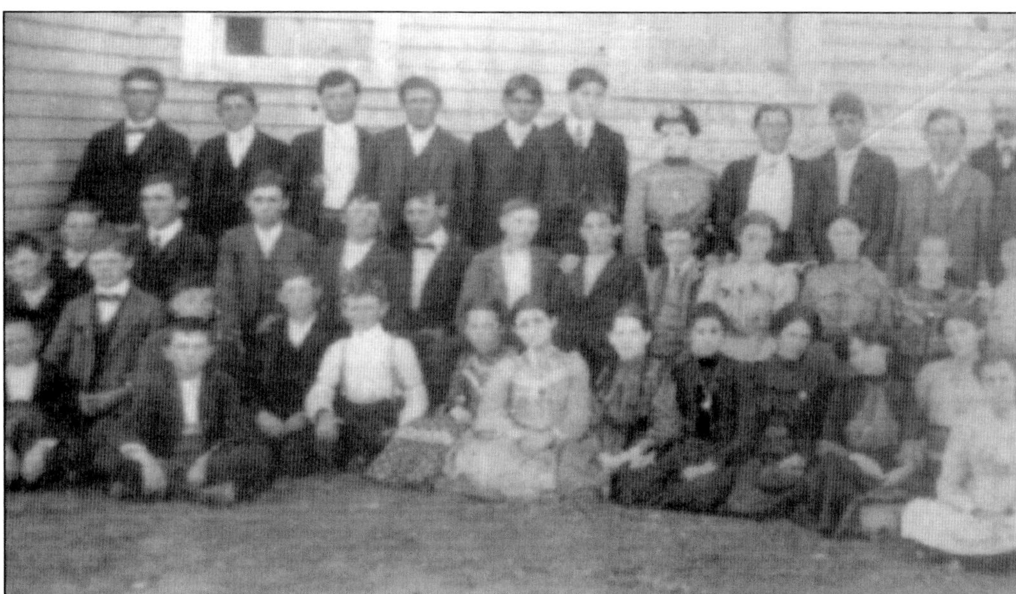

Professor Scarbourogh stands with his pupils at Ada's first school. It was located on Eighteenth and Stockton Streets and was also referred to as the Scarbourough Institute. (Courtesy of Alberta Blackburn.)

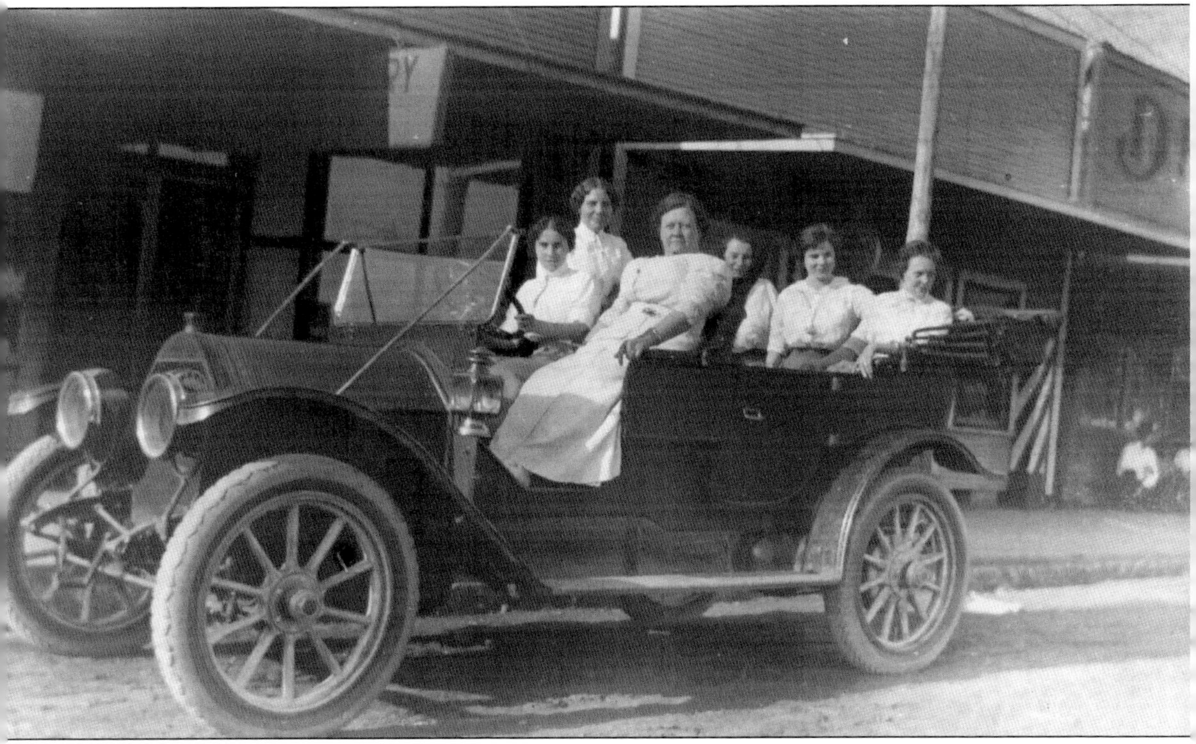

The steering wheel of this car is oddly placed in the middle of the dashboard. Men sitting in front of the barbershop look on while these ladies have their photograph taken. (Courtesy of Gary Haney.)

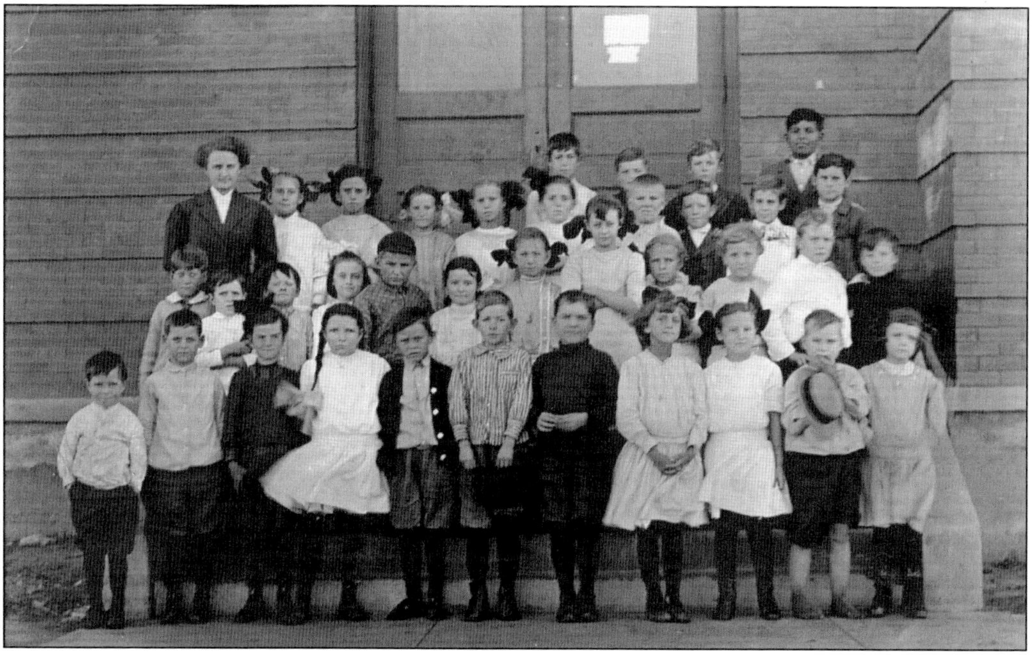

This unidentified school seems to have a good attendance. There seems to be a fashion for pigtails and big black bows. The facial expressions of these children are precious. (Courtesy of Gary Haney.)

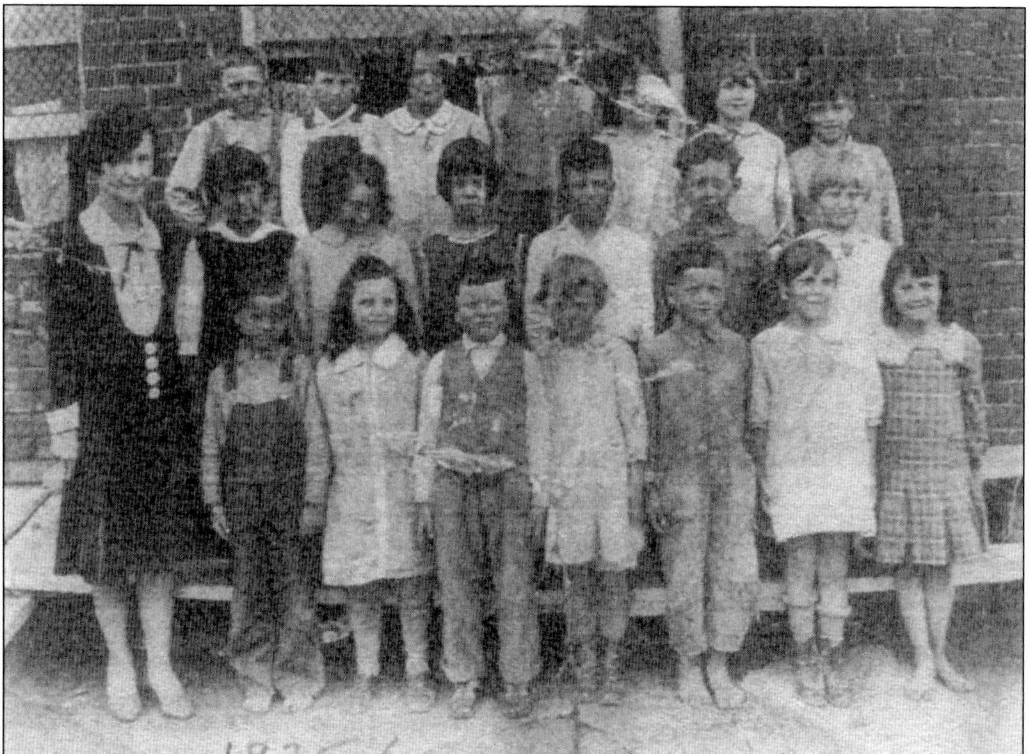

Mrs. Mallory stands proudly with her 1925–1926 class. (Courtesy of Alberta Blackburn.)

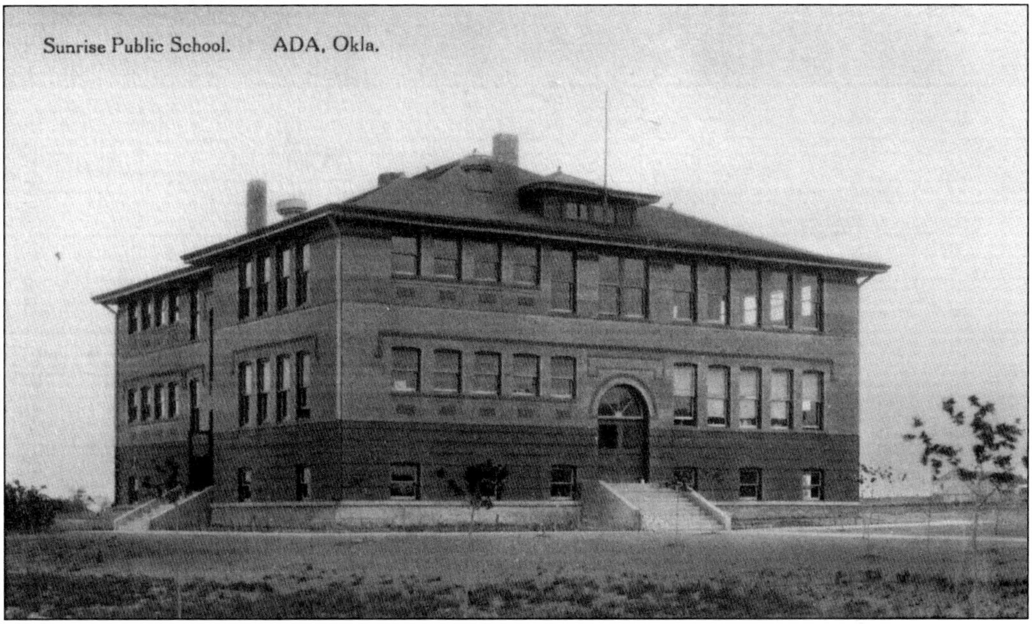

The Sunrise School was an early elementary school. (Courtesy of Gary Haney.)

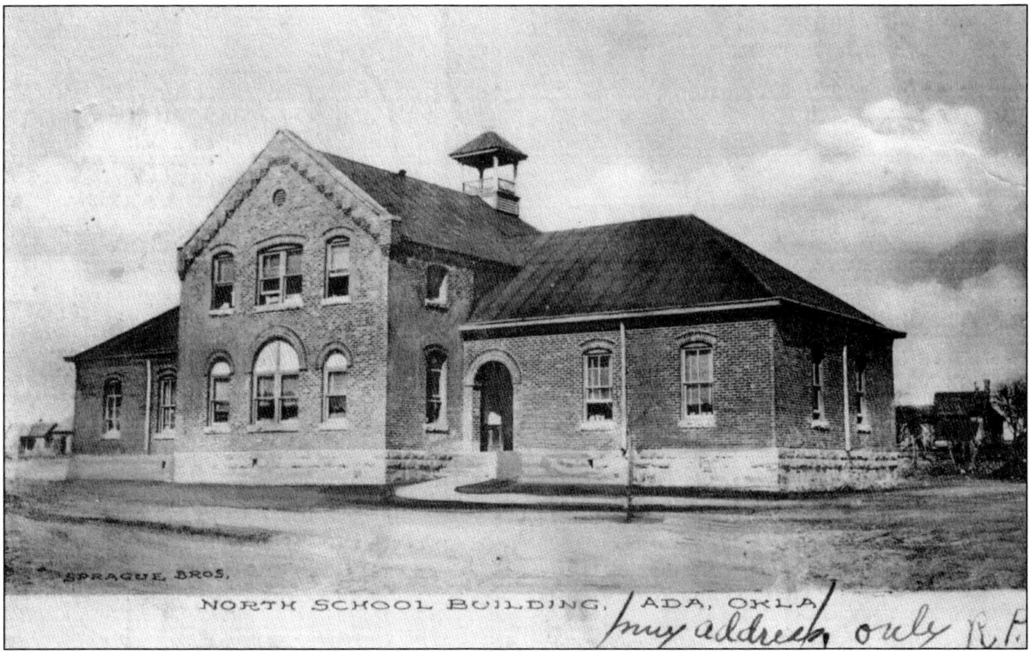

The North School building had a lookout tower. Maybe the truant officer used it to look for students who skipped out on school. (Courtesy of Gary Haney.)

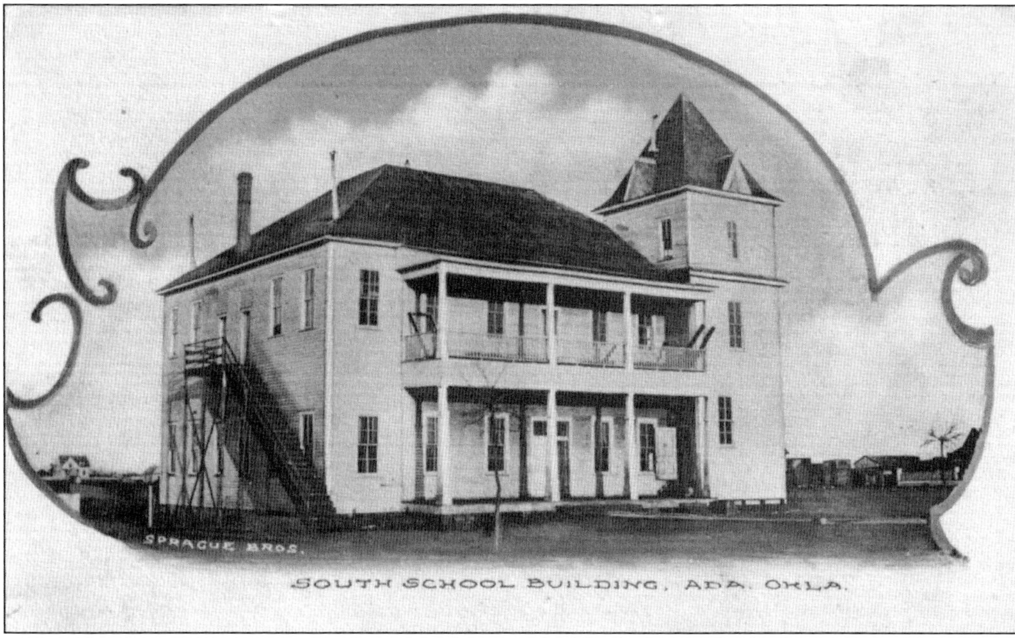

The South School had a fancy, elaborate schoolhouse. (Courtesy of Gary Haney.)

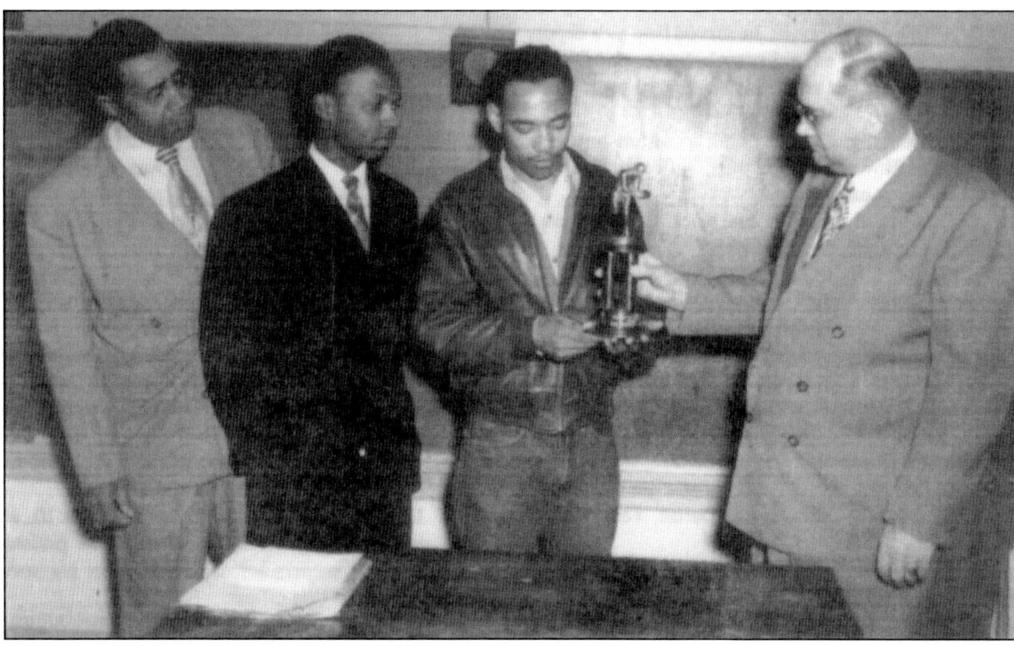

J. A. Richardson (right), president of the Ada Chamber of Commerce, awards Clifford Logan, of Napier School on North Broadway Avenue, a trophy for his part in the 1950 state football championship. His principal, C. R. Buford (far left), and coach, C. E. Black (second from left), observe the ceremony. (Courtesy of Alberta Blackburn.)

Four

MIDWAY

Ada became a very busy town in the mid-20th century. The Pontotoc County seat attracted shoppers from surrounding towns and communities. On Saturdays, the sidewalks were crowded. Uniformed policemen were stationed on every block to keep jaywalkers in check by making sure that pedestrians crossed at the lights. Policemen also worked the streets and kept traffic in order.

Men wearing overalls and worn fedoras gathered on corners to catch up on country life and its rewards and trials. Laughter, car horns, and police whistles were considered part of the Saturday experience. Main Street smelled of popcorn and chocolate from open candy bins in the five and dime stores, and pickup trucks full of feedbags for farm animals were always visible.

Stores were open until 9:00 p.m. on Saturday nights. The brightly lit window displays were turned on one by one to illuminate the streets. The numerous movie theaters brought world news to Ada, which kept people up to date.

Main Street started as Grand Avenue on what is now Twelfth Street, and Eleventh Street is now Main Street. Ada started in the northwest area of the present city. For easier access to trade, the town moved closer the railroad. East Central University started with one building and has grown not only in size but also in reputation.

The streets of Ada have changed drastically over the decades. Some buildings are completely gone, and others so different they are unrecognizable. A pictorial tour of the town that was determined to survive showcases these changes.

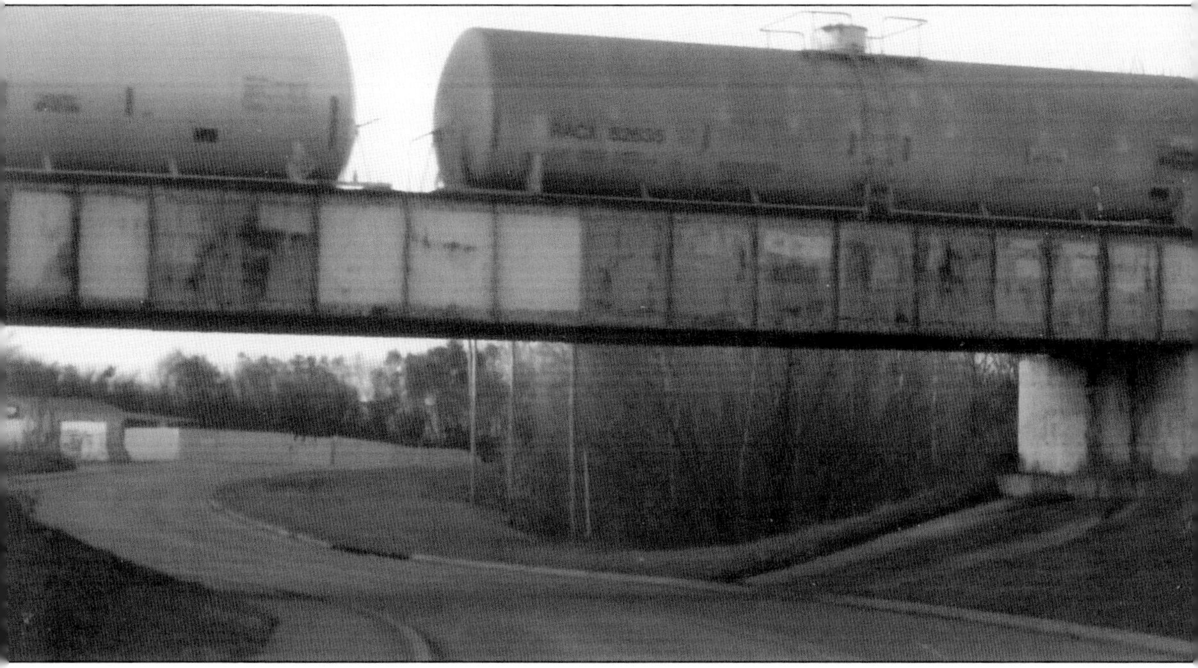

For decades, the underpass on Constant Street was the only way to get to the north side of Ada when trains were still in service. In 2008, the city put a new, wider road under the trestle. (Author's collection.)

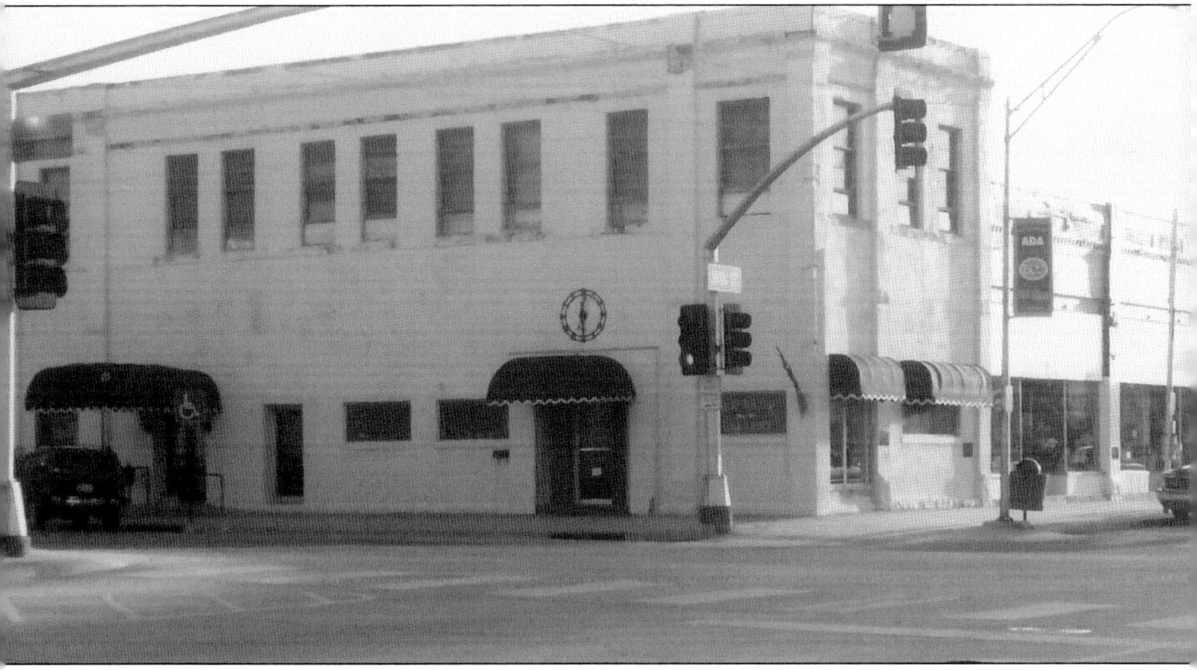

The Oklahoma State Bank was on the corner of Main Street and Townsend Avenue. In later years it has housed other businesses, including an antique shop. At present it is the Old Bank Fine Art Gallery. (Author's collection.)

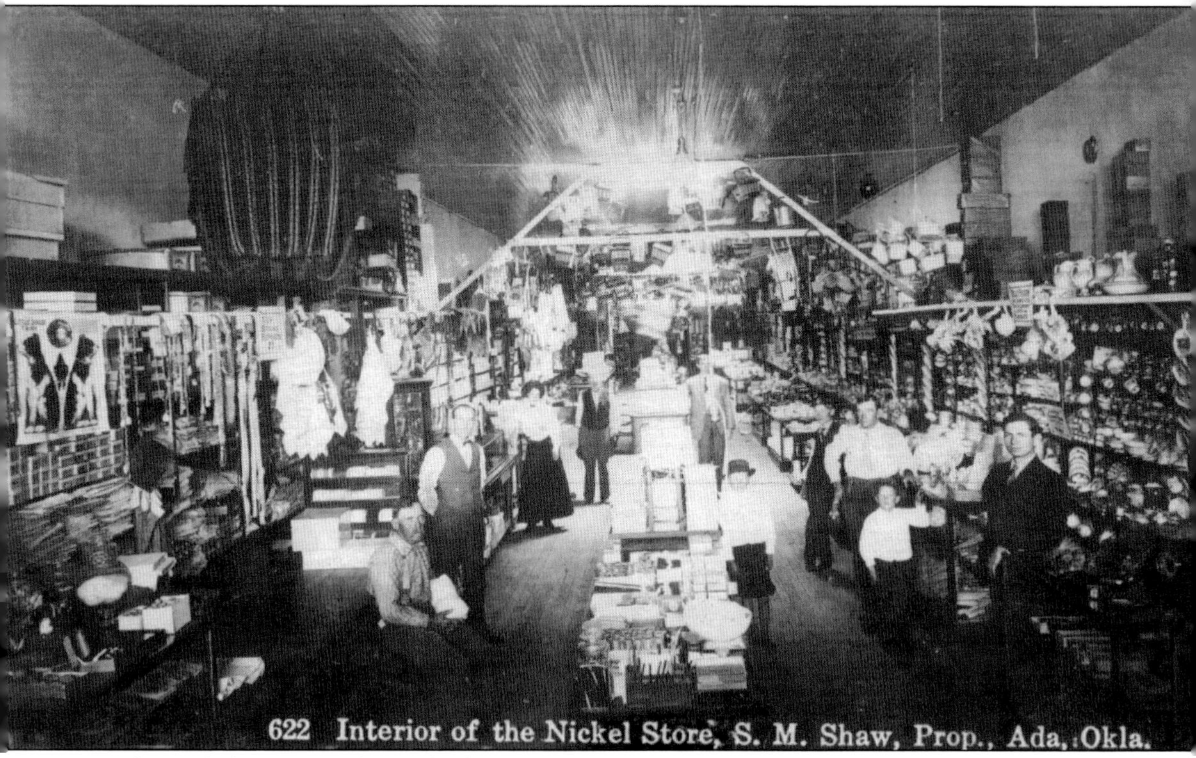

The Nickel Store, or Shaw's, had a very large inventory. At a nickel a piece, it evidently added up. Shaw's was a very popular store. (Courtesy of Gary Haney.)

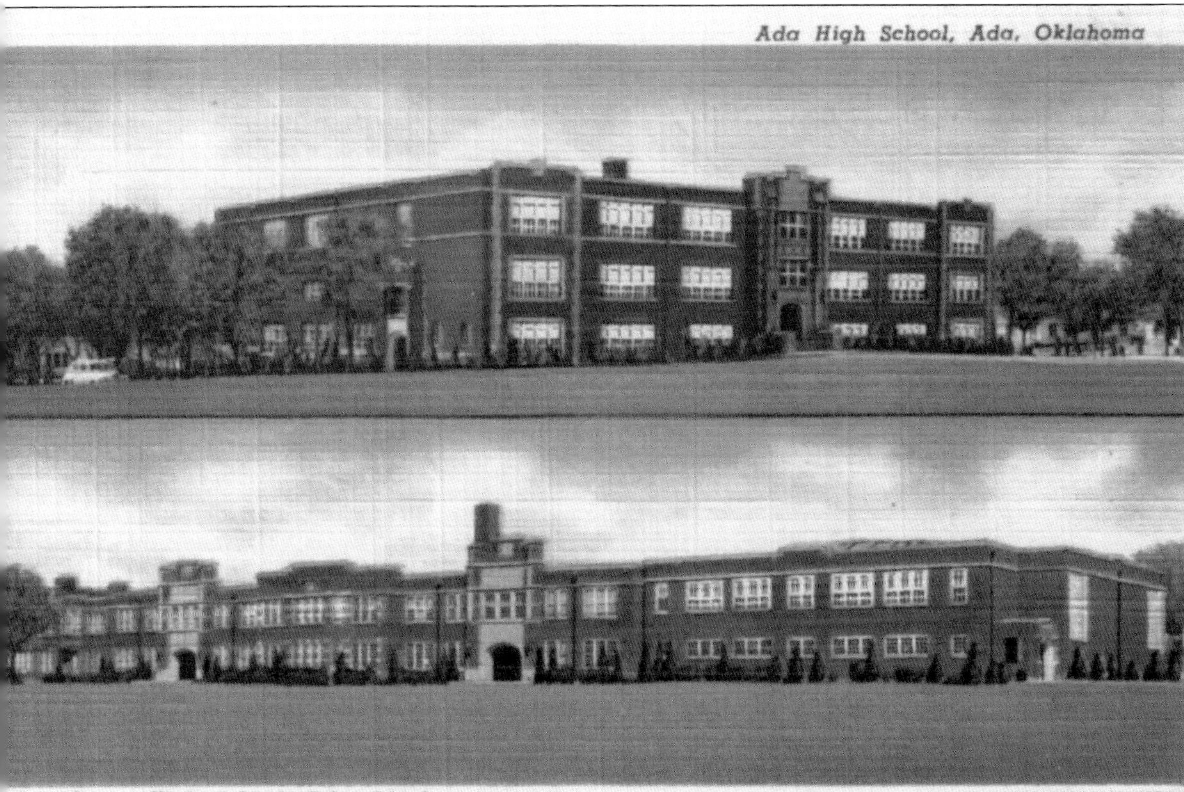

This early postcard shows two schools in Ada, the high school and the junior high school. (Courtesy of Gary Haney.)

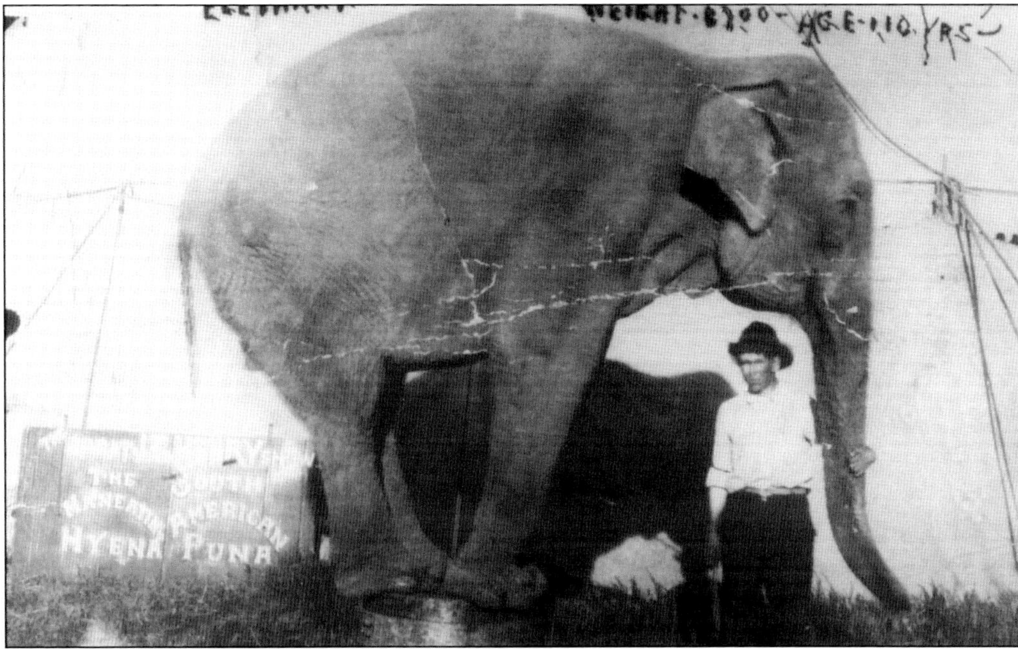

Ada had its own circus, which was owned by Honest Bill Newton. It wintered at the fairgrounds. This elephant was 110 years old and could possibly be the same elephant that was buried south of town. The location of the elephant burial is under the hill from the ECU Police Headquarters. (Courtesy of Bud Throne.)

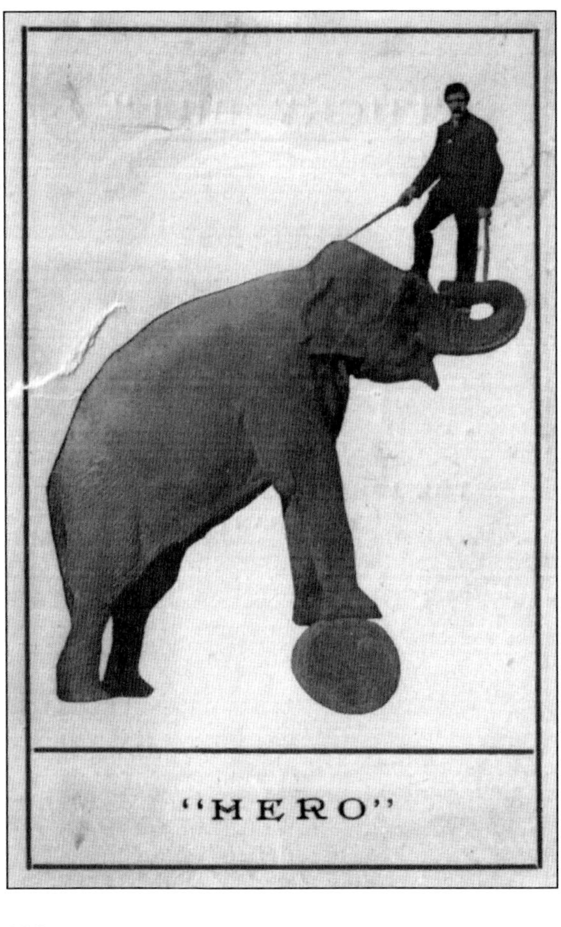

The Ada Circus had a fine band that was conducted by Harry James. Harry's son, Harry Jr., attended Willard School and was an outstanding trumpet player. (Courtesy of Gary Haney.)

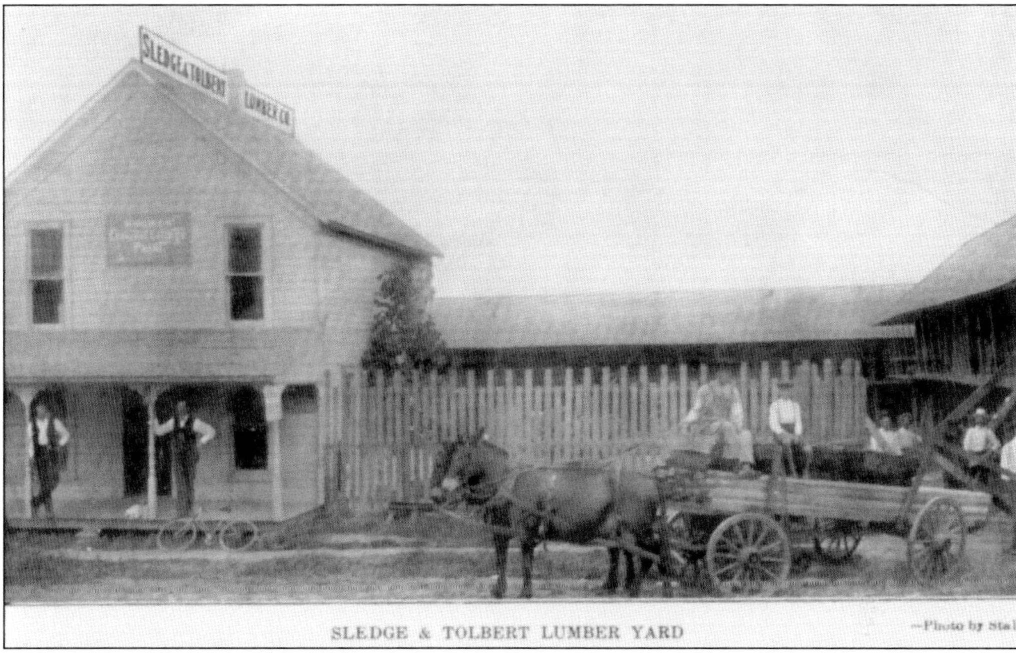

Men fill up a wagon in front of the Sledge and Tolbert Lumber Company. Just like Frances Wintersmith, Molly Sledge was an active woman in Ada politics. (Courtesy of Bud Throne.)

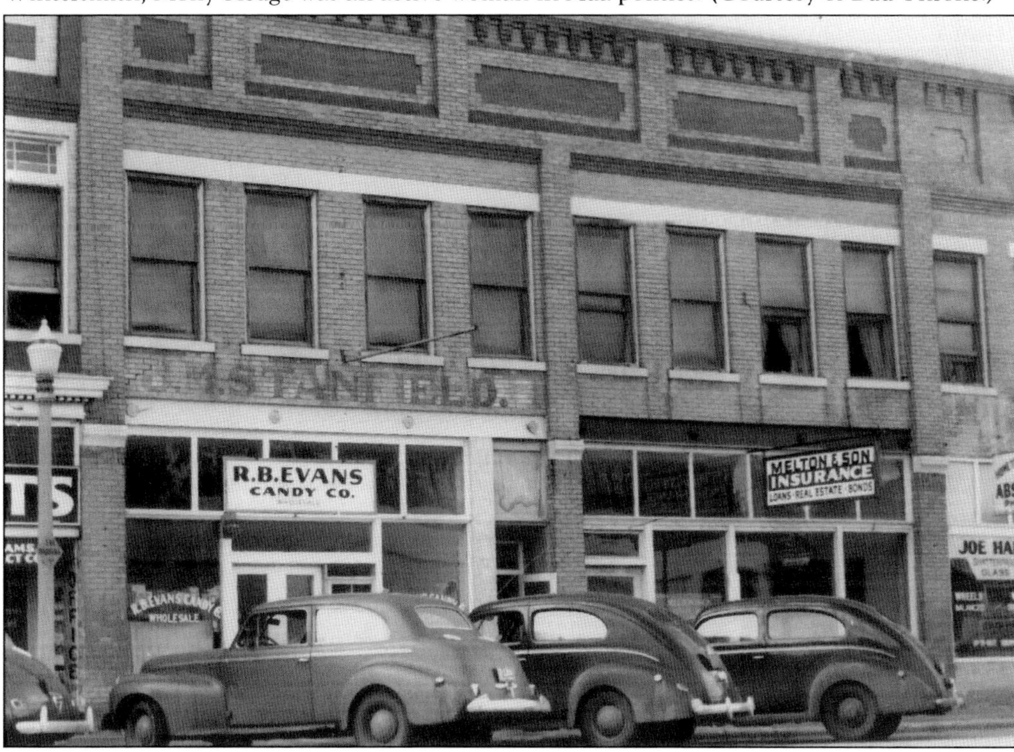

Argo's Cafe was once downtown but was moved west, closer to Glenwood Park. The Glenwood school kids would sometimes go under the school's underpass to have sandwiches for lunch at Argo's. (Courtesy of Bud Throne.)

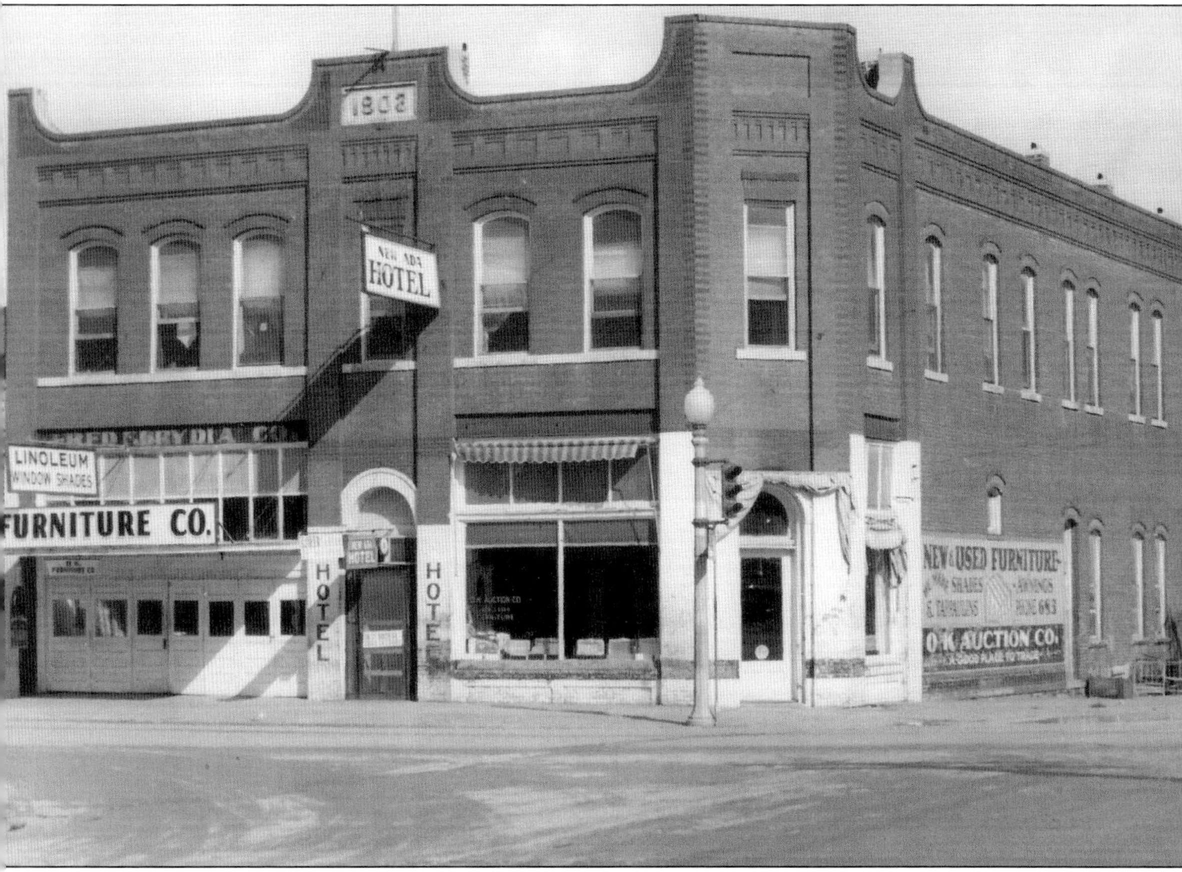

The northwest corner of Townsend and Main Streets has had many inhabitants. The Ada Hotel was once situated there, next to OK Furniture Store. It has been rumored that the door around the corner of the building had stairs that led up to an opera house. Built in 1802, the OK Furniture Store expanded two stores over and occupied both the upper and lower floors. It was on the east corner of "The Blood Bucket" block and across the street from the McSwain Theater. (Courtesy of Bud Throne.)

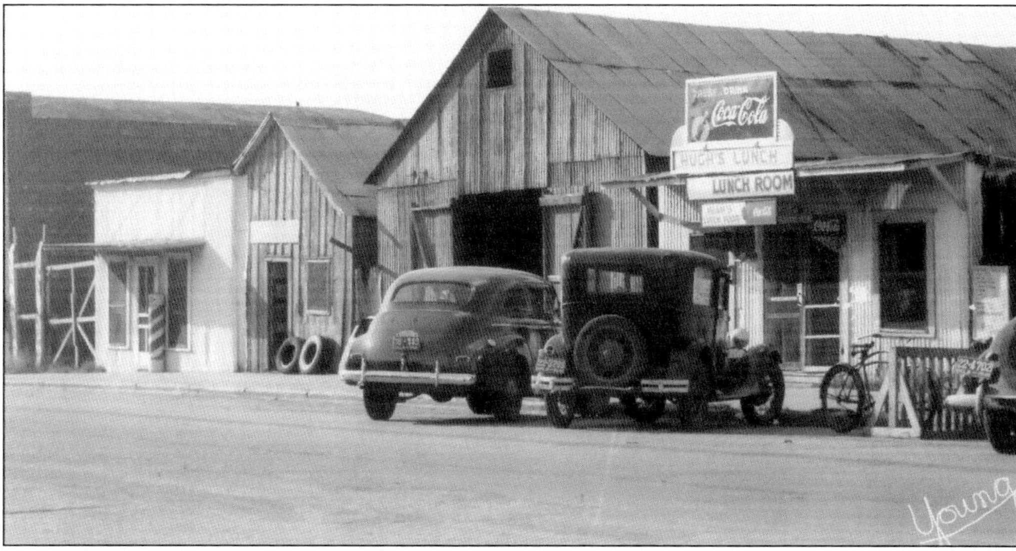

Located where the First United Bank parking lot is today, these buildings were across from M&P Grocers. This middle portion of the block is now an overflow parking lot for Polo's Mexican Restaurant. From the looks of the cars, Hugh must have served good lunches. (Courtesy of Bud Throne.)

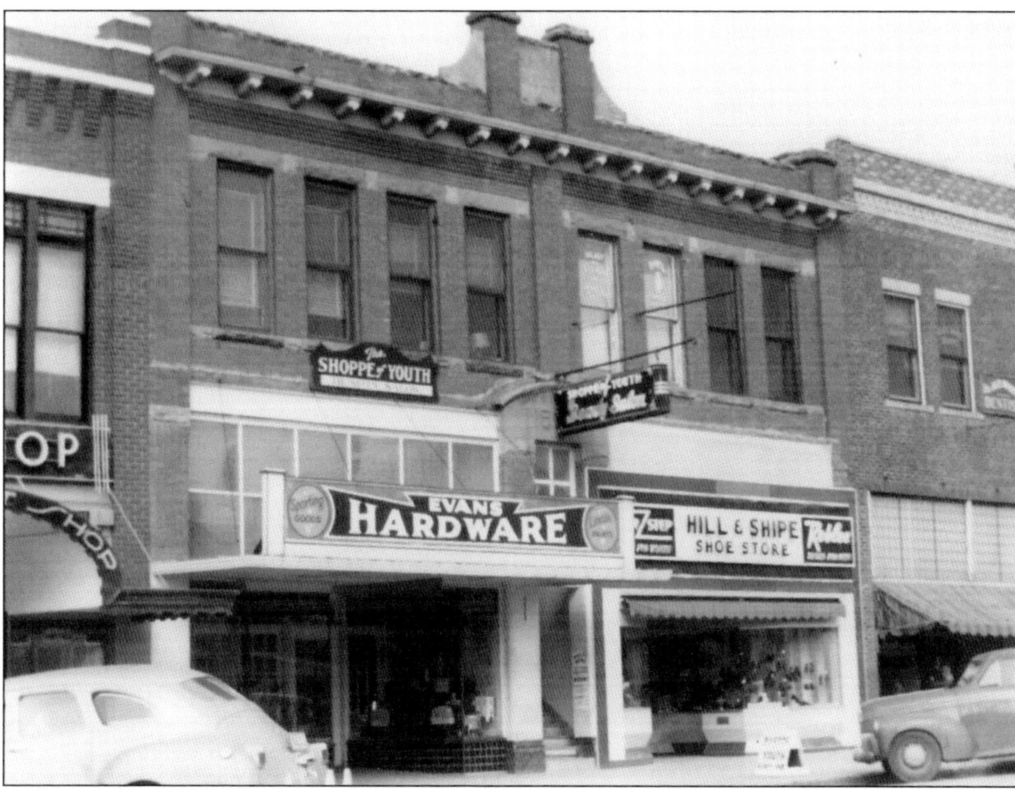

Evans Hardware and Hill and Shipe shoes lasted a long time on the 100 block of North Main Street. The Shoppe of Beauty was above Evans Hardware, which is now a flower shop, and the shoe store was renovated in 2009 into Cara's Central Dance. (Courtesy of Bud Throne.)

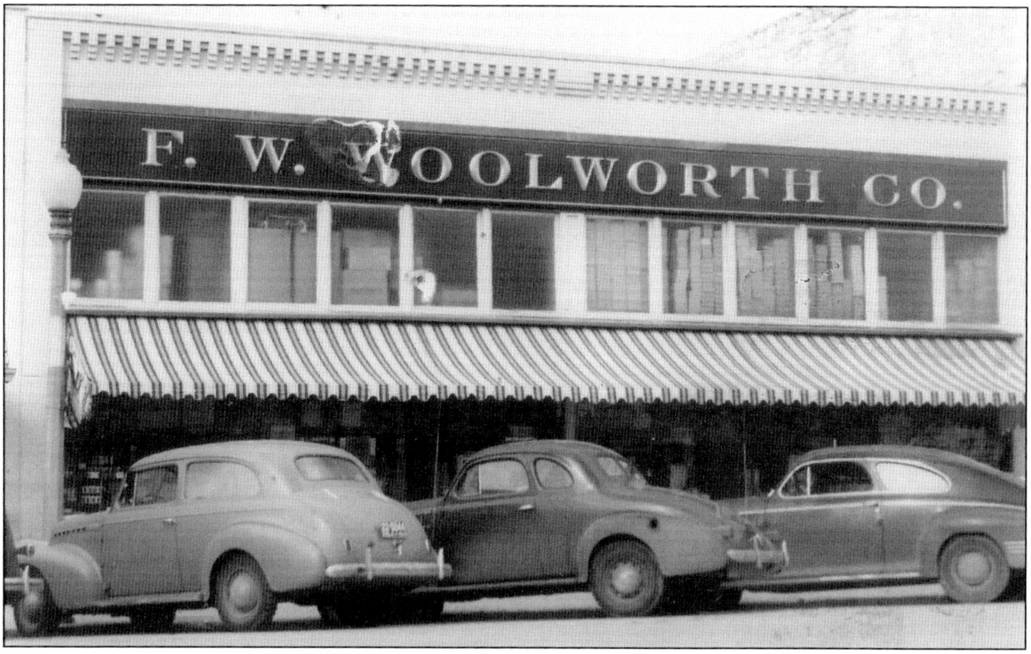

The F. W. Woolworth's became Duke and Ayers, a furniture shop. Duke and Ayers burned down, and the building was turned into the beautiful Central Park, located between Fields Clothing and JC Penney's. The Leader Shoe Store was on the corner. It combined with Fields Clothing next door and became the Corner Drugstore. (Courtesy of Bud Throne.)

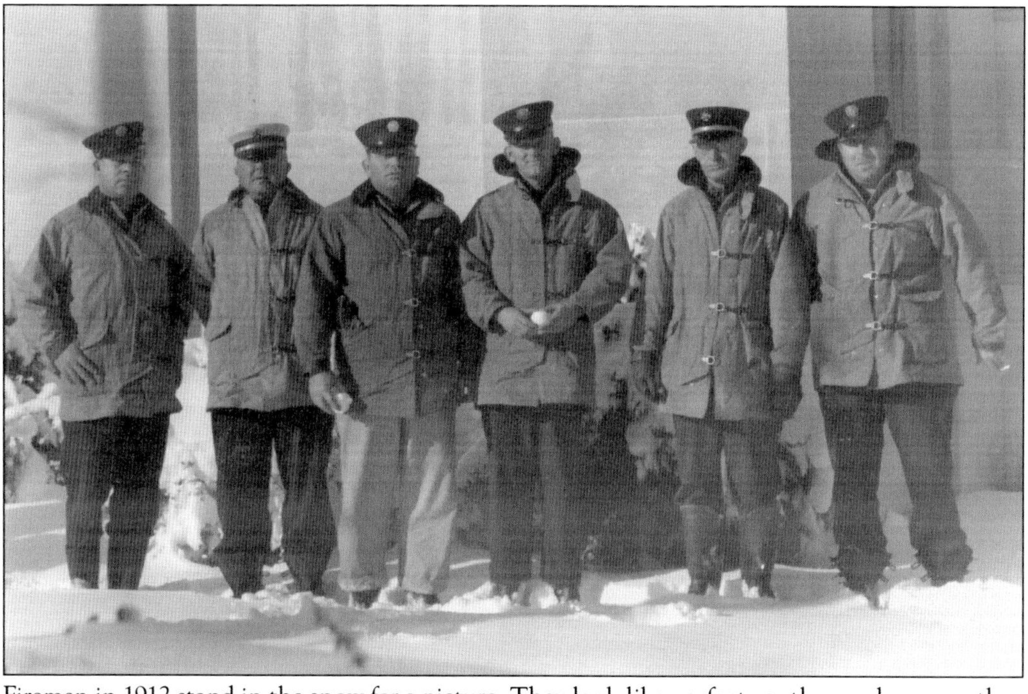

Firemen in 1912 stand in the snow for a picture. They look like perfect gentlemen; however, they are all holding snowballs. They are Elbert Reed, Allen Standfield, Jack Maxey, Somer Jones, and John Chauncy. (Courtesy of Bud Throne.)

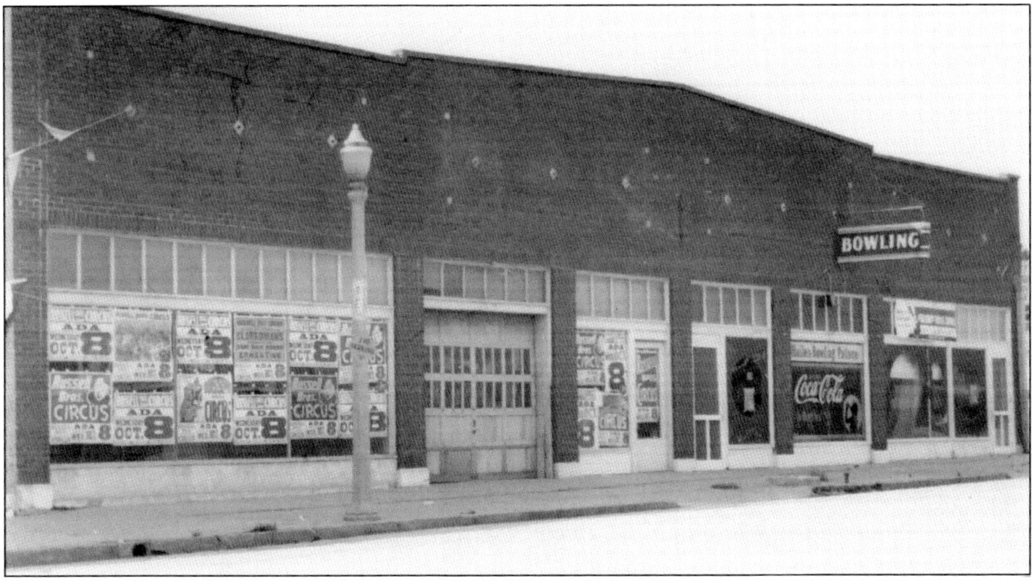

Hailes Bowling Palace was on the southeast corner of Main Street and Constant Avenue. A Pontiac dealership was just to the east. Flyers for the Russell Brother's Circus in Ada are posted in the windows. (Courtesy of Bud Throne.)

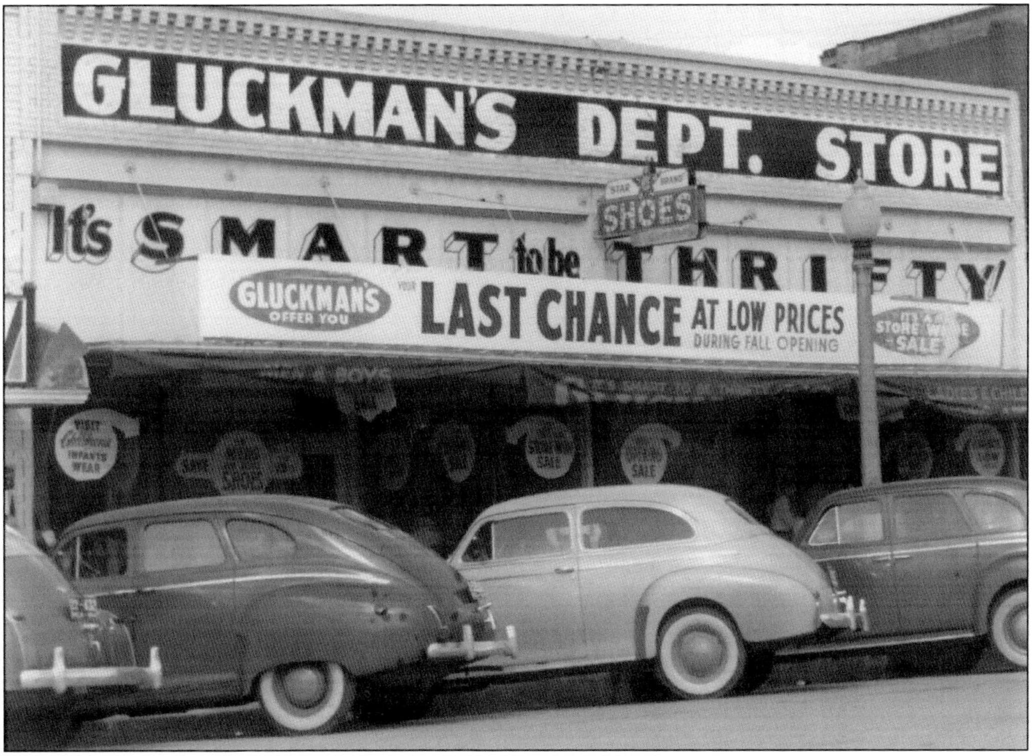

This building housed Gluckman's Department Store. On the north side of block 200 on Main Street, it had some nifty, smart, and thrifty signs and carried just about anything an Adan could want. It was located in the area where the Shaw Center is now, next to the House of Health. (Courtesy of Bud Throne.)

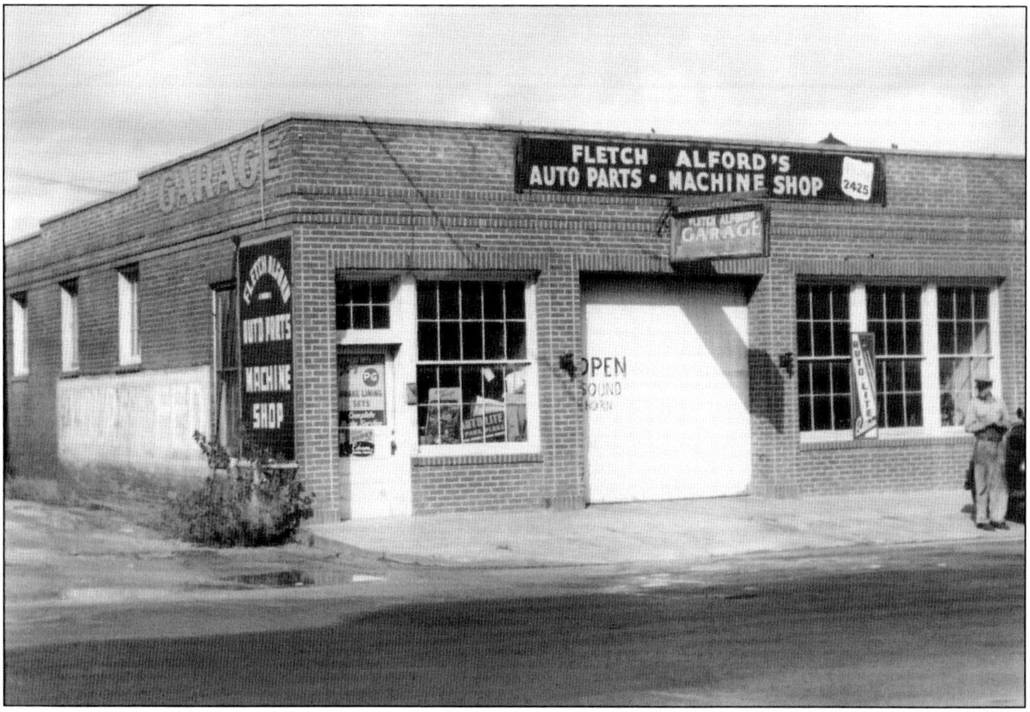

Located on North Townsend Avenue, between Main and Tenth Streets, this garage had a grocery store to the north that sat next to the infamous stable. The alley to the left led to the Frisco Depot, which was turned into offices for the Ada Chamber of Commerce decades later. (Courtesy of Bud Throne.)

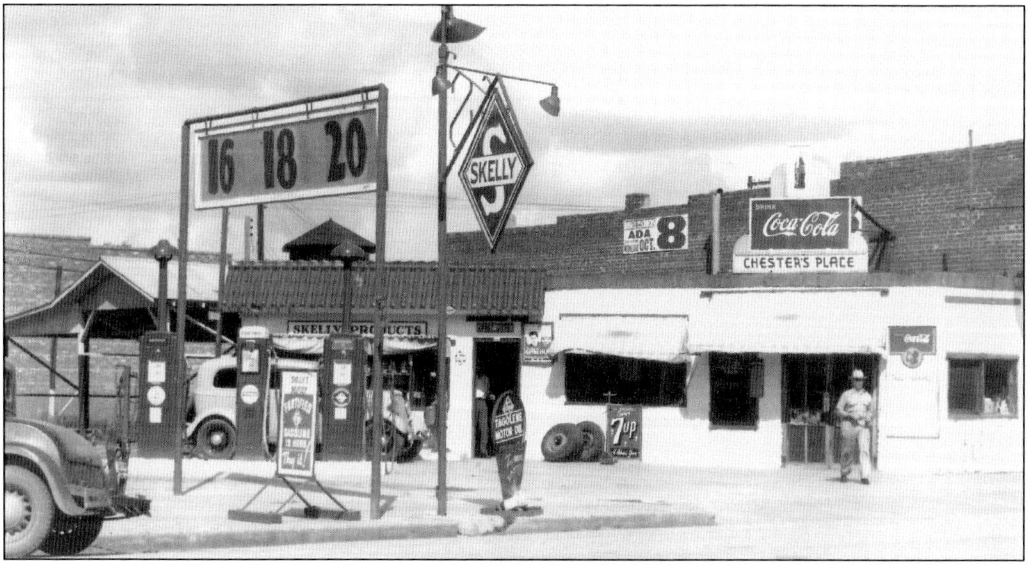

This area was located on Main Street, near the Frisco Depot parking lot. These two businesses were tacked onto where Yerby's Appliance is. The gasoline was cheap, and a sign says this A-1 Skelly station had just acquired fortified Skelly gasoline. Chester had a popular corner at the end of the 200 block. The two businesses were later demolished, leaving a clean wall for the next building. (Courtesy of Bud Throne.)

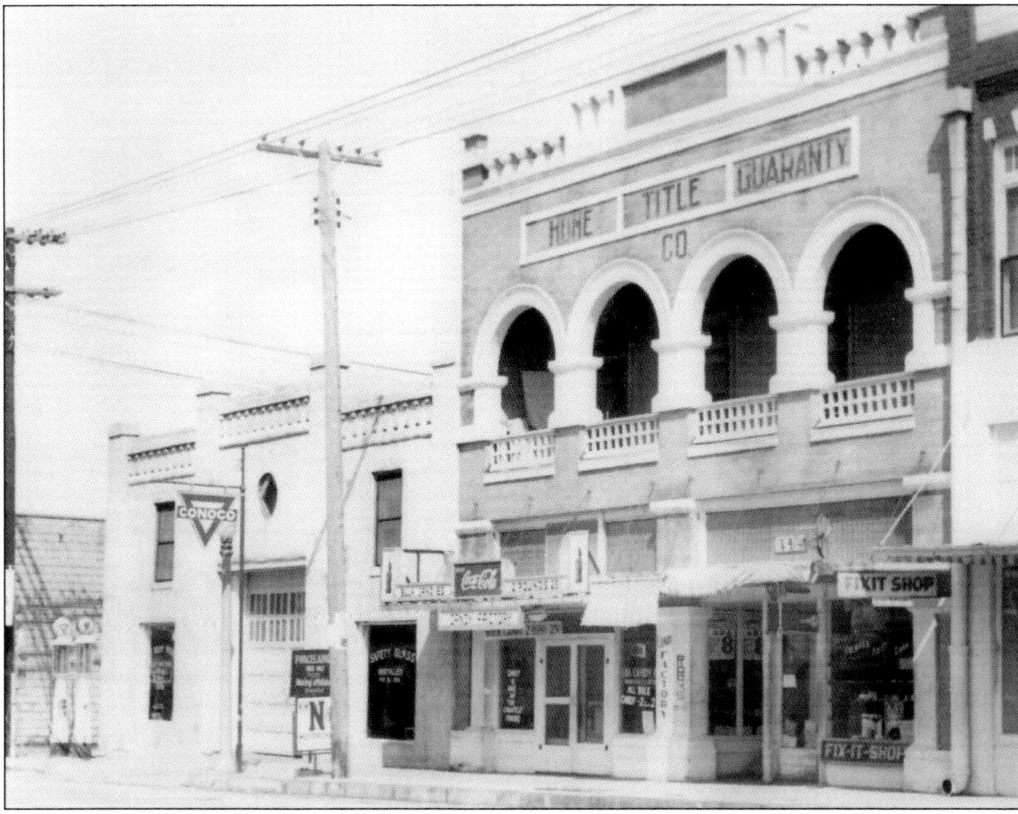

On Townsend Avenue, the garage, the Evans Candy Company, Home Title Warranty Company, and the Fix-It shop are no longer there. They were demolished to make a parking lot for overflow traffic. The parking lot is across the street from Citizens Bank. Area farmers now sell fresh fruits and vegetables every Wednesday under the row of trees at the edge of the lot. (Courtesy of Bud Throne.)

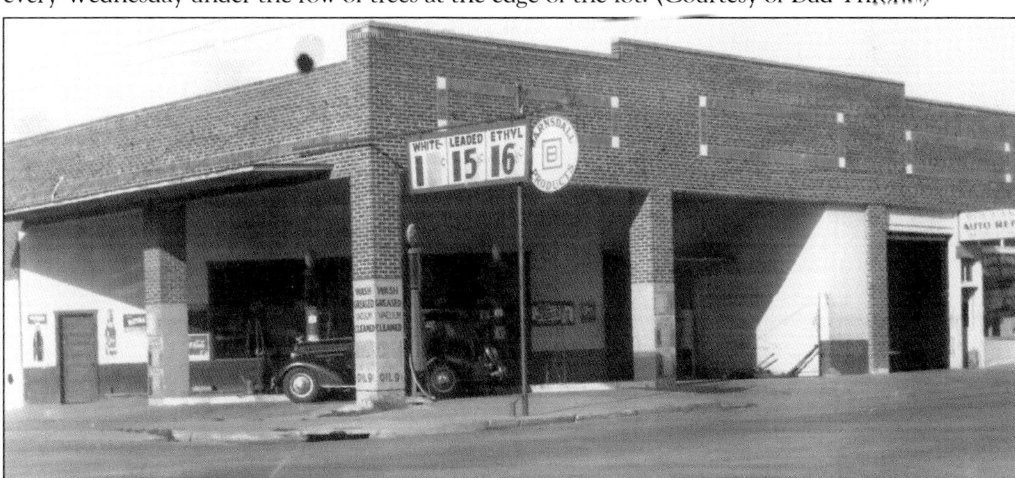

This corner now houses a rent-to-own service. It was Lee's Paint for years. At the time this picture was taken, it was Roy Rane's Auto Repair. Located on the northwest corner of Main Street and Constant Avenue, the Coffee Pot Cafe, a barbershop, and the Ritz Theater were just down the block to the west and across the street from the Ada Movie Theater. (Courtesy of Bud Throne.)

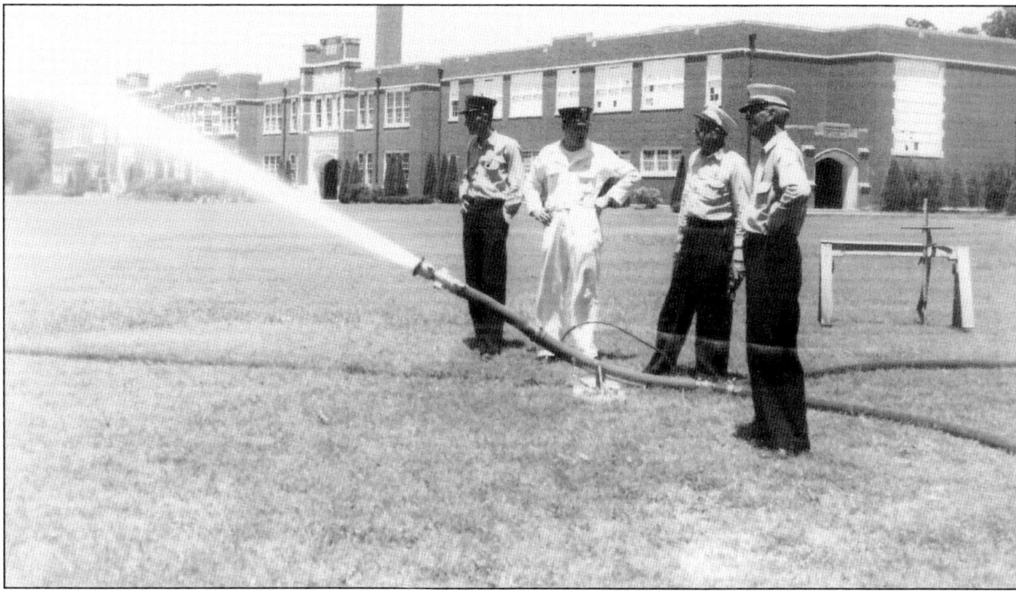

Ada firemen show the students at the high school how water pressure works. (Courtesy of Bud Throne.)

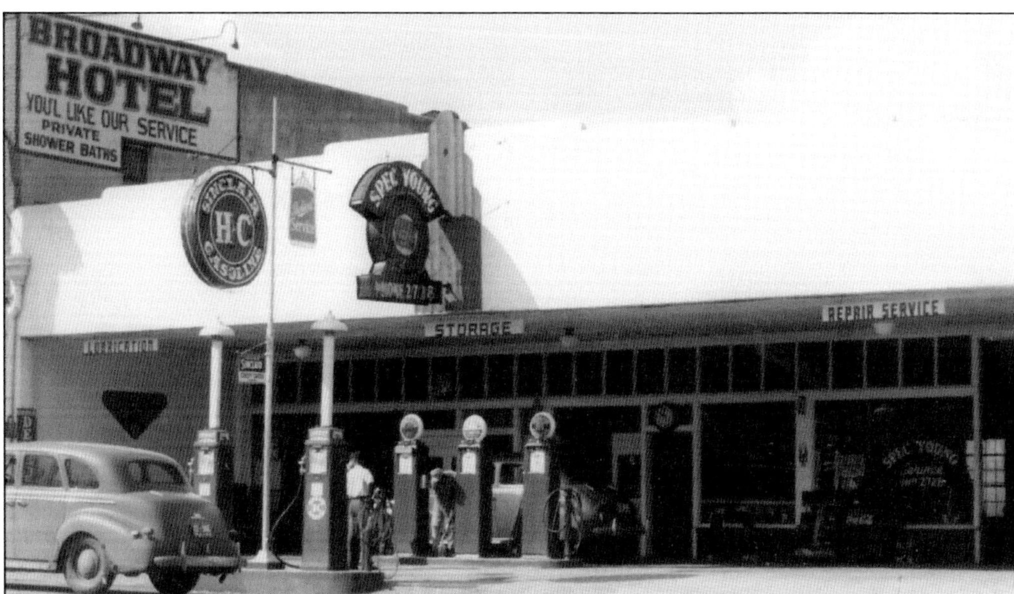

Spec Young was a well-known name in Ada for years. On the 100 block of North Broadway Avenue, he had a Nash Rambler dealership, just north of his service garage. Spec Young's Garage and Gas Station was located across from the present Ada News Building and parking lot. (Courtesy of Bud Throne.)

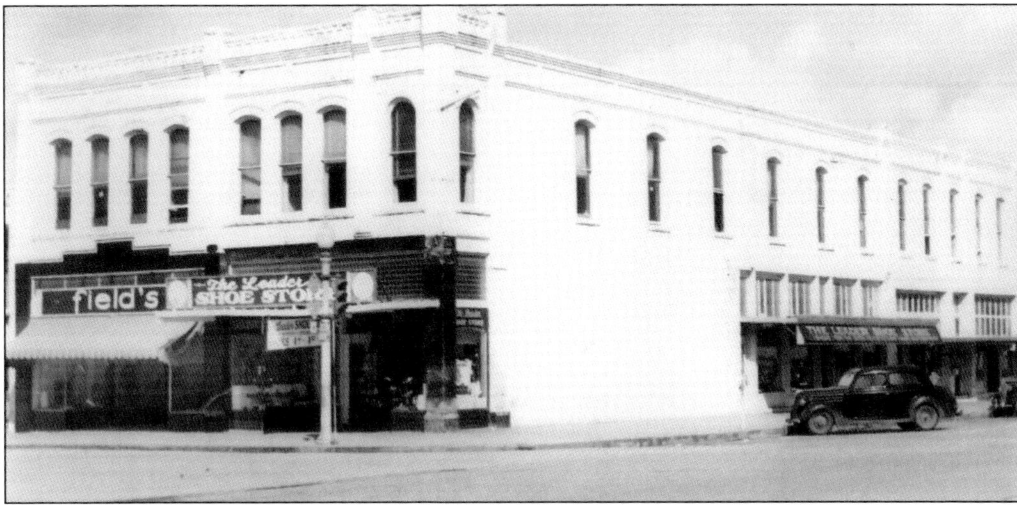

The Leader Shoe Store was on the northwest corner of Main Street and Broadway Avenue. The shoe store was very busy in its great location. It later became the Corner Drugstore and expanded into Fields Clothing. (Courtesy of Bud Throne.)

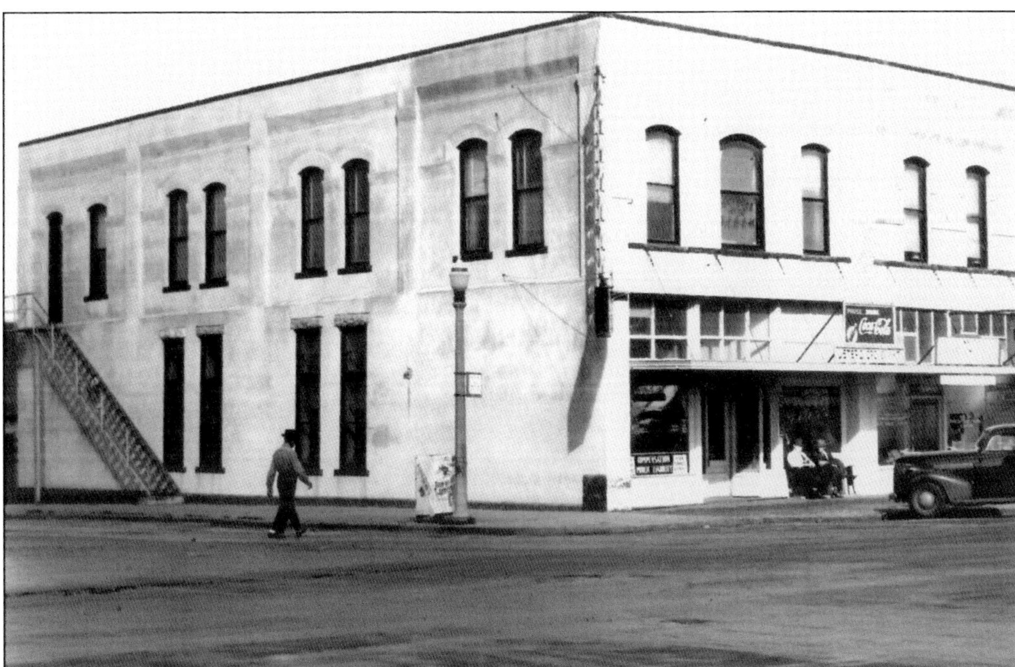

This building stands at Twelfth Street and Broadway Avenue, across the street from the Central Fire Station. The Masons were known to have meetings here on the second floor. The lower floor houses offices, and now the upper floor is home to the Childers family. Homer W. Peay put a large, vertical neon sign on the building to advertise his insurance office. The steps now lead to the Childers home. (Courtesy of Bud Throne.)

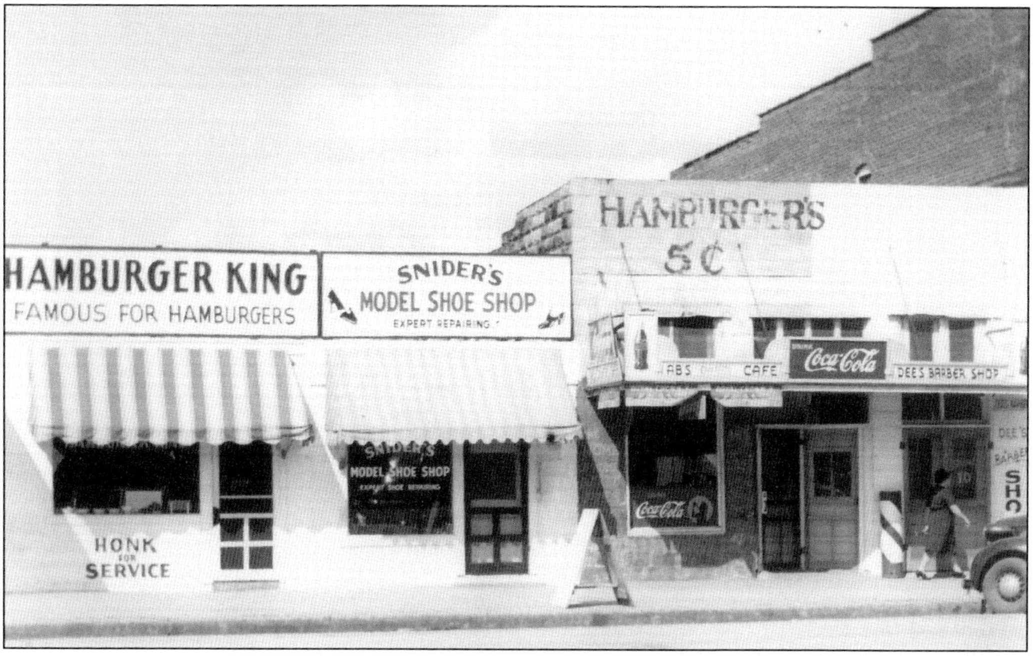

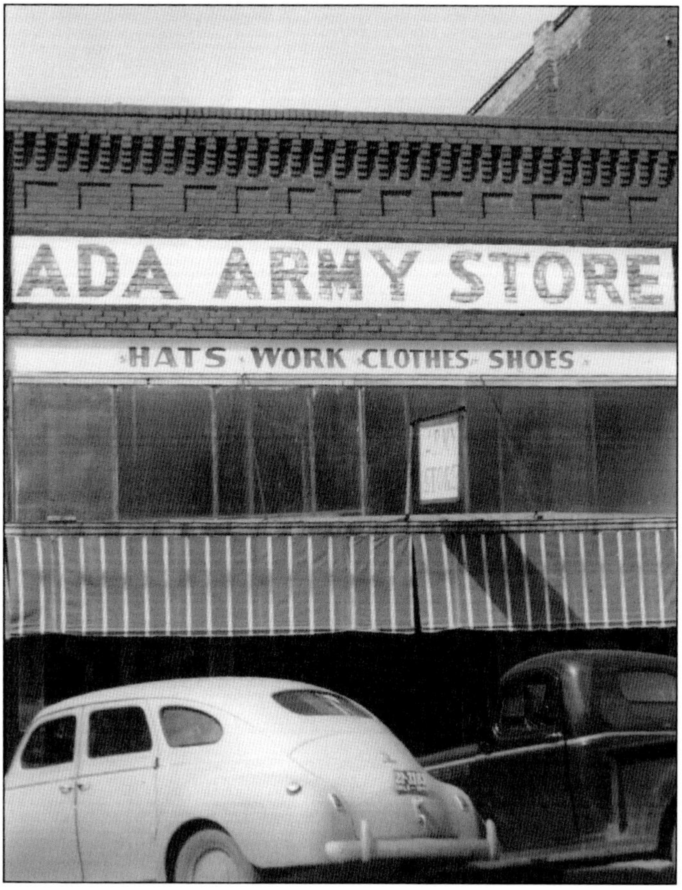

Everything about this west end cafe was tough, except for its hamburgers. Opening early and staying open late, it has endured through the years, and its old-time atmosphere is still intact. Many hamburgers have been consumed here, and countless songs have been chosen from the jukebox selectors at each table. The Hamburger King does not have a drive-through window, but dining-in is like a trip back in time. (Courtesy of Bud Throne.)

In the middle of the 100 block of West Main Street, the Army Store was in a busy spot. Jeans, shirts, socks, and work boots were sold there. The floor was swept with sawdust oil to keep the boards conditioned. The scent of denim and oil gave this neatly kept store a fragrance of its own. (Courtesy of Bud Throne.)

This is just one of the water towers in Ada, located just south of the Ada Middle School. One other water tower is located by Valley View Hospital. It is nice to be a two-tower town. (Author's collection.)

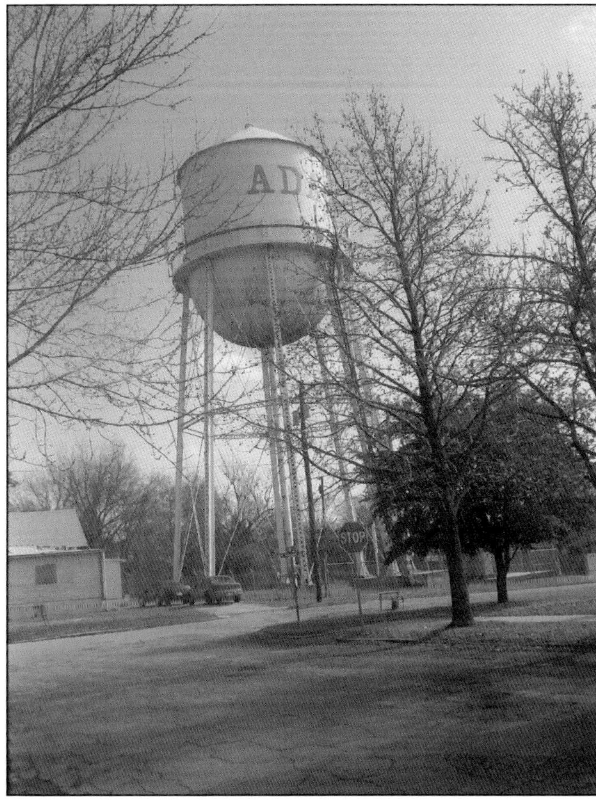

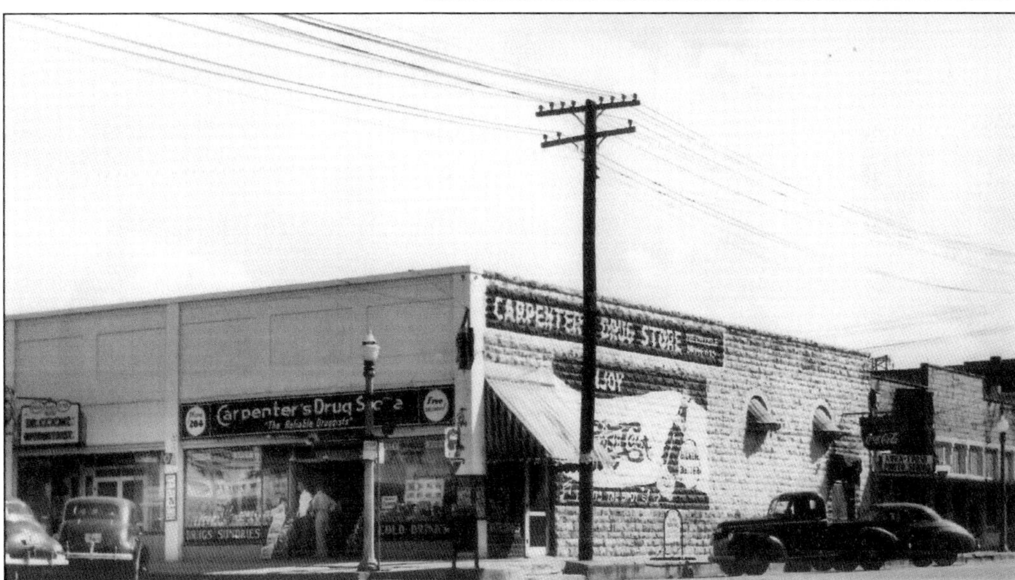

Located on the corner of Main Street and Townsend Avenue, the Carpenter Drugstore later became Bob McCurley's Corner Drug. It had a soda fountain and was a popular watering hole and meeting place. Just behind the store on Townsend Street, there was a small photograph shop that took quick pictures behind a curtained wall. It is now Sharpes clothing store. (Courtesy of Bud Throne.)

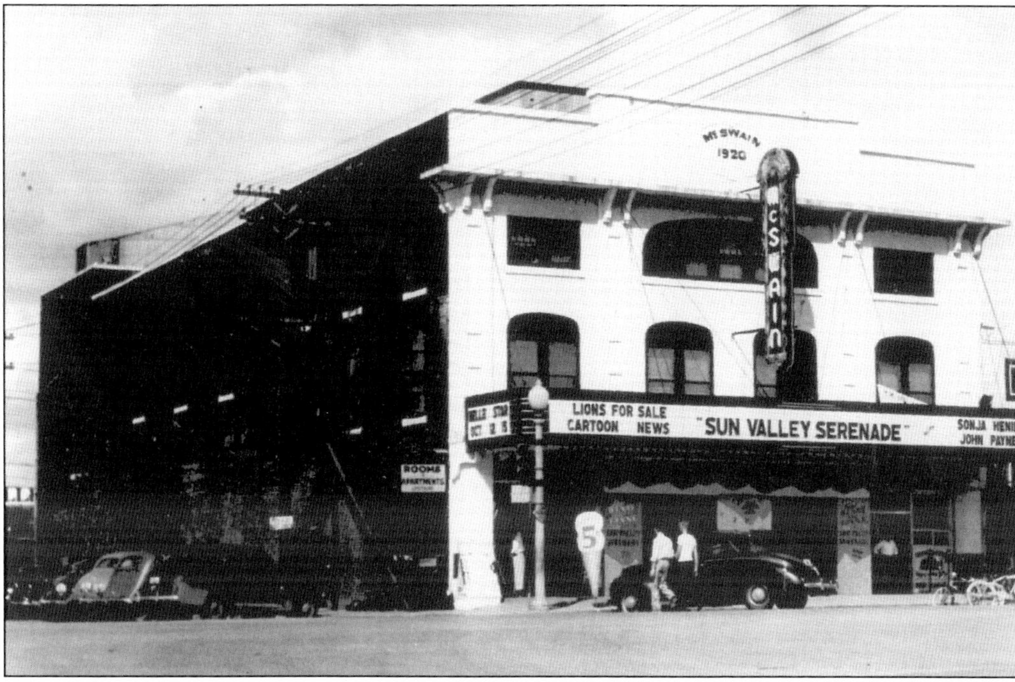

This is a picture of the McSwain Theater. At that time, there were rooms and apartments for rent on the upper floors. The clearing directly in front of the theater was a no parking zone and was solely reserved for bicycles. (Courtesy of Bud Throne.)

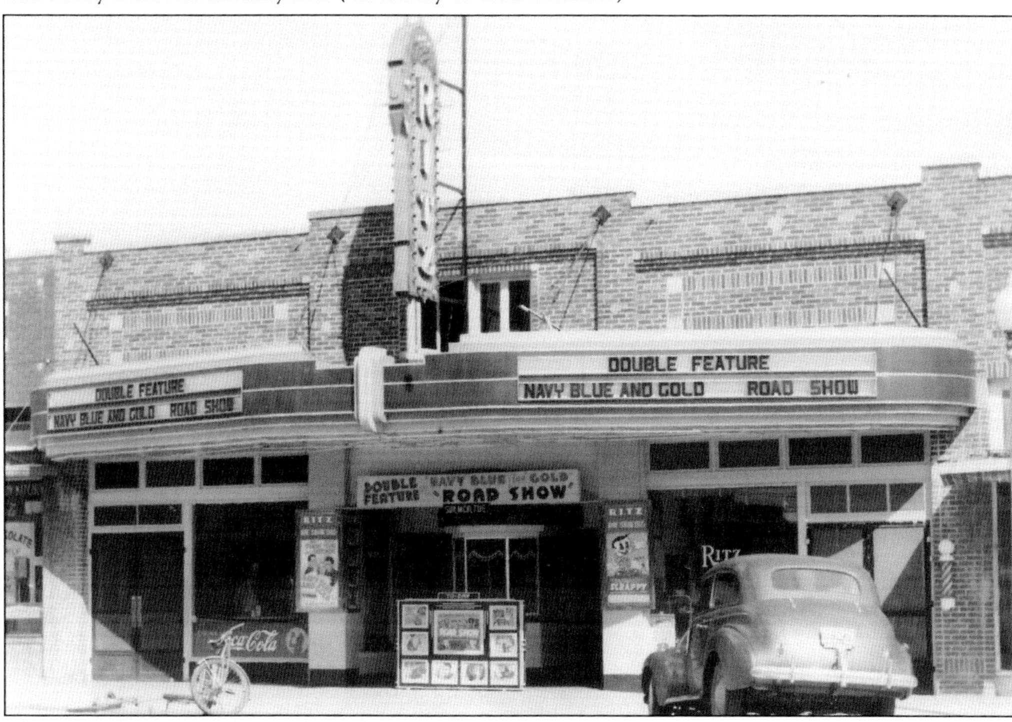

The Ritz Theater was located on the 300 block of East Main Street. When this picture was taken, a double feature was being shown—two for one! (Courtesy of Bud Throne.)

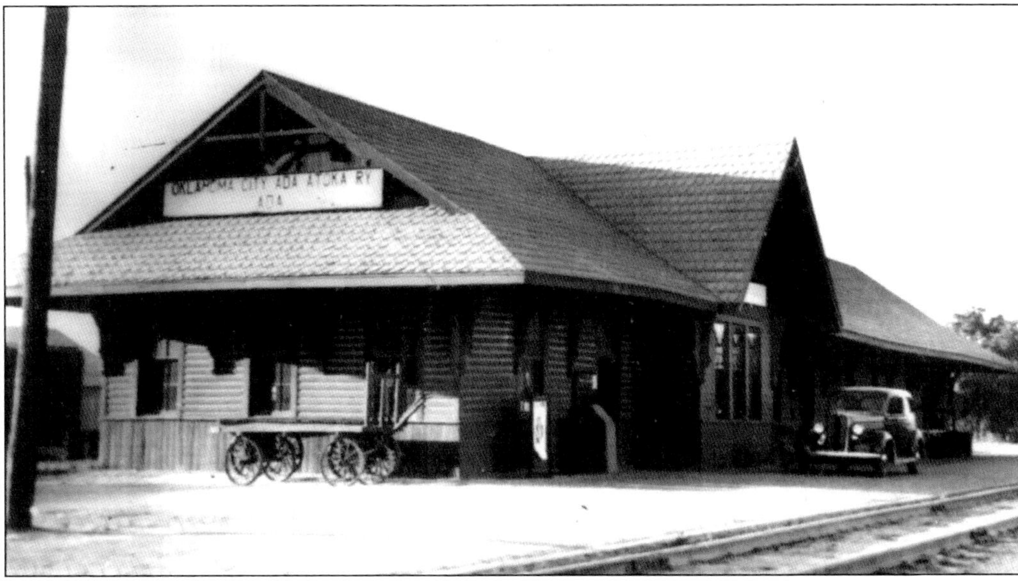

On the west side of the tracks on West Main, the Oklahoma City, Ada & Atoka depot was ready for the next train. The depot is now an antique and gift shop. (Courtesy of Gary Haney.)

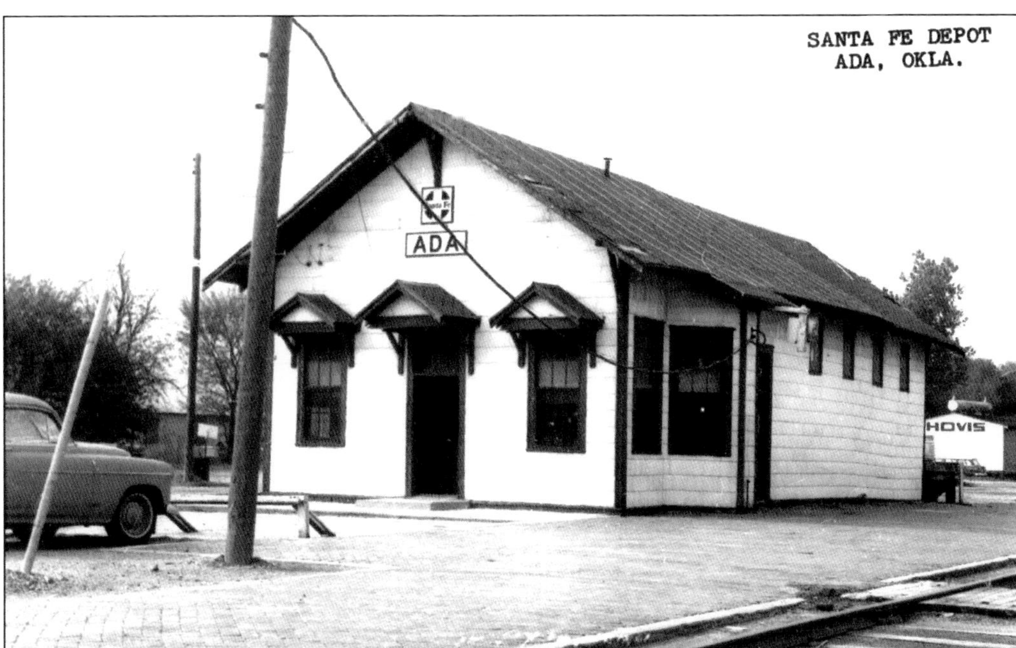

On East Main Street, the Santa Fe depot sat patiently. (Courtesy of Gary Haney.)

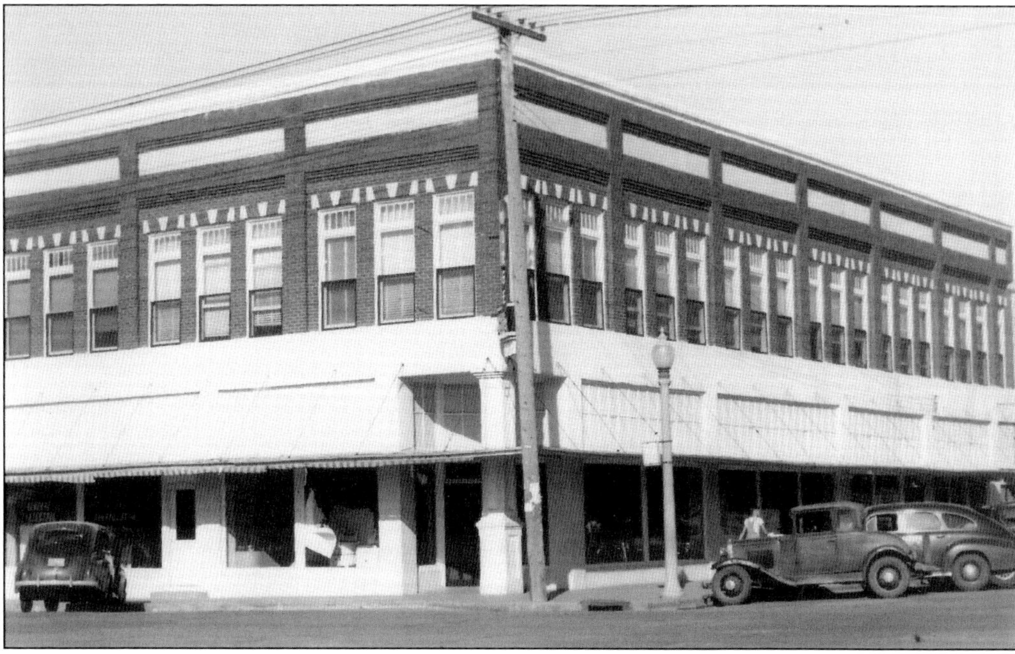

This is an early picture of the building on the corner of Townsend and Main Streets. It is located at the east end of "The Bloody Bucket" block. (Courtesy of Bud Throne.)

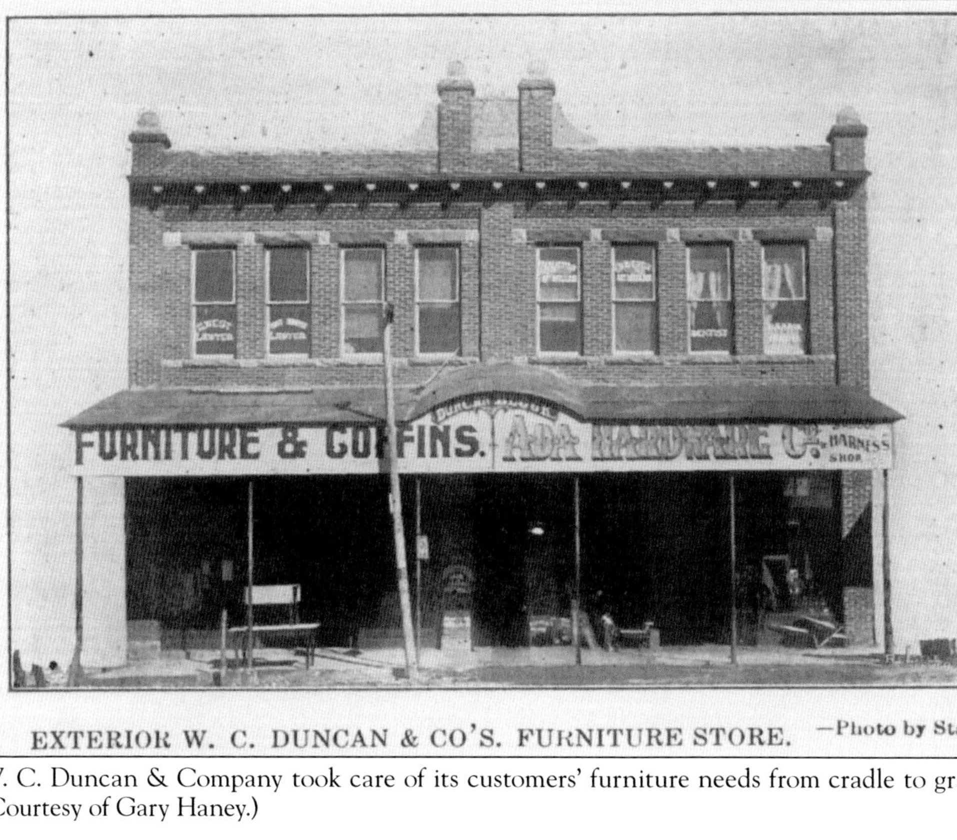

EXTERIOR W. C. DUNCAN & CO'S. FURNITURE STORE. —Photo by Stall

W. C. Duncan & Company took care of its customers' furniture needs from cradle to grave. (Courtesy of Gary Haney.)

Clower and Duncan Drugstore had a lot to offer. Steffen's Ice Cream, Coca-Cola, sodas, and cigars were all sold at the drugstore. Clower and Duncan offered curbside service as well. (Courtesy of Bud Throne.)

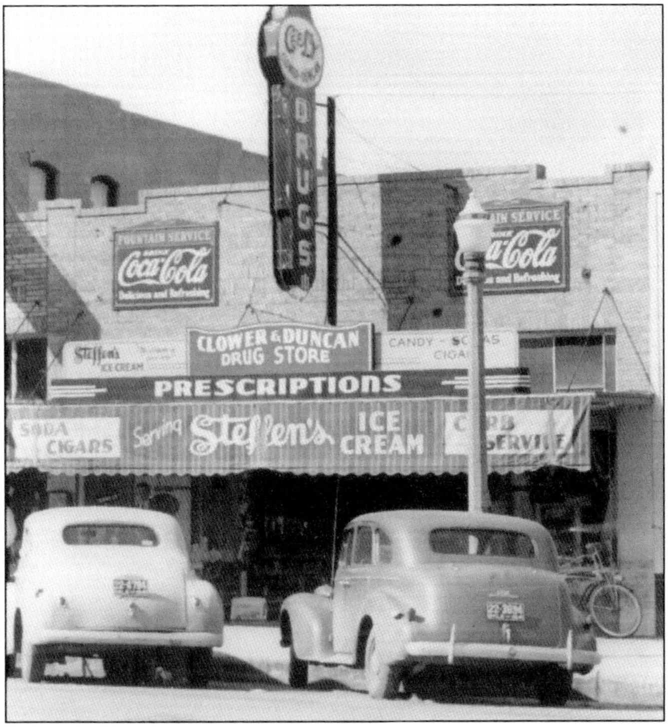

Cunningham Furniture sold furniture and upholstered used pieces for their customers. Located by the Ritz Theater, it was in a good spot for business. (Courtesy of Bud Throne.)

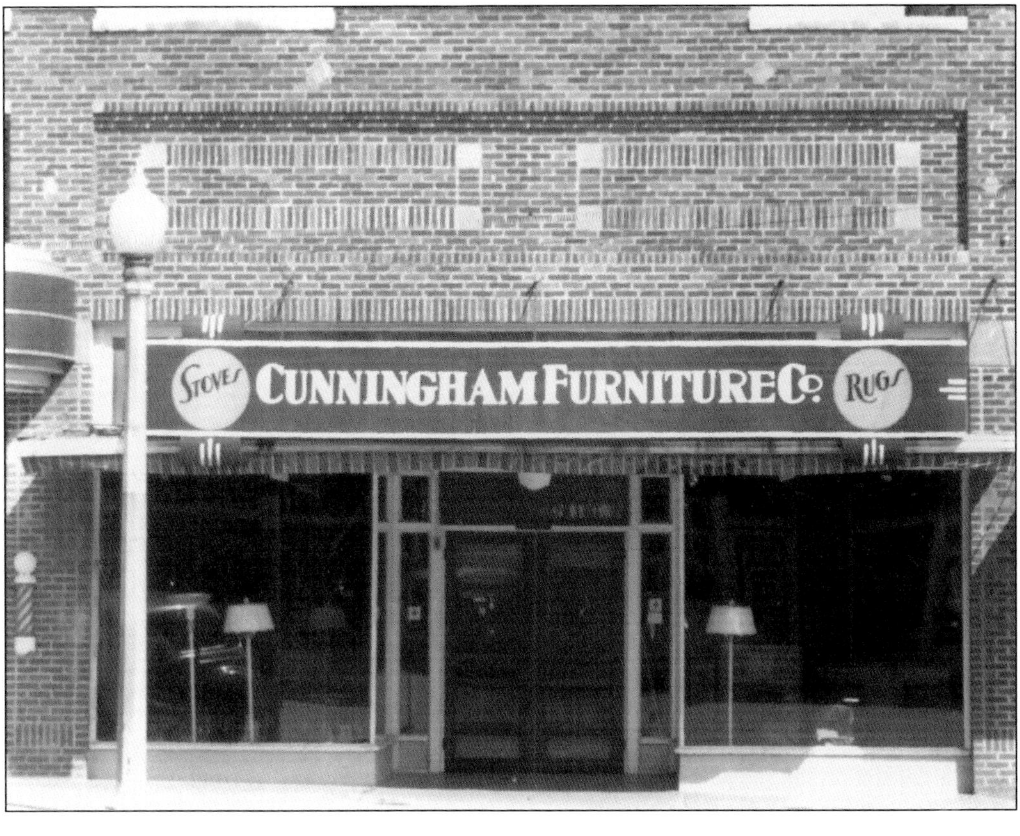

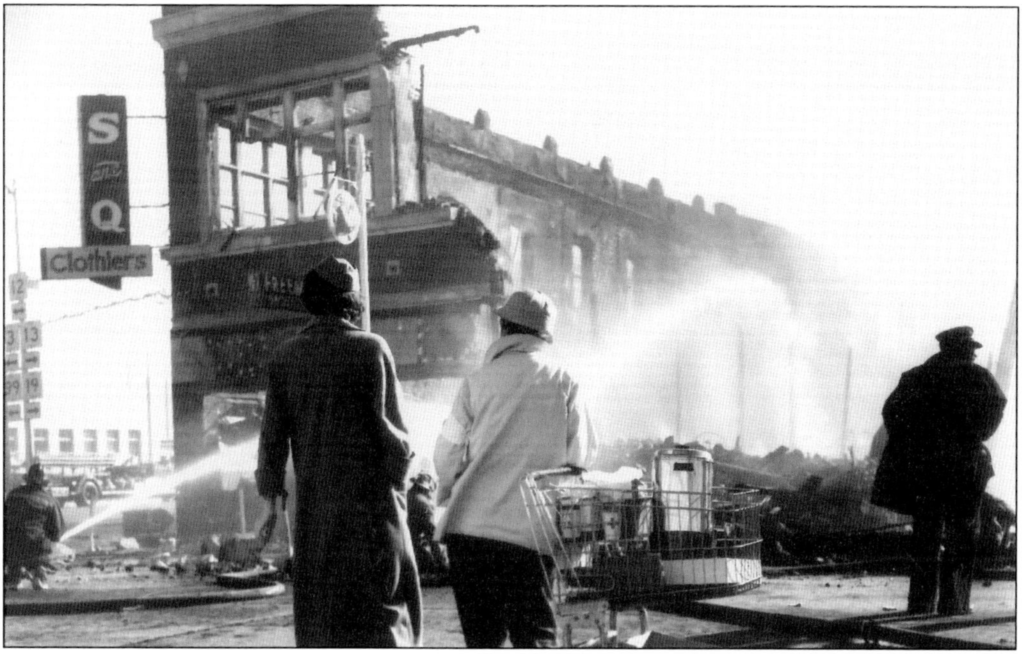

About half of the 100 block of West Main was destroyed by fire in January 1961. S&Q Clothiers, located on the corner, was a large store that was totally destroyed. Several adjoining stores down the block were also ruined. Observers watch from a safe distance. (Courtesy of Bud Throne.)

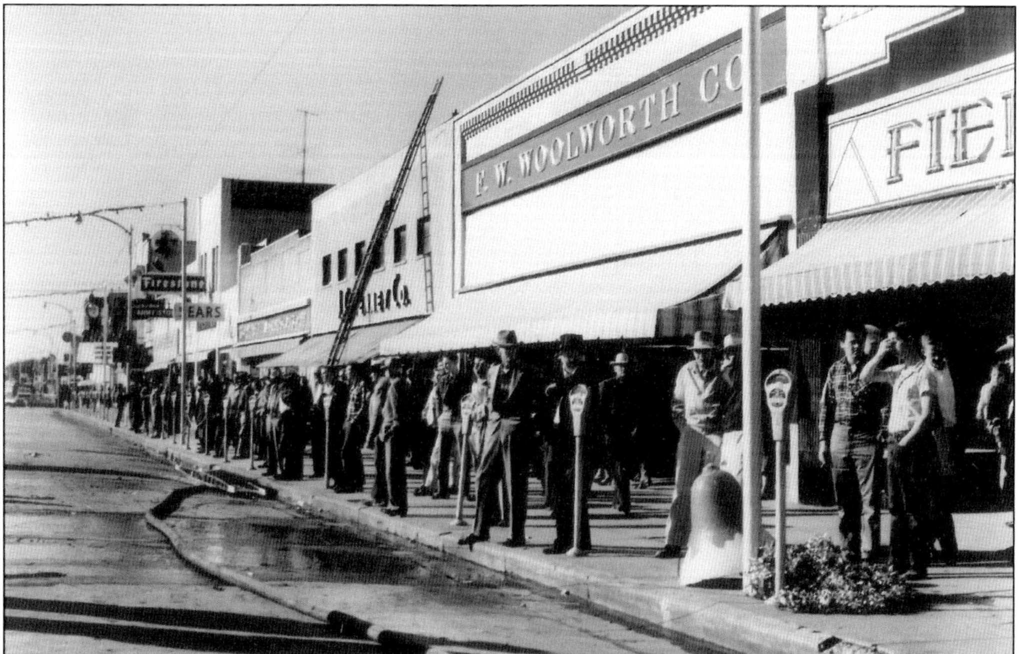

The fire in 1961 drew a crowd across the street. The entire block was filled with onlookers watching as the large fire changed Main Street forever. At the far west end of the block is the McSwain Theater. (Courtesy of Bud Throne.)

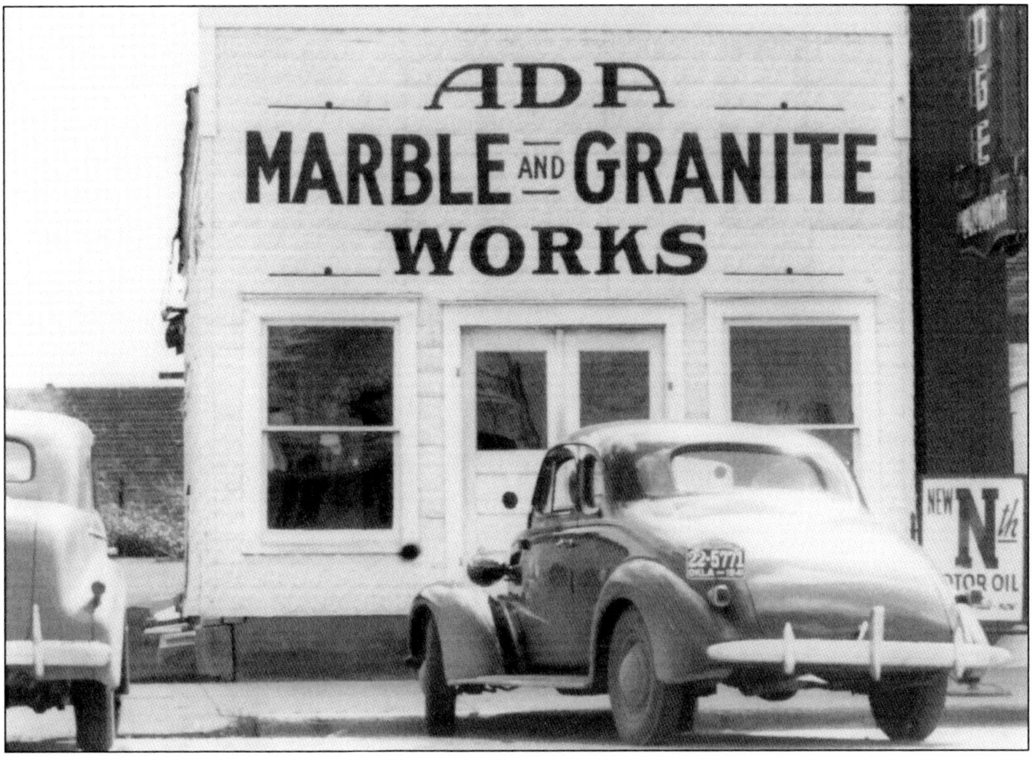

The Ada Marble and Granite Works looks small in its location. Dodge Plymouth Chrysler was located next door. They had the new Nth Motor Oil advertised on their sandwich board between the businesses. (Courtesy of Bud Throne.)

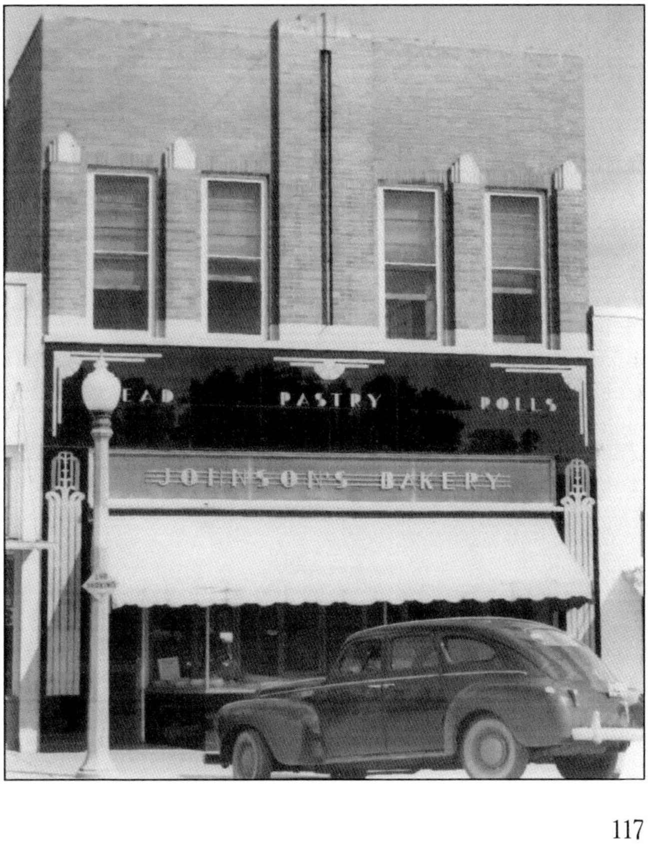

Johnson's Bakery had pastries, rolls, and fresh bread, and their enticing aromas lured customers from all directions in Ada. (Courtesy of Bud Throne.)

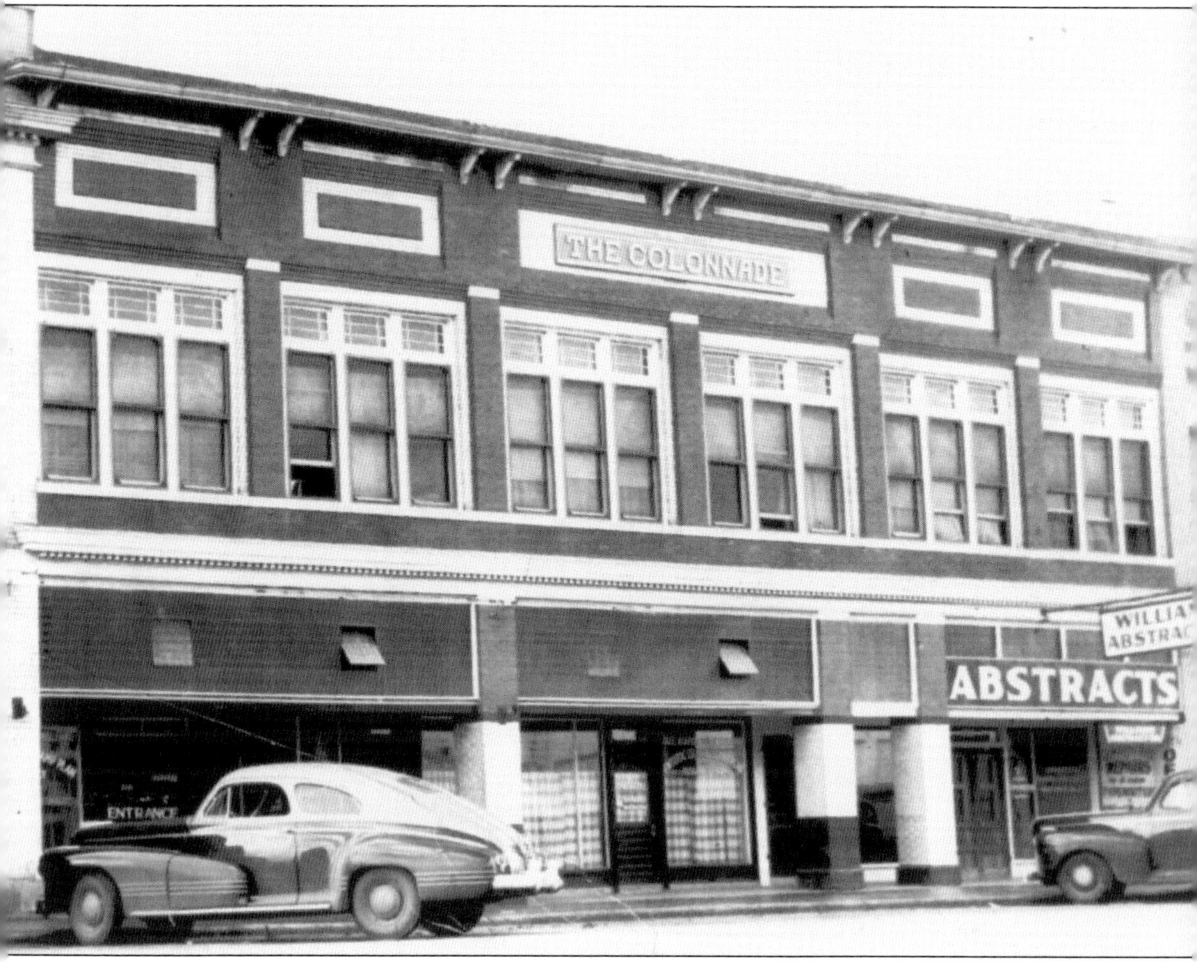

Williams Abstracts was well advertised on its storefront. Transom windows were used for ventilation. An abstract company is located in the same building today. (Courtesy of Bud Throne.)

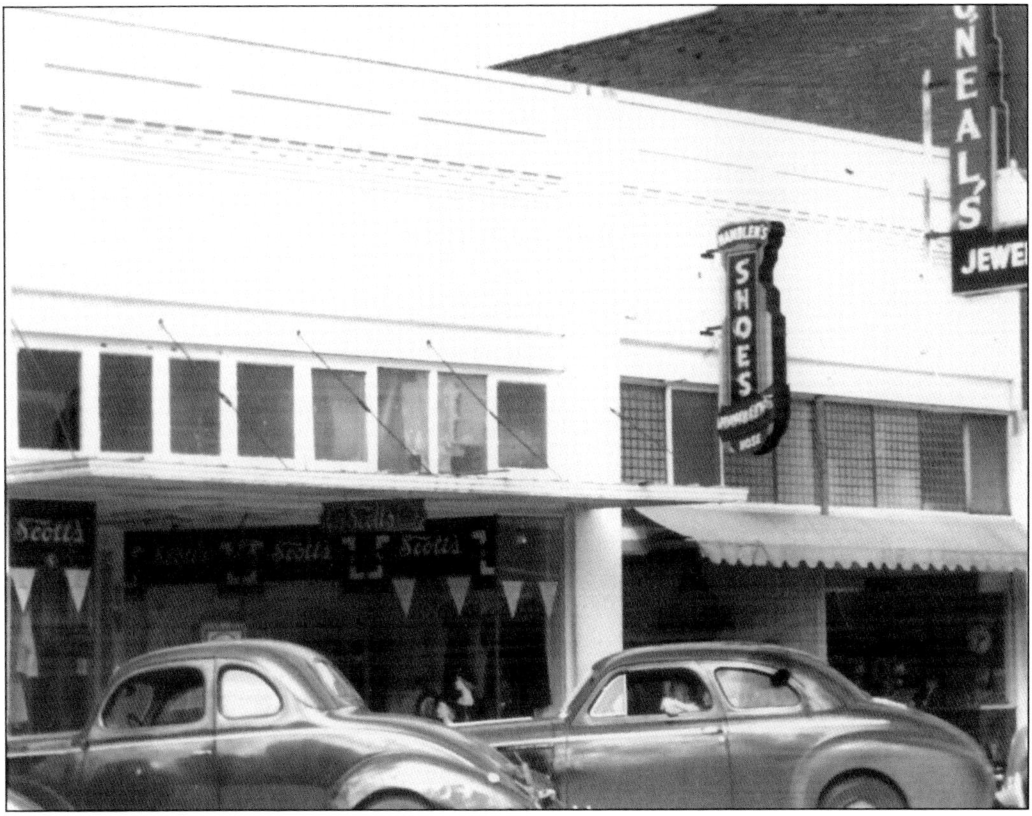

Scotts Clothing was a store that catered to all sizes. Their friendly clerks were always ready to help. A woman could dress up, go next door to find matching shoes, and then peruse diamonds at O'Neils jewelry. (Courtesy of Bud Throne.)

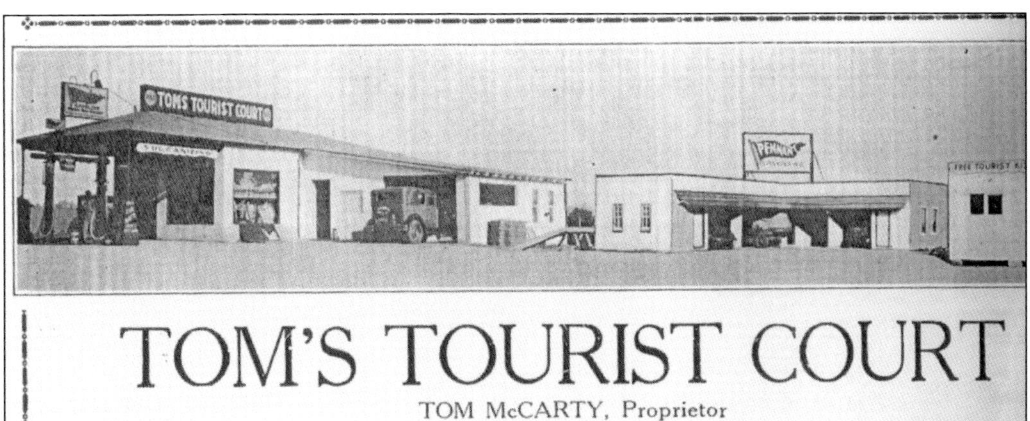

Tom's Tourist Court was located at the end of West Main Street, nestled in the "Y" of intersecting roads leading into Ada. It was a full service business and even had a free kitchen for tourist use. (Courtesy of Bud Throne.)

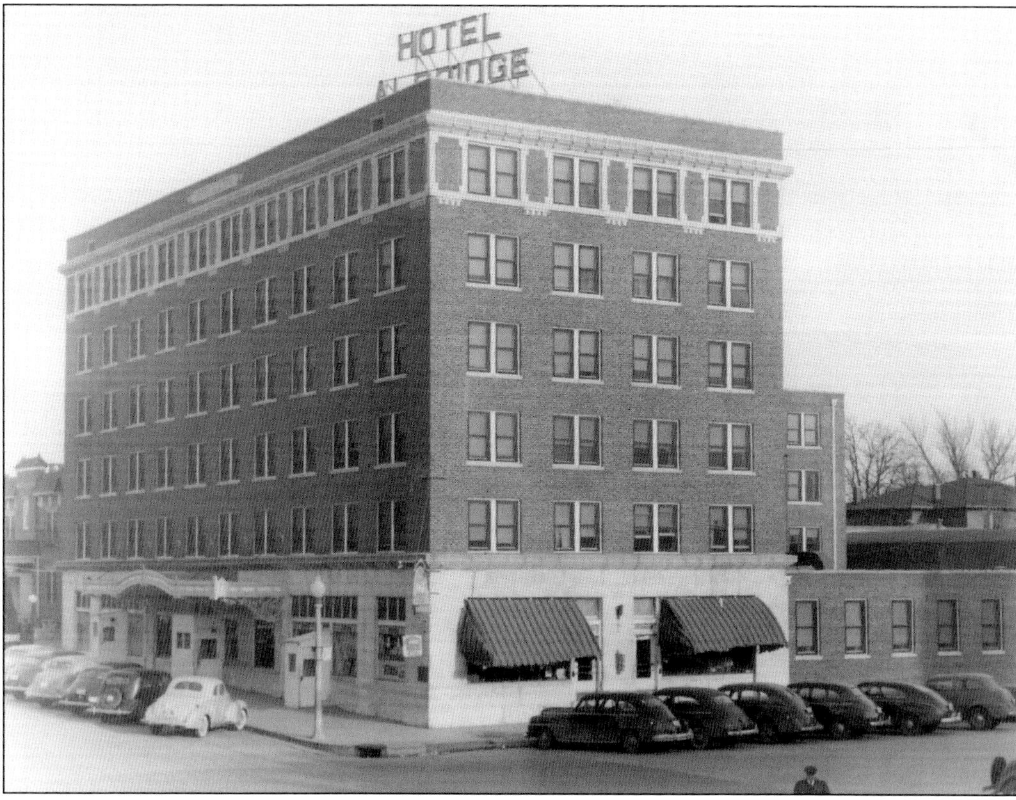

Once crowned by an extremely large sign on its roof, the Hotel Aldridge still stands but is now low-income housing. The original coffee shop still attracts a crowd at breakfast and lunchtime. It is also a popular meeting place for businessmen in the mornings. (Courtesy of Bud Throne.)

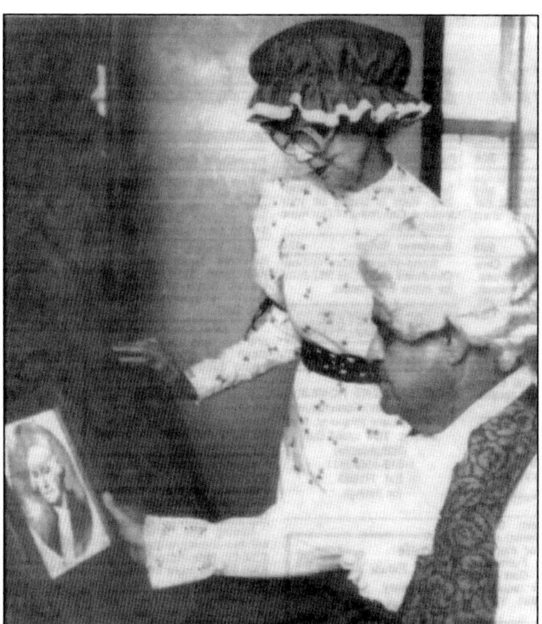

Alberta Blackburn and Ed Brooks dress in character as they celebrate an American holiday. (Courtesy of Alberta Blackburn.)

Five
ECHOES

The mystery in the blue skies filled with cloudy shapes and wood smoke seemed about to speak. The lazy swooping of an eagle against the glare of the sun, making eagle keening from afar gave notice to the listener. It was beautiful and mystic. The empty forest was running rampant with seeing eyes from behind anything visible. Ghosts of a virgin land kept by spirits that became part of the forest itself were in the breeze as was the land, the sky, and the eagle.

This was the essence of what man didn't understand. They cut down trees to build and invaded the valleys of tranquility with the noise of prosperity. It was inevitable. This new land of rolling plains was viewed differently in the eyes of the pioneer. This land where the wind came right behind the rain filled with people that came right behind the wind. That wind blew the dust up behind the horses and covered wagons, as they lay claim to the ground beneath the thundering hooves and wheels of the future. They settled on the plains and prepared to grow waving wheat.

A very large plot of land in the Indian Territory became Ada, Oklahoma. It was named for a daughter of one of the pioneers who claimed to be the founder of this new town. It survived because of pure courage and determination.

Today this city has taken on a beauty few others have acquired. All over the city, the Chickasaw Indians have brought their natural beauty and spirit into the mix of prosperity. Under the leadership of Chickasaw governor Bill Anoatubby, they have placed the beauty and natural mystique back into Ada and have gently and gloriously integrated themselves into Ada's progress.

This city is inundated with beautiful landscapes. The Chickasaws honor their history and take pride in it. The buildings that house their government might behold their spirit. Adans are grateful for all that the Chickasaws do for their city.

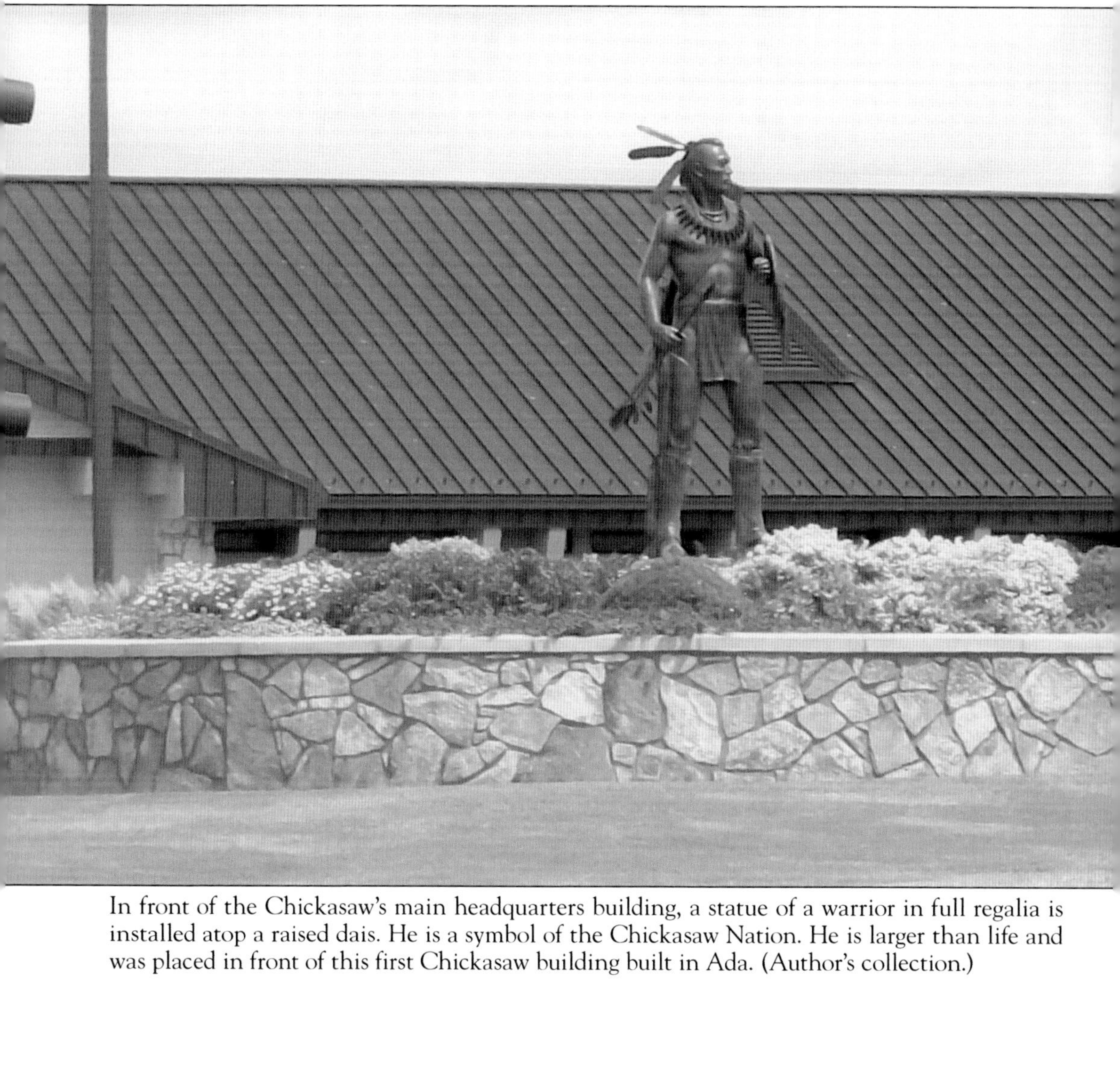

In front of the Chickasaw's main headquarters building, a statue of a warrior in full regalia is installed atop a raised dais. He is a symbol of the Chickasaw Nation. He is larger than life and was placed in front of this first Chickasaw building built in Ada. (Author's collection.)

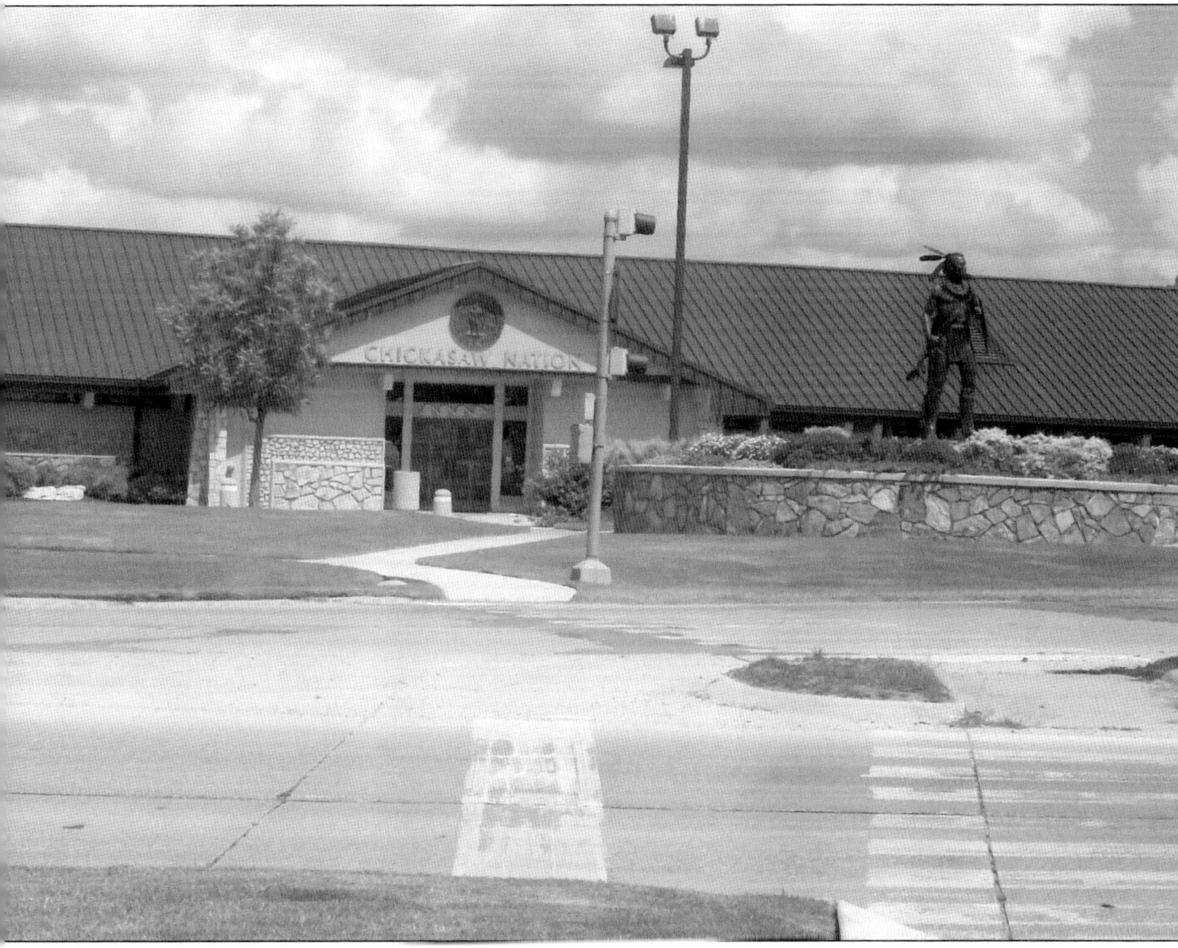

The first Chickasaw headquarters is located at the corner of Arlington and Mississippi. This building set the style for all future Chickasaw structures in the area. Similar architecture and stone facades emphasize the Chickasaw's reverence for nature. Each building is framed with beautiful landscaping. (Author's collection.)

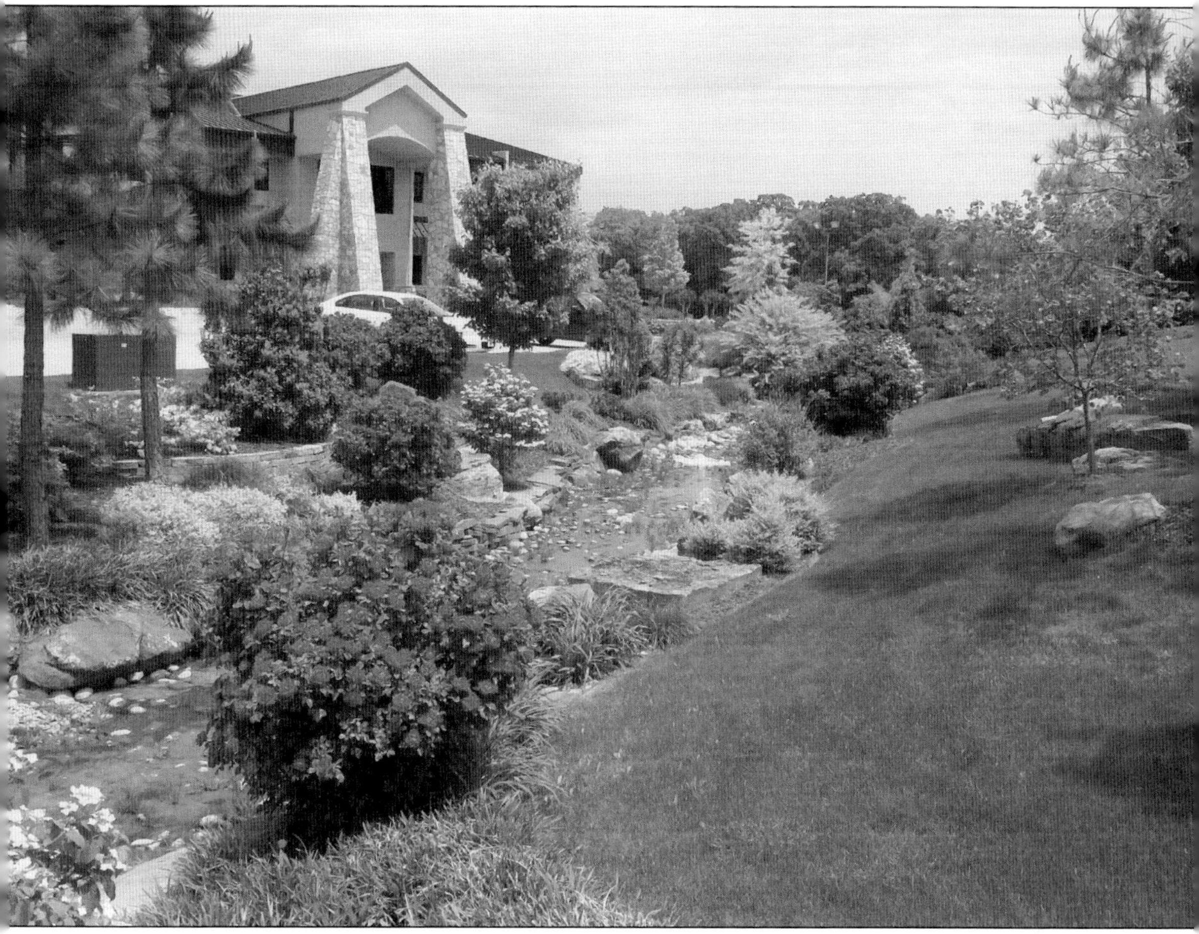

The Chickasaws purchased a large manufacturing facility on Lonnie Abbott Boulevard, remodeled it, and placed their signature look on not only the structure, but the surrounding area. Every building is encircled by a natural garden. (Author's collection.)

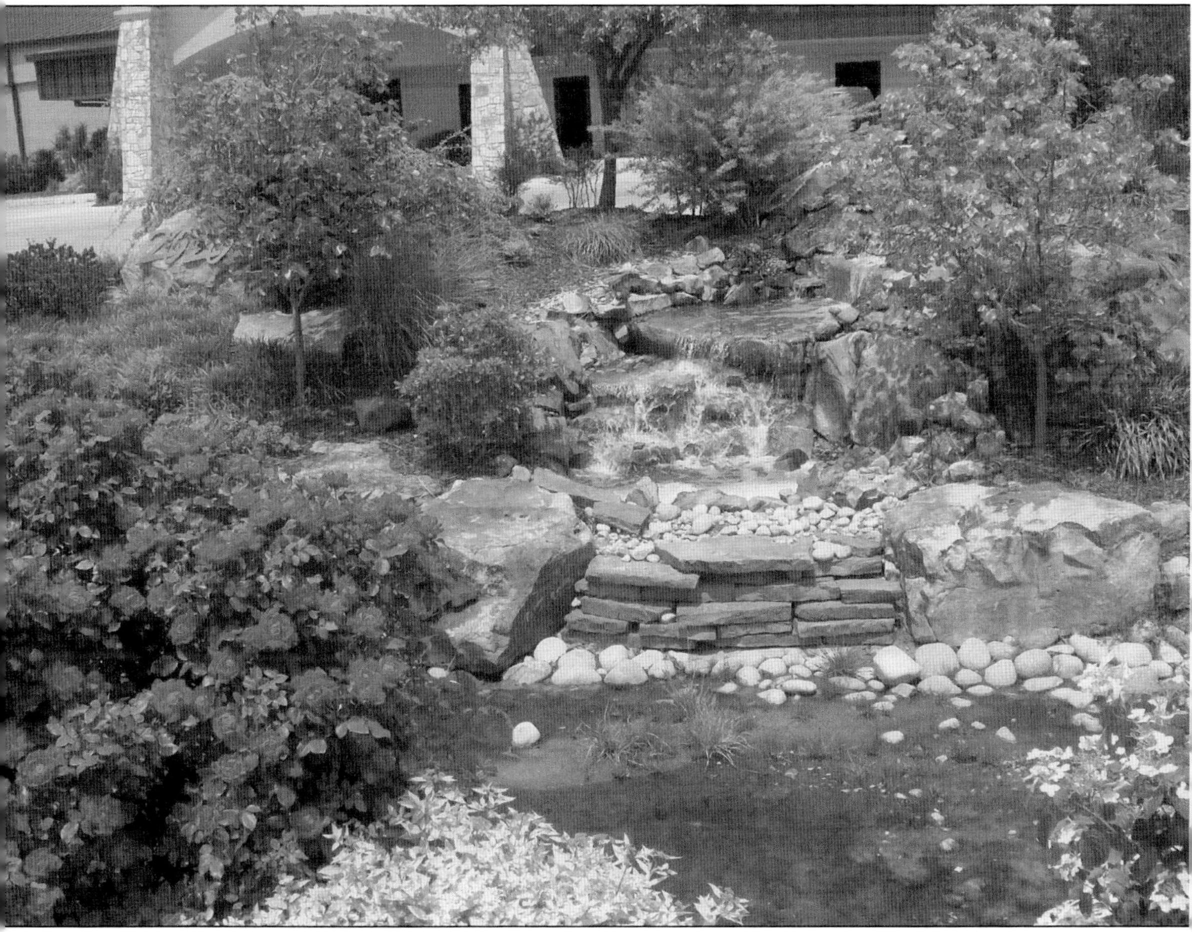

The beauty of everything the Chickasaw Nation has done for Ada is apparent in this photograph of a "Chickasaw Bar Ditch." This is characteristic of their attention to detail. The ever-changing colors of Oklahoma on display here complement the city of Ada in every season. (Author's collection.)

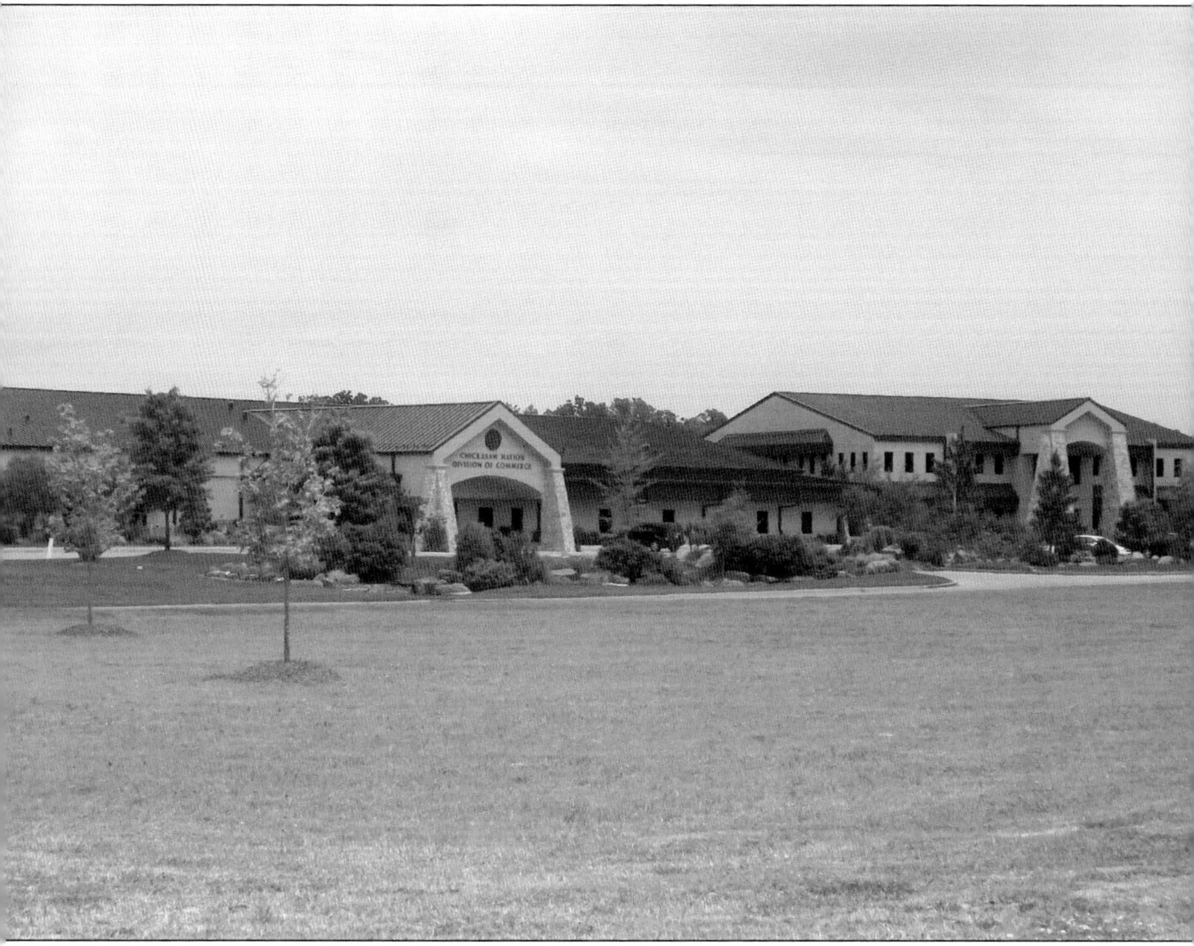

This huge transformed Chickasaw building is yet another example of how they use beautiful, natural landscapes to enhance their buildings, which add an element of pride to the city of Ada. (Author's collection.)

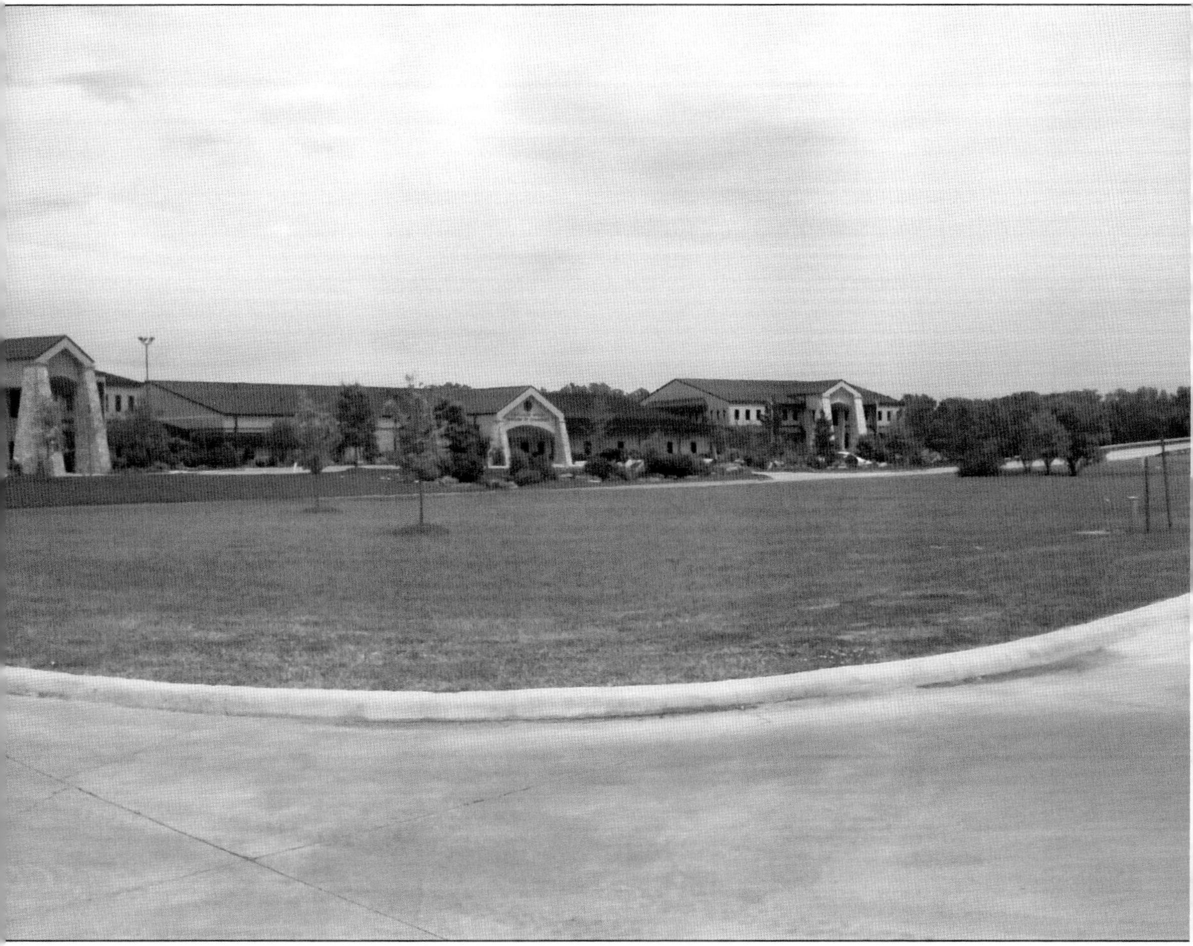

The central building of the huge complex on Lonnie Abbott Boulevard and its landscaping are characteristically associated with the Chickasaws. The Chickasaw seal above the entrance is used on all of their buildings. Again the landscaping represents the Chickasaws' connection to nature. In addition to beautifying the city of Ada, the Chickasaw Nation is one of the largest employers and contributors to Ada's economy. (Author's collection.)

Discover Thousands of Local History Books Featuring Millions of Vintage Images

Arcadia Publishing, the leading local history publisher in the United States, is committed to making history accessible and meaningful through publishing books that celebrate and preserve the heritage of America's people and places.

Find more books like this at
www.arcadiapublishing.com

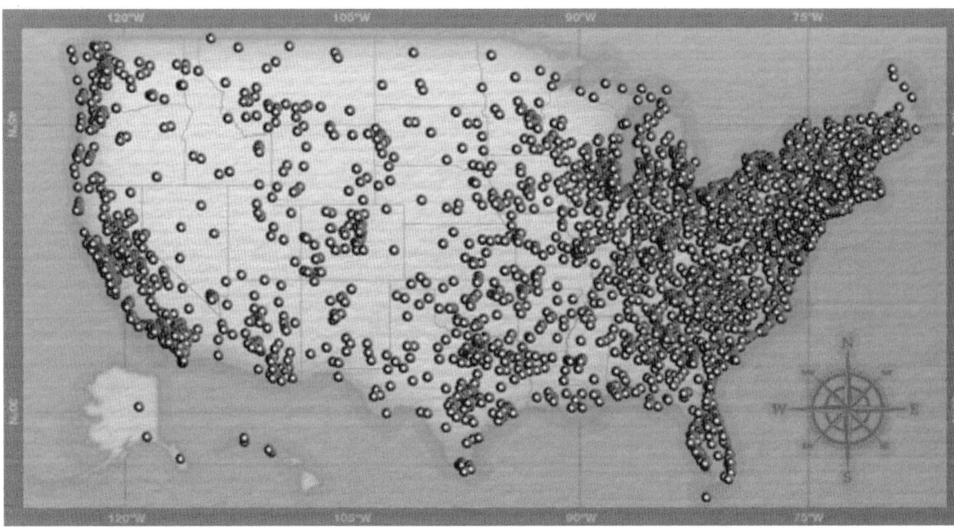

Search for your hometown history, your old stomping grounds, and even your favorite sports team.

Consistent with our mission to preserve history on a local level, this book was printed in South Carolina on American-made paper and manufactured entirely in the United States. Products carrying the accredited Forest Stewardship Council (FSC) label are printed on 100 percent FSC-certified paper.

MADE IN THE USA